Mystical Body ❦ Mystical Voice

Encountering Christ in the Words of the Mass

Christopher Carstens, MA
Douglas Martis, PHD, STD

LTP
LITURGY
TRAINING
PUBLICATIONS

Nihil Obstat
Imprimatur
+ Most Rev. J. Peter Sartain
Bishop of Joliet, Illinois
September 22, 2010

MYSTICAL BODY, MYSTICAL VOICE: ENCOUNTERING CHRIST IN THE WORDS OF THE MASS © 2011 Archdiocese of Chicago: Liturgy Training Publications, 3949 South Racine Avenue, Chicago IL 60609; 1-800-933-1800, fax 1-800-933-7094, e-mail orders@ltp.org. All rights reserved. See our Web site: www.LTP.org.

This book was edited by Kevin Thornton. Carol Mycio was the production editor. The design is by Anna Manhart, and the typesetting was done by Mark Hollopeter in Garamond. Cover photo: Denis McNamara; the Cathedral of Saint Joseph the Workman, Diocese of La Crosse, Wisconsin.

Printed in the United States of America.

Library of Congress Control Number: 2011920587

ISBN 978-1-56854-932-3

MBMV

Contents

Appendix

Bibliography   257

Index   259

Preface

God became man so that man might become God.

Saint Athanasius

By condescending to our level and assuming our nature, Saint Athanasius is telling us, we ourselves might be taken up into the heavenly places. Salvation is not only of the soul, but of the whole person and, as such, every part of him—including his language.

The topic of this book is the liturgical language of the Roman Rite Mass: how it praises God and, in praising, sanctifies those who speak it. Returning to the hero of the Council of Nicaea, we adapt Saint Athanasius's dictum to sacred language: "God speaks like us so that we might speak like him." The Second Person of the Holy Trinity—who is himself speech, the Word of the Father—has restored the once-broken dialogue of love between heaven and earth. In the Mystical Voice of the Church at Mass, this dialogue of love resounds in human and divine ears.

The Second Vatican Council (1962–1965), while seeking to preserve the use of the Latin language in its liturgies, allowed the use of the mother tongue to be broadened (*Sacrosanctum concilium*, 36). In a short period of time, nearly all of the texts of the Roman Rite were said in vernacular languages, including English. The Church was here faced with a novel, though happy, dilemma about *how* to translate the traditional Latin language into local languages. She found herself asking, Which translation principles—to this point in history undeveloped by the Church—would best effect a language consonant with the "true and authentic spirit" of the Roman Rite liturgy (ibid., 37) and, at the same time, be clear, noble, and simple for particular groups and peoples (ibid., 34, 38)?

Now, nearly fifty years after the Second Vatican Council, a third edition of *The Roman Missal* has been translated into the English language. This English edition is the fruit of pastoral practice, magisterial guidance, and the maturation of the Council's brief but substantial principles on translation. The first and second editions of *The Roman Missal* connected English speakers with the Voice of God in an effective and real way. The third edition, incorporating the benefits of its predecessors, contains a liturgical vernacular worthy of the mystery of God and accessible to those who use it.

What remains for its users—those who pray, sing, and hear the texts—is to encounter Christ and his saving Voice in the words of the Mass. In this age of the Church, Christ acts through sacramental signs. To hear the words of the Mass is to hear Christ himself, the Word of God; to pray with the Church's language is to join our voices with the same Word, now praising the Father in heaven in the Holy Spirit. The sacramental approach to the words of the Mass is the overarching theme of the present work. Because the liturgy is essentially a sacramental reality, the sacramental understanding can yield the most fruitful insights to the Truth of the Mass' texts.

Mystical Body, Mystical Voice: Encountering Christ in the Words of the Mass aids our hearing and praying by showing how Christ continues to speak in the Church's voice at prayer. Part I, "The Liturgical Primer," helps foster the sacramental outlook, showing how Christ is present in the Church's sacramental signs, especially in her language. Examining the particular texts of the Mass in Part II, "The Language of *The Roman Missal*," we learn to hear how Christ speaks in them with his Church.

Only when the sacramental perspective is achieved will the meaning of the Mass' words (or any other of its sacramental symbols) become clear. The sacramental approach to liturgical catechesis—also called mystagogical catechesis—is not only called for by the modern papacy, but has been applied in parishes and classrooms by the authors. Mystagogy is the best way to reveal Christ, the reality of every sacramental sign, and the liturgy as a whole. And when Christ is revealed clearly, we have the occasion to be transformed by him—to become heavenly, as Saint Athanasius says—and to "Go and announce the Gospel of the Lord" to the world (dismissal formula for Mass).

For the assistance in making this book possible, we wish to thank in a particular way the students and faculty of the Liturgical Institute at the University of St. Mary of the Lake/Mundelein Seminary. Their faith and vision have helped attune our own sacramental senses. For whatever insights the present book contains, they themselves deserve proper credit. We are also grateful to those who have helped in the production of this book, including Joseph O'Brien for tireless editing and thoughtful suggestions to the drafts; Deacon Owen Cummings for offering theological clarifications and suggestions; and Kevin Thornton for editing and encouragement.

Abbreviations

The Church has provided many documents over her long history to teach and instruct the faithful. Some of these are encyclicals, some are letters, and some are documents that come from councils. These documents carefully and clearly lay out the Church's teaching on particular issues relating to the words we use at Mass. In this book, we refer to the following documents by the abbreviations in this list. Although the relevant passages of these documents are cited in the text, we encourage you to read the documents in their entirety.

AAS   *Acta Apostolicae Sedis* (Rome, 1909–ff.)

ASS   *Acta Sanctae Sedis* (Rome, 1865–1908)

CT   *Catechesi tradendae*

CCC   *Catechism of the Catholic Church*

DCar   *Deus caritas est*

GIRM   *General Instruction of the Roman Missal*

GS   *Gaudiam et Spes*

LA   *Liturgiam authenticam*

LI   *Liturgiae instauarationes*

LG   *Lumen gentium*

MD   *Mediator Dei*

NMI   *Novo millennio ineunte*

MF   *Mysterium fidei*

MND   *Mane nobiscum Domine*

PL   *Patrologia Latina*, J. P. Migne, ed., (Paris: 1841–1855)

RT   *Ratio translationis*

SC   *Sacrosanctum concilium* (Constitution on the Sacred Liturgy)

SCar   *Sacramentum caritatis*

SS   *Spiritus et Sponsa*

TLS   *Tra le sollecitudini*

VL   *Varietates legitimae*

VQ   *Vicesimus quintus annus*

Introduction

And the Word became flesh and made his dwelling among us,
and we saw his glory, the glory as of the Father's only Son,
full of grace and truth.

John 1:14

At the center of history stands the God-become-man, Jesus Christ, who bridges the gap between a world fallen by its sin and a Heavenly City, the New Jerusalem. The material of this great bridge connecting heaven and earth is the wood of the cross. These outstretched arms embrace the whole world and then, like a "cosmic hoist," bear all up into the heavenly places.[1] Giving shape to our salvific link to heaven—and making the wood of the cross a living conduit of divine life—is the Word of God hanging upon it. Having taken to himself human nature at his Incarnation, the divine Word of God speaks the response the Father has longed to hear since the *non serviam* (I will not serve) of the first Adam: he proclaims an unequivocal "yes" to the Father's will. It is a response which he has spoken for us on Calvary, and it is a response which he speaks for us today at every Mass. In a synthesis of the natural and the divine, the saving cross and the Word enlivening it are presented before our eyes and ears in a drama played out in sacramental signs. Here the divine and human "yes" to the Father—the dramatic reunion of heaven to earth—is heard in the sacramental and mystical voice of his Body, the Church, in her own language. The more we come to recognize the saving work of Christ in the Mass, the greater is our ability to participate with him in his sacrificial "yes" to the Father, to grow in holiness after his image, and to glorify God in body and mind.

This book prepares the Catholic faithful to encounter the Word of God, the Second Person of the Holy Trinity. Liturgically speaking—literally!—this preparation focuses on the Mass' prayers, dialogues, and ordinary texts (e.g., *Kyrie*, Creed, *Agnus Dei*).

So that our liturgical encounter with Christ will be authentic, our approach begins by laying a solid foundation upon some of the Church's most fundamental theological principles. In fact, it is only in light of a larger, overarching understanding of these principles that the particular words of the Mass take on their full meaning. Participation in the liturgy is not simply a matter of saying words—whether new or familiar. Words mean something, and in the context of the Church's prayer, her words are meant to make us think of scriptural and spiritual and holy things.

Like many arenas of human life—medicine, accounting, or sports—the Church's liturgical language has a distinctiveness all its own, and very often it sounds different from other types of speech. But should it be different? If so, to what degree? Why does liturgical language have the characteristics and qualities that it does? Furthermore, the texts we use to pray the Mass are to be faithful translations of the Latin original text (see *Liturgiam authenticam*, 20). But why should this be so? Ought twenty-first century Americans be expected to pray at Mass with a language characterized by that used by Saint Jerome or Saint Augustine—or Cicero? To answer these and other questions about the Mass' language, it is necessary to step back, look at the "big picture," and see that our liturgical senses are attuned rightly to things as they are. In this way we can more fully encounter Christ as he is, present today in the sacraments.

Building a solid foundation in our approach to the liturgy requires effort, patience, and perseverance. But, like the wise builder of Jesus' parable (Matthew 7:24–27), the final product of such labor endures amid the tempests and temptations. Taking to heart this prudential approach to understanding the liturgy, we ought to resist the urge to turn directly to the texts themselves; rather, we should form a foundation based upon the larger theological mind of the Church. Specifically, this foundation includes the following:

Sacramentality: The words of the Mass—in fact, every element of the Mass—are essentially sacramental realities. The ultimate, yet unseen, reality of the Mass and of the sacramental elements that comprise it is Jesus Christ, the Word of God, and the grace of his Paschal Mystery. The Mass is our portal to heaven—it is where Christ and his grace are encountered by us today in outward, sacramental signs. In particular, the Eucharistic bread and wine are sacramental signs par excellence of Christ, for in these outward and sensible signs abide the substance of Christ's body, blood, soul, and divinity. But the priest, too, is a sacramental sign of Christ, as is the altar, the candles, the church building, the sacred music—in fact, the entire assembly; these are sacramental signs of Christ. In the following pages we will examine how the words of the Mass "sacramentalize" Christ (make the invisible, visible); we will also study how hearing, praying, and singing them rightly leads us to encounter the Word of God in them.

Ecclesiology: Closely connected to the sacramental character of the Mass' words is the ecclesial nature of these words: that they are spoken by the Church and her members. The Church is herself a sacrament of Christ, especially when gathered at the celebration of the Mass, for in the celebration of her rites, Christ, now seated at the right hand of the Father in heaven, is most clearly manifest. For this reason, after Saint Paul, the Church is called the Mystical Body of Christ. (Here, *mystical* might as easily be replaced by the term *sacramental*, for both express the reality of Christ presented in divinely instituted signs.) As Christ and his work are now present and active in his Body, the Church, so too is the voice with which he proclaimed his unreserved love for the Father. The Mystical Body speaks this same "Mystical Voice" of loving praise to the Father in the Holy Spirit. To pray the words of the Mass, consequently, is to pray with the voice of Christ now resounding in his Church.

Inculturation: Like the Christ, the Church exists among particular peoples at a given time and place, and never in any kind of abstract sphere. In her dealings with men and women of every age, the Church offers to them the saving truths of God in a way understandable to their cultural surroundings, while at the same time the Church takes to herself whatever in a particular culture can help her to articulate and celebrate the Mystery of Christ more fully. The "double movement" between the culture of the Church and the culture of men and women is also at play in the English language used in the celebration of the Mass. The texts used by English-speaking Catholics today are the product of the union between the supernatural faith of the Church and the English-speaking peoples of the Roman Church. To pray at Mass is therefore to cultivate our own identity not only with the present circumstances of our earthly culture, but also with the eternal and abiding culture of the Heavenly Jerusalem.

Eschatology: While one result of inculturation is the incarnation of Christ's Gospel into the cultures of the present world, the ultimate fruit of inculturation is the transformation of the city of man into the City of God. The Word's becoming flesh is an unfathomably glorious event, but even greater than the divine becoming man is the possibility of man becoming divine—that is, of the earthly denizens becoming heavenly citizens. "God became man," writes Saint Athanasius, "so that man might become God." By condescending in the Incarnation to be circumscribed by human words, the Word has, at the same time, elevated human words and human beings to the eternal heights. God speaks like us—if we can paraphrase Saint Athanasius's dictum—so that we might speak like him. Our English-language Mass texts, therefore, are not only of this world (offering the best of vocabulary, composition, and style), but also of the heavenly world. To pray with Christ and his Body at Mass is to pray with the heavenly host today and to learn to be like them who live eternally in the City of God.

Mystagogy: Christ the Word, the Mystical Body, and the Heavenly City are all accessible to those who participate in the Mass; in fact, these *are* the realities of the Mass, and to look for anything else is to miss the point of the Mass. But seeing and hearing what is there is not always an easy task, for it requires formation and training, and our senses, which live rather comfortably in the surrounding natural environment, are not always attuned to the supernatural realities offered at Mass. To apprehend supernatural realities requires supernatural senses, and their formation is a mystagogical one, where we are led from the sign to the signified, the sacrament to the mystery, the ritual to the Christ. In linguistic terms specifically, mystagogy means not only hearing the words of the celebration, but also hearing in them Christ's own voice of sacrificial love for the Father and for us. Mystagogical hearing means, in addition, that our own words, folded in prayer with the Church, are at the same time the words of *the* Word, Jesus Christ, restoring the unity of heaven and earth, which had been destroyed by the divisive power of sin.

Sacramentality, ecclesiology, inculturation, eschatology, and mystagogy: each of these elements creates a foundation and a context for the individual texts of the Mass. As this book demonstrates, by establishing this foundation and understanding this context, the faithful will hear more clearly, grasp more authentically, and participate more fully in the Holy Sacrifice and Wedding Feast of the Lamb.

The book is divided into two main sections: the first establishes the ground and context needed to appreciate the meaning of the Mass' language, while the second looks to the particular words of the Mass with a view to the encounter with Christ that they facilitate. Part I, the "Liturgical Primer," begins in chapter 1 with a review of liturgical theology (relying greatly on the writings of Cardinal Ratzinger, now Pope Benedict XVI), which is particularly appropriate for our current task of examining liturgical language. Called "A Logical Look at the Liturgy," this first chapter focuses on the

Second Person of the Trinity's *Logos*-character, or Word-character, and how all of salvation history—from creation and the Fall, to the Incarnation of the Logos and his sacrificial work, to the Church's continued work until the end of time—bears a decidedly Logical, or Word-based, character. Chapter 2, "The Sacramental Nature of the Liturgy," demonstrates how the Mystery of Christ is now carried out in the sacraments of the Church. The chapter follows God's own "divine pedagogy" (CCC, 1145), and it uncovers the origin and meaning of sacramental signs, which explain in large part how Christ the Logos is present and active in the liturgy's signs. While the Mass comprises many different sacramental signs, it is sacramental words in particular that chapter 3, "The Use of Words in the Church's Liturgy," examines. Like other sacramental signs, the words used in today's Mass have roots in a many-layered soil from which they enjoy a fruitful and organic growth. Once again, it is by examining the origins of the Mass' words that we are better able to hear the Mystical Voice of Christ's Church in them.

For those tempted to skip over this aspect of our study, keep in mind that an examination of any part of the liturgy—be it sacred architecture, the various ministers, or words—necessitates a first look at the fundamentals of liturgy. This examination now begun, Part II looks in greater detail at the words of the *Roman Missal*. Chapter 4, "Vatican II and the Third Edition of the *Roman Missal*," analyzes the founding principles of the *Constitution on the Sacred Liturgy*, which govern the reform and restoration of the sacred liturgy. The chapter then examines how these principles, and particularly those pertaining to translations, unfolded during the papacy of John Paul II, especially in his apostolic letter *Vicesimus quintus annus*, on the 25th anniversary of the *Constitution on the Sacred Liturgy*, and the curial document *Liturgiam authenticam*, the Fifth Instruction on the proper implementation of the *Constitution on the Sacred Liturgy*. We are then in a better position in chapters 5, 6, and 7 to uncover the authentic meaning of the words of the Mass—the Introductory Rites, the Liturgy of the Word, the Liturgy of the Eucharist, and the Concluding Rites—which, in the end, signify nothing other than Christ. Finally, chapter 8, "Liturgical Catechesis for Active Participation," provides suggestions for liturgical formation that can be used by pastors, catechists, and each of the lay faithful.

In fact, it is for each of these groups—pastors, educators, and laity—that this book is written. The pedagogy employed here—which is a mystagogical pedagogy—is the same invoked by both John Paul II and Pope Benedict XVI for a greater active participation by all. Mystagogy leads us from the signs to the signified; textually, mystagogical catechesis leads us from the Mass' words to the Word, Jesus. About the mystagogical approach to catechesis, Pope Benedict teaches:

> A mystagogical catechesis must also be concerned with *presenting the meaning of the signs* contained in the rites. This is particularly important in a highly technological age like our own, which risks losing the ability to appreciate signs and symbols. More than simply conveying information, a mystagogical catechesis should be capable of making the faithful more sensitive to the language of signs and gestures which, together with the word, make up the rite. (SCar, 64; emphasis added)

While mystagogical catechesis is based first and foremost in the experience of the liturgy itself, this book provides insights that assist pastors and their flocks to enter more deeply into a relationship with the Person of Christ alive in the Mass.

The most effective way to use the present book is in conjunction with the attentive and prayerful celebration of the Mass. "The best catechesis on the Eucharist," says Pope Benedict, "is the Eucharist itself, celebrated well" (SCar, 64). A Eucharist "celebrated well" is marked by sacramental signs and symbols that radiate their meaning. In other words, before one can encounter the signified Christ, he must first encounter the sacramental signs of the Mass. The "art of celebrating," or *ars celebrandi*, is attentive to the signs and symbols of the rite, such as vesture, actions, silence, music, and language. When these signs—and, for our purposes here, language—speak clearly and authentically, the faithful are drawn to a fuller and more active collaboration in the work of Christ, the Word of God. Based upon the primary celebration of the Mass, our work in the following pages will help Catholics to gain a greater understanding of the prayers of the Mass and foster an intelligent participation in them.

This book is suitable for individuals, large groups, and classrooms. The Questions and Answers section in chapter 8 is designed to reinforce the principle points of each chapter and to shape the sacramental and ecclesial perspective necessary to understand as fully as possible the words of the Mass. But a word of proviso. While this book examines the Mass' texts in some detail, it does not offer an exhaustive treatment of any one text. In fact, the infinite Mystery of Christ made present during the Church's liturgy is incapable of being entirely grasped, at least in this life. Nevertheless, the sacramental approach and the mystagogical formation offered by *Mystical Body,*

Mystical Voice provides valuable training for those students of the Church's prayer, seminarians, and their teachers who desire to participate more fully in the sacramental liturgy and wish above all to hear and understand every text more clearly.

Finally, a note about the sources we used is in this book. The most fundamental texts are those of the Mass themselves, followed in close succession by the Sacred Scriptures that inform them. Next in order of importance, the guiding documents of the Magisterium are invoked as often as possible to demonstrate that the sacramental words of the Mass belong to the Church (of which we are a part), and that the voice of the Church at prayer is truly our "Mother's tongue." Among the documents we have used to unearth these sacramental words are the following: the Second Vatican Council's *Constitution on the Sacred Liturgy (Sacrosanctum concilium)*; the papal documents commemorating the *Constitution's* promulgation, on the 25th anniversary (*Vicesimus quintus annus*) and the 40th anniversary (*Spiritus et Sponsa*); and the curial documents on the proper implementation of the *Constitution*, on inculturation (*Varietates legitimae*) and on translation (*Liturgiam authenticam*). All of these documents form us and our language to be heavenly, suitable to sing with the angels now and, God willing, for all eternity. The historical information of the book is supplied by three of the modern era's best liturgical historians: Joseph Jungmann and his works *The Mass of the Roman Rite: Its Origins and Development* (1951) and *The Mass: An Historical, Theological, and Pastoral Survey* (1976); Johannes Emminghaus, *The Eucharist: Essence, Form, Celebration* (1978, revised 1997); and Robert Cabié, *The Eucharist* (1986). Since each of these works provides detailed development of the Roman Rite Mass, readers seeking further historical background on the development of the Mass through the centuries will benefit from reading any of these authors' works.

Finally, as stated above, the works of Cardinal Joseph Ratzinger contribute significantly to the liturgical theology presented in *Mystical Body, Mystical Voice*. The clearest and most original voice of the current liturgical movement—and it's no small significance that this same author is now Pope—Joseph Ratzinger provides insights particularly relevant to the reality of liturgical language. *The Feast of Faith: Approaches to a Theology of the Liturgy* (1986), *A New Song for the Lord: Faith in Christ and Liturgy Today* (1996), and *The Spirit of the Liturgy* (2000) present Christ in his inmost reality, the Logos of the Father, his Word, who gives meaning and purpose to all things. While as Incarnate as the Word made flesh, the liturgy of the Mass is also characterized by the Logos and celebrated "according to the Logos." The words of the Mass, in essence, belong to *the* Word, the Logos. Christ gives meaning to the liturgy's words, and by praying them with the Church we right our relationship to the Word and, through him, to the Father.

The Word was made flesh, dwelt among us, and showed us his glory. The same Word dwells among us today, in many forms. In a preeminent way Christ the Word is alive for us in the liturgy of the Church, especially in her Mystical Voice of prayer to the Father animated by the Holy Spirit. As we begin to attune our ears to this Mystical Voice, may the words of the Mass resonate in our hearts so that as the Word dwells among us today, we may dwell with him in the Eternal City to come.

Endnotes

1. See Joseph Ratzinger, *The Spirit of the Liturgy,* trans. John Saward (San Francisco: Ignatius Press, 2000), 183.

PART I

THE LITURGICAL PRIMER

Catholics today are the beneficiaries of more than a century's worth of work by the liturgical apostolate. Figures of the European liturgical movement, such as France's Prosper Guéranger (1805–1875), Belgium's Lambert Beauduin (1873–1960), and Germany's Romano Guardini (1885–1968), exposed the riches and beauty of the liturgy to the Church's members in a new and exciting way. Under the direction of the Magisterium, the liturgical apostolate focused on the active and intelligent participation of all in the Eucharistic celebration, on the Paschal Mystery and priesthood of Christ, and on the corporate nature of the Mystical Body of Christ. In the United States subsequent leaders, such as Virgil Michel (1883–1938), Martin Hellriegel (1891–1981), and Reynold Hillenbrand (1904–1979), applied the movement's goals in an immanently practical way, seeking to transform parish life and, by extension, the life of society as a whole.

Instaurare omnia in Christo ("To restore all things in Christ") was the motto of Pope St. Pius X, a liturgical promoter of the highest order, and one, consequently, that gave a degree of authority to the goals of the early liturgical movement. In 1903, the first year of his pontificate, he wrote the following on the liturgy and, for the first time in an ecclesiastic document, introduced the idea of "active participation":

> Filled as we are with a most ardent desire to see the true Christian spirit flourish in every respect and be preserved by all the faithful, we deem it necessary to provide before anything else for the sanctity and dignity of the temple, in which the faithful assemble for no other object than that of acquiring this spirit from its foremost and indispensable font, which is the active participation (*participatione attiva*) in the most holy mysteries and in the public and solemn prayer of the Church. (*Tra le sollecitudini*)

Sixty years later, the Second Vatican Council would approve its *Constitution on the Sacred Liturgy*, insisting that the "full and active participation (*participatio actuosa*) by all the people is the aim to be considered before all else" (SC, 14).

A generation after Pius X, Pope Pius XII further clarified the nature of the liturgy. Following his encyclical on the Mystical Body of Christ, *Mystici Corporis Christi*,[1] he devoted a second encyclical entirely to the liturgy, *Mediator Dei* (MD).[2] In it the Holy Father both cautions against "over-eager and novel practices" (MD, 8) and commends the initiatives of sound reformers (MD, 4–5). A number of the liturgical movement's themes find expression in *Mediator Dei's* articulation of the liturgy: "The sacred liturgy is the public worship which our Redeemer as Head of the Church renders to the Father, as well as the worship which the community of the faithful renders to its Founder, and through him to the heavenly Father. It is, in short, the worship rendered by the Mystical Body of Christ in the entirety of its Head and members" (MD, 20). Such an understanding of the liturgy was quite different from that held by many Catholics who at that time viewed "liturgy" as only outward ceremonial or as the rubrics governing the rite (MD, 25). Pius XII's encyclicals and liturgical reforms, such as the restoration of the Easter Vigil in 1951 and the entire Holy Week in 1955, helped all in the Church to see the liturgy afresh by leading Catholics to the heart of the Paschal Mystery.

The fruit of the early liturgical apostolate was realized in the *Constitution on the Sacred Liturgy (Sacrosanctum concilium)*. The liturgy, it says, echoing Pius XII, "is considered as an exercise of the priestly office of Jesus Christ. In the liturgy the sanctification of the man is sig- nified by signs perceptible to the senses, and is effected in a way which corresponds with each of these signs; in the liturgy the whole public worship is performed by the Mystical Body of Jesus Christ, that is, by the Head and his members" (SC, 7). Since the promulgation of the *Constitution on the Sacred Liturgy* in 1963, the Magisterium has produced five documents on its proper implementation, reflections on its 25th and 40th anniversaries, and completed the *Catechism of the Catholic Church*, which expounds the nature and celebration of the liturgy with great depth and beauty.

Despite the work of the early liturgical movement, the popes, the Second Vatican Council, and subsequent pastoral efforts in this arena, confusion still exists about the nature of the liturgy. To a 1985 plenary meeting of the Congregation for Divine Worship and the Discipline of the Sacraments, Pope John Paul II raised a number of questions:

> The liturgy! Everybody speaks about it, writes about it, and dis- cusses the subject. It has been commented on, it has been praised, and it has been criticized. But who really knows the principles and norms by which it is to be put into practice? The Constitution *Sacrosanctum Concilium* referred to the liturgy as the "source" and the "summit" of the Church's life; what is being done to make this sublime definition a reality?[3]

John Paul II, as Bishop and active participant at the Second Vatican Council, strove in his writings to promote a clearer understand- ing of the Church's liturgy. Drawing on insights from a phenomeno- logical and personalist philosophy, he constantly put before the Church the truth that our liturgical encounter is a *personal* one, a meet- ing between oneself and the Person of Jesus.

As a theological expert (*peritus*) at the Council and later as Prefect of the Congregation for the Doctrine of the Faith, Joseph Ratzinger wrote extensively on the nature of the liturgy and its place in the life of the Church. In *The Spirit of the Liturgy* he intends "to assist this renewal of understanding" of the liturgy, to offer "an aid to the understanding of the faith and to the right way to give the faith its central form of expression in the liturgy."[4] As the Roman Pontiff, he leads the Church and her members deeper into the mystery of our faith, which is Christ himself.

As the extensive writings of the liturgical movement and Magisterium attest, there are a number of insightful ways to look at the liturgy, and when taken together they help us to see what the Church herself sees in this reality. So, relying on the insights of the popes, the *Constitution on the Sacred Liturgy*, and the *Catechism of the Catholic Church*, let us refine our "mystagogical senses" and build a solid foundation upon which we can examine fruitfully the language of the liturgy. These magisterial and theological works provide a particularly acute vantage for "the renewal of our minds," so that we may "discern what is the will of God, what is good and pleasing and perfect" in our spiritual worship (Romans 12:1–2).

Endnotes

1. AAS, 35 (1943).

2. AAS, 39 (1947).

3. In Denis Crouan, *The History and the Future of the Roman Liturgy* (San Francisco: Ignatius Press, 2005), 15.

4. Joseph Ratzinger, *The Spirit of the Liturgy,* trans. John Saward (San Francisco: Ignatius Press, 2000), 8.

Chapter 1

A Logical Look at the Liturgy

The only way we can be saved from succumbing to the inflation of words
is if we have the courage to face silence and in it learn to listen afresh to the
Word. Otherwise we shall be overwhelmed by "mere words" at the very
point where we should be encountering the Word, the Logos, the Word of
love, crucified and risen, who brings us life and joy.[1]

Joseph Ratzinger

Where does one begin to look at the liturgy? The Code of Canon Law? The rubrics of the rite? The assembly and priest? The historical precedent? All are all possible starting points. But, like most answers to Catholic questions, we will start—and end—with Christ himself, who is *the* beginning and end, the Alpha and Omega.

Christ is the Logos, the Word of the Father. Our look at the liturgy is therefore a *Logical* one, in the sense that it is centered on the Logos. Since a principal aim of this book is to examine the texts of the Mass, it will be beneficial to begin with the ultimate meaning of all liturgical words, the Word of the Trinity.

Theology of the Trinity: "God Himself Is Speech"[2]

The mystery of the Most Holy Trinity is the central mystery of the faith, the "source of all the other mysteries of faith, [and] the light that enlightens them" (CCC, 234). The same is true in our present consideration of the liturgy and its language, for the Trinitarian mystery explains and contextualizes the liturgical mystery, shedding light upon the liturgy's essential meaning.

What is the Trinity? God. *Who* is the Trinity? Father, Son, and Holy Spirit. "It is the Father who generates, the Son who is begotten, and the Holy Spirit who proceeds."[3] This foundational mystery of the three Persons in one

God is "dialogical."[4] According to its etymology, *dialogue* means "to speak" (*logein*) "across" (*dia*). God the Father "speaks of himself," has a knowledge of himself, and this speaking and knowing is called his idea, thought, or word: *Logos*.

Unlike the idea that I have of myself, the Logos of God is perfect, complete. When I think of myself—who I am and what I am like—I find that the image never quite matches the reality. In some instances, the idea of myself can be seriously flawed (if I thought I was George Washington or Saint Michael the Archangel, for example). But even if my mind and other faculties *are* functioning perfectly, my mind's image will never be identical to my actual existence. As Walker Percy remarks, the stranger who passes me by in the street has a view of me that I am incapable of having (this is why, he suggests, the first person I look for in a group photo is myself).[5] The infinite God, however, is not limited as I am. The image that the Father generates of himself is perfect, lacking nothing of his own being. Since God has an idea of himself, "this idea must be totally adequate, in no way less than the Being of which it is the Idea, lacking nothing that the being has. The Idea must contain all the perfection of the Being of which it is the Idea. There can be nothing in the Thinker that is not in His Thought of Himself, otherwise the Thinker would be thinking of Himself inadequately, which is impossible for the Infinite."[6] In short, the identity of the Son with the Father, the Word with the Speaker, is so perfect that the only distinction between them is their "relations of origin" (CCC, 254), the Son "born of the Father before all ages."[7]

The third Person of the Trinity is the Holy Spirit, "who proceeds from the Father and the Son."[8] Here again, the loving relationship between the Father and the Son is unique to the Godhead. True love is something totally given over to the other, so that the one loving holds nothing back. When total love is mutual, it is perfect. Yet in human loving there is often self-interest, where the love expressed does not contain the whole of the lover. Even when human love *is* total and genuine—as between a loving married couple (e.g., Blessed Zelie and Louis Martin, parents of Thérèse of Lisieux) or the willing sacrificial death of one for another (e.g., Saint Maximilian Kolbe for Auschwitz prisoner Franciszek Gajowniczek)—the relation between the two persons remains disparate, for it is impossible to give everything to the other. The husband and wife of the holiest marriage, giving themselves totally to one another, remain individuals who continue to possess themselves and not wholly the other; so, also, in the self-sacrifice of the martyr. While the bond of true love unites two persons, each continues to remain distinctive. With God, the Love that exists between the Father and the Son is so real and perfect—the Father giving all to the Son and the Son returning all to the Father—that another Person, the Holy Spirit, is breathed or "spirated" from them both. In short: "The Father is that which the Son is, the Son that which the Father is, the Father and the Son that which the Holy Spirit is, i.e., by nature one God"; while, at the same time, "he is not the Father who is the Son, nor is the Son he who is the Father, nor is the Holy Spirit he who is the Father or the Son."[9] An alternate formulation of trinitarian faith sees the Breath, which is the Spirit, and the Word, which is the Son, uniting in an eternal hymn of praise to the Father.[10]

Before looking to the Trinity's special significance for the liturgy and its language, two observations are in order. First, the Son's very identity is Word or Logos. Partly because of the limitations of our minds in the face of such a mystery, and partly because of Christ's own mission, we ascribe to the Son various names: Jesus, Christ, Redeemer, Temple, Good Shepherd. Yet each of these titles—true as they are—*describe* Christ, especially as he carries out God's plan in time. But to call the Second Person of the Trinity the *Word* is to speak to his identity within the Trinity. Second, the Word who is Christ differs significantly from the ordinary words that we speak. He is not literally a word like those we use to speak to one another. His identity as the Logos is not therefore analogous to our words, except from our own perspective. The Son of God is Word in the truest sense, fully identical to the Meaning of all things, while our own words are approximations of the eternal Word. This relationship is similar to that signified by his title as Son: I, too, am a son, but not a son like *the* Son. And to say that the Sonship of the Second Person of the Trinity is different from the sonship I have in relation to my natural father is not to lessen his Sonship in the comparison, but, on the contrary, to see how my own is a likeness to his. In short, *God* is the standard, *we* are the analogy. Similarly, the Logos is not a word similar to human words, but our words are like the primordial and fundamental Word of God.

The Logos-character of the Trinity is particularly meaningful for the liturgy, for just as the Word is an essential part of the Trinity, so too is the Word the essence of the liturgy and its prayer. "Only because there is already speech, 'Logos,' in God can there be speech, 'Logos,' to God. Philosophically we could put it like this: the Logos in God is the onto-*logical* foundation for prayer."[11] In other words, we can speak to God and listen to God because "God himself is speech, word. His nature is to speak, to hear, to reply . . . ."[12] Consequently, when we participate in the liturgy, we not only share in Christ's "dialogue with God," but "we can share in the dialogue which God *is*."[13] The Logical character of the Trinity is the character of the Church's liturgy. The "Logical" is also, as we shall see next, the character of the entire economy of salvation, the Church herself, and the Christian life.

Creation and the Fall: God Speaks, but Man Does Not Listen

In *The Acting Person: A Contribution to Phenomenological Anthropology*,[14] Karol Wojtyla ties human anthropology to human action: a man *is* how he acts and *acts* according to who he is. In a similar way, the actions of God in the world reveal something of his innermost being, while God's Trinitarian nature enlightens for us his actions in the world. Accordingly, the Church's Tradition speaks of *theology* when referring to the life of the Trinity in itself, and *economy* when considering God's creation from himself and his governance of the cosmos back to himself (see CCC, 236). *Logically* speaking, this means that the dialogical character of the Trinity is expressed in God's work of creating and redeeming.

Saint John the Evangelist begins his Gospel account this way: "In the beginning was the Word, and the Word was with God, and the Word was God . . . . All things came to be through him, and without him nothing came to be" (John 1:1, 3). The Father's Logos "is a voice which entered the scene at the very beginning of creation, when it tore through the silence of nothingness."[15] The Word that is spoken eternally by the Father within the Trinity is now spoken by the Father at the beginning of time; the uncreated Word of the Trinity is the creative Word of the cosmos; and the dia-*logical* character of the communion of divine persons is the logical source of the unity of creation and creator. "In the beginning . . . , God *said*, 'Let there be light,' and there was light" (Genesis 1:1, 3, emphasis added). Together with "the mighty wind [that] swept over the waters" (Genesis 1:2), the Son and the Holy Spirit are considered the Father's "creating hands"[16] and his divine "artisans."[17]

In addition to *how* God created all things—that is, through his Logos— the Church's catechesis on creation also teaches us *why* God created. "Scripture and Tradition," the *Catechism of the Catholic Church* says, "never cease to teach and celebrate this fundamental truth: 'The world was made for the glory of God'" (CCC, 293). Closely related to this purpose of the creation—the glory of God—is another; namely, the sanctification of human beings and, with them, all of creation. What does it mean that God creates for his own glory? Citing Saint Bonaventure, the *Catechism* explains that "God created all things 'not to increase his glory, but to show it forth and to communicate it'" (CCC, 293). In other words, God's glory does not consist of his accruing praise, worship, and glory to himself—since he needs none of these—but, rather, in bestowing, sharing, and manifesting his goodness to us. God's glory and our sanctification are so closely related that we might say they are two sides of the same coin, for if we wish to glorify God to the best of our ability, we need to become saints. At the same time, if we wish to become saints, we must glorify God in all that we do. Saint Augustine, speaking of the life of prayer, captures this reciprocal relationship when he says that "God thirsts for us so that we might thirst for him" (see CCC, 2560). Or again, following the beautiful phrase of Saint Irenaeus, "The glory of God is man fully alive; moreover man's life is the vision of God."[18] In short: God is glorified in his creation, and creation is divinized in its God.

Liturgy reflects these truths of creation. As the Logos is at the center of natural creation, so too is he the source of the new creation found in the liturgy. Worship, Saint Paul writes to the Romans, is *Logical: logikē latreía* (12:1). The words of the liturgy are also Logical, that is, they express *the* Word. Also, just as the purpose of creation is the glory of God through the sanctification of his people, the purpose of the liturgy and its language strives ultimately to glorify and sanctify. In short, we speak according to the Logos, and we do so to become saints unto the glory of God.

Because Adam spoke with God and listened to him, he was destined to be "fully 'divinized' by God in glory" (CCC, 398). God told Adam, for example, how to live according to the divine economy: "You are free to eat from any of the trees of the garden except the tree of knowledge of good and bad. From that tree you shall not eat; the moment you eat from it you are surely doomed to die" (Genesis 2:16–17). *Economy* means literally "the management of a household," and when applied to the divine plan, it includes the creation of all things by God (what the Tradition calls the *exitus*) and the return of all things back to God according to his design (called the *reditus*). God's commands to Adam and Eve are, in other words, his appeal to "listen to my plan for you and for all of creation." When all was working "according to plan," there existed order, peace, harmony, and beauty in the cosmos. Such harmony, order, and beauty existed even between and within man and woman. As long as Adam and Eve listened to God with their intellects and wills, their bodies and all of their desires listened to them. The word used to describe such *listening*, whether of man to God or man's body to his soul, is *obedience*, from the Latin *ob-audire*, "to hear" or "listen to" (see CCC, 144). As long as Adam was obedient to God's voice, Original Justice reigned.

And yet we know that Adam's freedom and willingness to follow God were tested; the original harmony fell into discord. Rather than choosing God's plan, Adam designed his own. "[H]e wanted to 'be like God,' but 'without God, before God, and not in accordance with God.'"[19] Adam did indeed want what was best: "to be like God." What greater thing, in his condition of original holiness, would he have fallen for? The problem was that he wanted to follow his own economy to achieve it. He stopped obeying God's voice and started listening to his own. He rejected the Lord's will to embrace his self-styled will. He quit thirsting for God and drowned his thirst in his own way of doing things. Adam rejects the *reditus*.

> But everything is bound up with freedom, and the creature has the freedom to turn the positive *exitus* of its creation around, as it were, to rupture it in the Fall: this is the refusal to be dependent, saying No to the *reditus*. Love is seen as dependence and is rejected. In its place come autonomy and autarchy: existing from oneself and in oneself, being a god of one's own making.[20]

This original sin is the reason why Christ came as our redeemer.[21] Wounded by sin, man is no longer able to accomplish the *reditus*, to choose or to return to the Creator with his whole being. No longer following the path of God, man now follows his own way, a way which terminates in dead-ends. What must happen in order for Adam and his race to reunite with God? Someone must come who has the power to say "yes" to the *reditus*, to thirst again entirely for the divine, to seek God's glory by following the Godhead's own economy. This person is the Word of God himself.

The dynamic of language—in its speaking and its hearing—is at the core of Adam's (and thus our) creation and fall. Man is created by the *Logos*, in his image and likeness. God *tells* him how to follow the divine economy and live. As long as Adam *listens* to God, *harmony*—"the concord of sounds"—reigns in all his relations. When he stops listening to God, when he *says* "no" to the divine plan, man disrupts the original dia-*logue*. This dialogue with God then devolves into mono-*logue*, a redundant monotony of man talking to himself. This same dynamic of language will be key to the plan of Christ's saving and restoring humanity to God.

The Old Covenant: Learning to Listen

The account of the Fall in Genesis includes a first indication that God will send a redeemer: "He will strike at your head" (3:15). And as the Fall consisted in Adam's disobedience to God's revealed plan, so redemption will be won by a second Adam's perfect obedience—that is, his *listening*—to God's will. The time of the Old Covenant thus becomes a time of *learning to listen*; a time of preparation for the coming of a man who will listen and respond with a "yes" to the *reditus;* a time of breaking the monologue and reestablishing a dialogue.

But why, it has been asked, did the Father wait so long to send the Word as our Redeemer? While he did promise a Redeemer who would crush the head of the serpent, could he have not done so immediately? The answer may be that in the course of salvation history until the time of Christ's coming we were simply not ready yet to receive him. If the Redeemer was to be that same Word which the Father spoke at the creation, then his reception would require "listening," "hearing," and "being obedient to." The age of the promises, of covenants, then, was a time to prepare humanity to receive the Word of God, to listen clearly this time and, unlike Adam, to respond with fidelity. When God speaks again, he wants us to hear properly. To do this, the Father shapes and "shakes our hearts"[22] both *by* and *for* the Word.

Part of the Chosen People's preparation for the redeeming Word comes through the mouths of the prophets. The voice of God is a key component to the covenantal relationship between God and his people. The prophets call out to God's household when it strays from his divine economy. In doing so they herald the fullness of the divine plan in the Messiah. Authorized by God to speak on his behalf, the prophets are essential to the biblical and redemptive dialogue, which is then completed in man's affirmative response.

Another essential aspect of human training to receive God's only Son, one closely related to the work of the prophets, is found in the sacrificial system of the Old Covenant. We find Cain and Abel giving sacrifice, as well as Noah, Melchizedek, and Abraham. As a part of the covenant made through Moses at Mt. Sinai, God prescribes in great detail the ways sacrifices are to be offered, especially the Paschal Sacrifice marking the liberation from slavery in Egypt. Like prophetic voices calling man back to union with God, the sacrifices of the covenant seek the same goal. This union with the divine, while at the core of sacrifice, often is either misunderstood or forgotten altogether.

What *is* sacrifice? Many think of sacrifice as something essentially painful and therefore to be avoided. In this vein we ask one another prior to the season of Lent, "What are you *giving up* this year?" and it is often the smaller sacrifices that we choose. While it is not entirely untrue to think of sacrifice in this light, to consider only these negative aspects keeps us from understanding the essence of sacrifice rightly. True and authentic sacrifice looks very different:

> It consists—according to the Fathers, in fidelity to biblical thought—in the union of man and creation with God. Belonging to God has nothing to do with destruction or non-being; rather, it is a way of being. It means emerging from the state of separation, of apparent autonomy, of existing only for oneself and in oneself. It means losing oneself as the only possible way of finding oneself (cf. Mark 8:35; Matthew 10:39). That is why Saint Augustine could say that the true "sacrifice" is the *civitas Dei*, that is, love-transformed mankind, the divinization of creation and the surrender of all things to God: God all in all (cf. 1 Corinthians 15:28). That is the purpose of the world. That is the essence of sacrifice and worship.[23]

True sacrifice is "union with God," "love-transformed mankind," and "divinization." It is, if you will, the flip-side of all the apparent negative aspects of sacrifice. It is not that pain and suffering having nothing to do with sacrifice; it's that they are not the heart of sacrifice.

Such an understanding is necessary to appreciate the sacrificial practices of the covenant and, ultimately, Christ's own sacrifice. It also helps clarify the pointed words of the prophets surrounding many of the sacrifices of the time. "Obedience is better than sacrifice," says Samuel (1 Samuel 15:22). "For it is love that I desire, not sacrifice," Hosea proclaims (6:6). "Do I eat the flesh of bulls or drink the blood of goats?" queries the psalmist. "Offer praise as your sacrifice to God" (Psalm 50:13–14). Does the God who first prescribed sacrifice as a part of the covenant relationship at the same time not wish them? What lies behind the "prophetic disquiet and questioning"[24] is the misunderstanding of sacrifice, the gift that is sacrificed, and the requirements made on the person who offers it.

The history of man and his religion is the story of his efforts to reunite himself with the divine. To bring about the reunion, man offers a gift to the gods, but in the end realizes that nothing less than the gift of himself will suffice. And insofar as man is not usually willing to offer his complete self to the deity, he searches to find a gift, an offering, a sacrifice that "represents" himself. A true representative gift is one in which the giver is in some way present in his gift; in this way the gift truly represents man in his attempt to give himself to God. Not all gifts, however, can be classified in this way, for in some gifts man is *not* present in the offering. These gifts are called by Cardinal Ratzinger "replacement gifts," where the offerer is not present in his gift, even though on the surface he believes himself to be.[25] The distinction, then, is this: the "representative sacrifice" truly symbolizes man's genuine and heartfelt desire to give himself over, to unite himself to God, to divinize himself: in a word, to "sacrifice." The "replacement sacrifice," on the contrary, is a mere empty sign or gesture of man's supposed desire for reunion; the replacement sacrifice is a replacement of man, and "worship with replacements turns out to be a replacement for worship. Somehow the real thing is missing."[26] It is these latter sacrifices that the prophets seek to correct.

God's intervention in salvation history is a movement following his own economy toward true and authentic sacrificial representation. What had made sacrifices in Israel unique is not only that they were offered to the one, true God, but also that the offerings approached true representation. What, after all, could be a more genuine representation and symbol of the giver than his very own son? With Abraham's sacrifice of Isaac, and later of Israel's sacrifice of its firstborn sons—both of which are represented, at God's own command, by a lamb—God sets Israel on a trajectory toward truly representational sacrifice and, consequently, true and authentic worship, which is the right way to relate to God.[27]

Like the Trinity, the creation, and the Fall, the period of the Old Testament is *Logical*. The prophets speak in accord with the Logos of God and call the household of Israel back to himself. The sacrifices offered represent the core of man's own being, symbolized in the lamb who takes the place of the firstborn son. The covenant's prophetic voice and priestly sacrifice look forward to the *Sacrifice* of the *Word* in the person of Jesus. But until his coming, the prophets and the ritual sacrifices prepare God's household to receive his Logos and finally, this time, to "listen to him" (Mark 9:7; Luke 9:35).

The Incarnation and Paschal Sacrifice[28]

We have seen that the dialogue of love that is the Trinity desired to express and share its own being and goodness. It accomplished this through the Logos in the creation of the universe. Despite human sin, the dialogue between God and man continued in partial ways (Hebrews 1:1). In "the fullness of time" (Galatians 4:3), when men and women were open and prepared to hear the divine message, God spoke again: "And the Logos became flesh" (John 1:14). With the Incarnation, the same eternal Logos (of the Trinity, of creation, and of salvation history) speaks again, now in the flesh, with the sound of a human voice. At the Incarnation, creation echoed the words of long-suffering Job: "I had heard of you by word of mouth, but now my eye has seen you." (Job 42:5).[29] Christianity is, then, not simply a spiritual and word-based religion, but also and essentially a bodily and incarnate one, both dimensions united completely and perfectly together after the model of Christ himself.[30]

Jesus Christ, the *Logos incarnatus*,[31] is a Word unlike any other. In human speech, words are formed of the air, in the mouth; they flee as soon as they pass the lips. Shakespeare's Falstaff asks of the word *honor*: "What is honor? A word. What is in that word honor? What is that honor? Air. A trim reckoning!" (Falstaff, in *Henry IV*, Part I, Act 5, Scene 1) Christ the Word, on the contrary, is not a "mere scutcheon" or mere symbol, but is a Word that does not pass away. The Logos of the dia-*logue* between God and men is a Person, substantial and abiding. He is nothing less than the "dialogue of grace."[32]

Saint Augustine pointed this out in comparing the voice of John the Baptist to Christ:

> The Lord *is the Word who was in the beginning*. John is the voice that lasts for a time; from the beginning Christ is the Word who lives for ever. Take away the word, the meaning, and what is the voice? Where there is no understanding, there is only a meaningless sound. The voice without the word strikes the ear but does not build up the heart.[33]

The dialogue of grace, now restored in Christ, "incarnate of the Virgin Mary,"[34] restores and perfects the initial dialogue interrupted by human refusal to listen. In taking on our nature, Christ elevates it and allows us to rejoin the dialogue with the Trinity: "God became man so that man might become God."[35] Another way to speak of the Incarnation, this time in an explicitly *Logical* way, can be found in *The Feast of Faith*: "he who is speech, Word, Logos, in God and to God, participates in human speech. This has a reciprocal effect, involving man in God's own internal speech. Or we could say that man is able to participate in the dialogue within God himself because God has first shared in human speech and has thus brought the two into communication with one another."[36]

We might say, therefore, that Christ is not only the *Logos incarnatus*, but the *Dia-logos incarnatus,* for in addition to being the eternal voice of the Father to men, he is also the voice of men to the Father. Because Jesus shares completely in both natures, only he can *represent* perfectly and authentically both sides of the dialogue, the "speaking across" the abyss that divides them. As God, his clear voice loses nothing in its delivery to us; as man, he listens obediently and unreservedly to the Father. The responding voice from men to the Father completes and restores the dialogue: as man, Christ speaks and sings the hymn of perfect praise to the Father; as God, his voice is heard in the dialogue of the Trinity. Man is thus freed from his self-centered monologue and is opened up in a new way to the Father. Representing man, Jesus says "yes to the *reditus*," yes to union with God, and yes to divinization.

Jesus "says" all of these things throughout his life, for he is the dialogue of God and men in the flesh. Nevertheless, it is in the obedience of the Paschal Sacrifice that his "yes" resounds most clearly and articulately. When the first Adam sins by "not listening" to the Father's voice, the Second Adam redeems by listening perfectly to the Father's voice: "by whose obedience we have been restored to those gifts of yours that by sinning we had lost in disobedience."[37] The Paschal Mystery of Christ—his suffering, death, Resurrection, and Ascension—is the longed-for response of love from man to God because it is the total return of self to the Creator.

What pleased the Father about Christ's sacrifice on the cross? What was it about the Paschal Mystery that satisfied God and won our salvation? "According to the Fathers, in fidelity to biblical thought,"[38] and contrary to the common view, what pleased God most in the sacrifice of Christ was not primarily his suffering, his precious blood, his physical, mental, and spiritual agonies, but the love he had for the Father, the thirst for him, and the union of wills of which all of his Son's passion is the perfect expression. It is not that Christ's agonies are by any means inconsequential; rather, what is more important is the interior union of wills with the Father.[39] If the first Adam said that he would not listen, would be disobedient, the second Adam is obedient and does listen to the Father's will. We chose our own economy, our own plan, instead of the Father's. Christ, by contrast, chose not his own will but his Father's. Although "he was in the form of God, [he] did not regard equality with God something to be grasped. Rather, he emptied himself, taking the form of a slave . . . " (Philippians 2:6–7). When we stopped thirsting for God, Christ came to be thirsty on our behalf. The act of contrition recognizes these two dimensions of sacrifice: We are sorry for our sins not simply because of the demands of justice ("the loss of heaven and the pains of hell"), but principally because they symbolize deficiencies in our love for Love itself ("but most of all because they offend you who are all good and worthy of all my love").

In the Incarnation our *Logical* look at the liturgy finds its core. The salvific work of Christ, like all else before and after it, is Word-based.

> The shepherd who rescues [man] and takes him home is the Logos himself, the eternal Word, the eternal Meaning of the universe dwelling in the Son. He it is who makes his way to us and takes the sheep onto his shoulders, that is, he assumes human nature, and as the God-Man he carries man the creature home to God. And so the *reditus* is possible. Man is given a homecoming.[40]

The Church and the Liturgy: Becoming One with the Logos

Jesus Christ, the *Logos incarnatus*, reunites us with the Father in the Paschal Sacrifice of the cross. Sacrifice is not the destruction of being but is "a way of being . . . : love-transformed mankind, the divinization of creation and the surrender of all things to God."[41] The essence of the "Logical Sacrifice" is Christ's obedient "yes" to the will of the Father, which reverses the *non serviam* (I will not serve) of the disobedient. While his victory is won, what remains to be realized is man's own identification with the Logos in his perfect response to the Father, which today takes place in the Church.

The restoration of the dialogical relationship of God and man, at one time actualized in the Incarnate Logos, lives now in his Mystical Body.

> This structure of Word and response, which is essential to the liturgy, is modeled on the basic structure of the process of divine revelation, in which the Word and response, the speech of God and the receptive hearing of the Bride, the Church, go together . . . God, the Revealer, did not want to stay as *solus Deus, solus Christus* (God alone, Christ alone). No, he wanted to create a Body for himself, to find a Bride—he sought a response. It was really for her that the Word went forth.[42]

Now, as he is seated in glory at the Father's right hand, Christ continues his saving work in and with his Bride and Mystical Body, the Church (see CCC, 1076).

To the question "Who Celebrates the Liturgy?" the *Catechism* identifies three categories of persons: the Trinity, the heavenly participants, and earthly participants of the sacramental liturgy (nos. 1137–1144). According to the visions of Isaiah, Ezekiel, and John, heaven is centered around a throne, upon which sits the Lord God (Ezekiel 1:26–28; Isaiah 6:1; Revelation 4:2). A slain Lamb also occupies the throne (Revelation 5:4), and flowing from both, the throne and the Lamb, is a "river of life-giving water" (Revelation 22:1). The Father, Son, and Holy Spirit are the liturgy's principal actors. We enter into their work when we, God's people, participate in the liturgy. Around the Persons of the Trinity, the book of Revelation identifies the liturgy's heavenly participants, those standing before the throne and worshipping God face to face: heavenly powers, four living beings, twenty-four elders, a woman, and a countless multitude. It is in this heavenly and eternal liturgy that the Church's earthly members join through the mediation of the sacraments.

Christ is called the liturgist (*leitourgos*) and his work, liturgical (see Hebrews 8:2, 6) because he performs a work—his sacrificial "yes" to the Father—in the name of and on behalf of his people (*pro populo*). His Church is likewise *leitourgos* (CCC, 1144), for through Christ she continues the restored dialogue of grace with the Father on behalf of her members and the entire world. The liturgy's heavenly participants are described as "recapitulated in Christ" (CCC, 1138), more literally, "re-headed" in Christ. They have, by cooperating with his grace, earned a permanent place under his headship. Christ is, for them as well as for us, the Head. Gathered under him, the Church exists as his own Mystical Body: he the Head, we the members.

The image of the Church as the Mystical Body of Christ comes to us from Saint Paul's First Letter to the Corinthians: "As a body is one though it has many parts, and all the parts of the body, though many, are one body, so also Christ. [. . .] Now you are Christ's body, and individually parts of it" (1 Corinthians 12:12–14, 27). The Body, like any body, takes its direction from the Head. And as Christ worked as prophet, priest, and king (what the Tradition calls the *munera Christi*, the offices of Christ) for the glory of God and the sanctification of creation, so also does the Mystical Body carry on with him his prophetic, priestly, and kingly *ergon* (work) for the salvation of the *laos* (people) unto God's greater glory. She, the Church, imitates her head in her activities—proclaiming the Good News of salvation, continually offering Christ's Paschal Sacrifice in the liturgy, and leading by serving the needs of all—yet, after the example of her Head, she speaks most clearly and effectively in her priestly work, where Christ's Paschal Sacrifice of praise is made present and active.

In her sacramental liturgy, particularly the Eucharist, Christ's sacrificial "yes" to the *reditus* and to God's will is made present: "Christ transformed his death into a verbal form."[43] In other words, the "eucharistic canon is a sacrifice in the form of the word."[44] And because the Eucharistic prayer is the re-presentation of Christ's sacrifice, it is the occasion for the Church to make it her own, her opportunity to join in the dialogue, to say "yes" along with him to the Father: "The Eucharistic prayer is an entering-in to the prayer of Jesus Christ himself; hence it is the Church's entering-in to the Logos, the Father's Word, into the Logos' self-surrender to the Father, which, in the Cross, has also become the surrender of mankind to him."[45]

The "Logical Sacrifice" of Christ now becomes the "Logical worship" of the Mystical Body. As Head of his Mystical Body, the Logos is the Mystical Voice, speaking on behalf of God to man and on behalf of man to God in the restored dialogue of "love-transformed mankind." All that the Mystical Body says and does is "in accord with the Logos," be it in the exercise of her prophetic office, her priestly office, or her kingly office. The Mystical Body's priestly activity in worship is particularly Logical. Her calendar, sacred music, and churches are all established "in accord with the Logos."[46] In a sacramental approach to the texts of the Mass, we notice that the Church *speaks* in accord with the Logos, and we, members of the Mystical Body, speak with her and, in so doing, are divinized after the image of the Logos.

Liturgical Participation: "Logifying Our Existence"[47]

The Mystical Body's liturgy sacramentalizes—which is to say makes present and active—the Paschal Sacrifice of the Logos. In the liturgy, the Mystical Body joins with Christ and speaks the Mystical Voice of praise and adoration to the Father. The Church's "worship in accord with the Logos" is the opportunity for members of the Body to unite themselves to the Logos, to, in the expression of Cardinal Ratzinger, "logify our existence"[48]: "we must still pray for [the Sacrifice of the Logos] to become *our* sacrifice, that we ourselves, as we said, may be transformed into the Logos, conformed to the Logos, and so be made the true Body of Christ."[49]

To "logify" is to become fully united to the Son in his union with the Father. The idea is expressed in the Letter of Saint Paul to the Romans: "I urge you therefore, brothers, by the mercies of God, to offer your bodies as a living sacrifice, holy and pleasing to God, your spiritual worship [*logikē latreia*]. Do not conform yourselves to this age but be transformed by the renewal of your mind, that you may discern what is the will of God, what is good and pleasing and perfect" (Romans 12:1–2). *Logikē latreia* here expresses the new reality of Christian worship established at the Incarnation of the Logos: after Christ, who is both Word and flesh, we are to worship according to the word and the flesh ("spirit, soul, and body" [1 Thessalonians 5:23]), identifying with Christ in mind and body. Following Christ (the fundamental *Logos incarnatus*) as members of his Mystical Body, we are to become *logoi incarnati*.

The primary and indispensable source of "logification" is our full, conscious, and active participation in the liturgy, especially the Eucharist.[50] Here we "ask that the Logos, Christ, who *is* the true sacrifice, may himself draw us into his act of sacrifice, may 'logify' us, make us 'more consistent with the word,' 'more truly rational,' so that his sacrifice may become ours and may be accepted by God as ours . . . ."[51] In the Church, especially at her liturgy, heaven joins earth, the invisible becomes visible, and the symbolic is the real (sign and reality). The ultimate purpose of this meeting of above and below, however, is the divinization of the created, the perfection of the fallen, and the consummation of restored communion. Pope Benedict XVI invokes Saint Augustine on this point, recounting his transformative dialogue with the Eucharistic Christ: "I am the food of grown men; grow, and you shall feed upon me; nor shall you change me, like the food of your flesh, into yourself, but you shall be changed into me" (SCar, 70). The liturgy makes us more fully human, precisely because it restores our likeness to God lost at the Fall, and transforms us according to the Logos, our ultimate goal.

Following our liturgical and sacramental identification with the Logos, we are impelled to "be transformed" in every aspect of our existence: "The Apostle's insistence on the offering of our bodies emphasizes the concrete human reality of a worship which is anything but disincarnate" (SCar, 70). The liturgical life, one lived according to the Logos, spends most of its time outside the walls of the church building and on "the front lines" of society and culture, as Pius XII says (see CCC, 899). Here we see also the liturgy's place in the "New Evangelization." As evidenced in the scriptures, evangelization always begins with an encounter with the living Christ, is followed by a *metanoia* or turning toward him and away from sin, and then the seemingly irrepressible desire to announce to the world the Good News. The New Evangelization promoted so energetically by Pope John Paul II is likewise founded upon a *new* encounter with Christ (most especially in the Eucharistic liturgy), a subsequent return to him, and the urgent desire to evangelize in the world.

The place of the Logos in our liturgical participation is paramount. To identify with the Paschal Sacrifice of the Logos made present in the sacraments is to hear the Father's clear voice, to listen perfectly to it, and to return a "yes" in concert with the Mystical Voice of Christ and his Church. Liturgical participation is therefore a listening and a speaking. Particular words sacramentalize the Word, so that our literal speaking is also a real participation in the Voice of Christ and his Church. There is a natural and supernatural affinity between the sacramental word on the one hand, and the Mystical Word on the other. Consequently, just as Christ is a particular Word who says a definite "yes" in a truly remarkable way, so too are liturgical words to say definite things in precise ways. The Son of God is not "just any old word," but the Logos of the Father; so too the sacramental words seeking to convey the Word must have a particular tenor, voice, and precision. While a rose, by any other name, would smell as sweet, the Logos of God, in many other words, would not sound as clear.

> Particular words sacramentalize the Word . . .

Because liturgical participation requires a hearing and a speaking, liturgical formation—like that of the Chosen People—is learning to hear the Word and learning to speak with the Word. In the process of this type of liturgical formation,

> . . . the language of our Mother becomes ours; we learn to speak it along with her, so that, gradually, her words on our lips become our words. We are given an anticipatory share in the Church's perennial dialogue of love with him who desired to be one flesh with her, and this gift is transformed into the gift of speech. And it is in the gift of speech, and not until then, that I am really restored to my true self; only thus am I given back to God, handed over by him to all my fellow men; only thus am I free.[52]

In short, the language that we use during the liturgy is the Mystical Voice of the Mystical Body, a "hymn of praise that is sung through all the ages in the heavenly places . . . brought by the High Priest, Christ Jesus, into the land of exile . . . " (Paul VI, *Laudis canticum*). This Voice is for us the means to divinization and union with God, and the instrument by which we hope to enter that divine dialogue of love, the Trinity.

Summary

There are, we said at the start, a number of ways to approach the liturgy in order to deepen our understanding of it. Based in large part on the writing of Joseph Ratzinger, now Pope Benedict XVI, we have looked at the liturgy from a particular angle, Christ as the Word of the Father. Here summarizes our "Logical Look at the Liturgy"—or, more accurately, our logical *listen* to the Liturgy:

> . . . the language that we use during the liturgy is the Mystical Voice of the Mystical Body . . .

- God himself is speech, a dialogue.
- God creates by his Word, and man sins by not listening to God's Word.
- The time of the Old Covenant prepares men and women, through the covenants with Israel, to listen once again to the Word of God.
- At the Incarnation, God speaks his Logos into the world. The redemption is Christ's perfect "yes" back to the Father from the cross.
- Christ associates his Mystical Body, the Church, in his dia-*logue* with the Father.
- Christians *logify* their existence by uniting themselves with the Logos in the Mystical Body. Together, Christ, the Church, and Christians speak the Mystical Voice of praise to the Father.

This Logos approach is singularly meaningful for our current task of understanding the words of *The Roman Missal* since the words of our sacramental celebrations approximate the very Word which is Christ himself. Ritual and sacramental language, to put it another way, should be consonant, harmonious, and corresponding with the Logos, for such language is, in truth, the Mystical Voice of the Mystical Body, of which Christ is the Head and spokesman. In the next chapter, we will consider how the liturgical reality is made present and active to us in the Church by way of sacramental signs and symbols (chapter 2). Then, before turning to the actual texts of *The Roman Missal*, we will examine how words in particular serve as sacramental signs of Christ and allow us to participate in his eternal dialogue in the Trinity (chapter 3).

Endnotes

1. Joseph Ratzinger, *The Feast of Faith: Approaches to a Theology of the Liturgy*, trans. Graham Harrison (San Francisco: Ignatius Press, 1986), 73.

2. Ratzinger, *The Feast of Faith*, 25.

3. CCC, 254, see Fourth Lateran Council (1215), DS 804.

4. Ratzinger, *The Feast of Faith*, 25.

5. Walker Percy, *Signposts in a Strange Land* (New York: Noonday, 1992), 127, 136.

6. Frank Sheed, *Theology and Sanity* (San Francisco: Ignatius Press, 1993), 61.

7. Niceno-Constantinopolitan Creed, *Missale Romanum*, third typical edition.

8. See CCC, 246 for a fuller discussion on the *filioque*.

9. CCC, 253–4; see Council of Toledo XI (675), DS 530:26.

10. Ratzinger, *The Spirit of the Liturgy*, 140.

11. Ratzinger, *The Feast of Faith*, 25.

12. Ibid.

13. Ratzinger, *The Feast of Faith*, 26.

14. Karol Wojtyla, *The Acting Person: A Contribution to Phenomenological Anthropology (Analecta Husserliana)* (Boston: D. Reidel Publishing Company, 1979).

15. XII Ordinary General Assembly of the Synod of Bishops, "Message to the People of God," October 24, 2008, 1.

16. CCC 292, 703; see St. Irenaeus, *Adv. hæres.* 2, 30, 9; 4, 20, I: PG 7/1, 822, 1032.

17. CCC, 1091; see Ratzinger, *The Spirit of the Liturgy*, 153–4.

18. See CCC, 294; Saint Irenaeus, *Adv. hæres.* 4, 20, 7: PG 7/1, 1037; Ratzinger, *The Spirit of the Liturgy*, 18.

19. CCC, 398; Saint Maximus the Confessor, *Ambigua*: PG 91, 1156C.

20. Ratzinger, *The Spirit of the Liturgy*, 33.

21. Did the Son of God become man only on account of sin? See Richard H. Bulzaccelli, "The Εσχατος Αδαμ and the Meaning of Sacrifice in the Theology of Joseph Ratzinger/Benedict XVI," *Antiphon* 13.1 (2009): 56–57.

22. Ratzinger, *In the Beginning: A Catholic Understanding of the Story of Creation and the Fall,* trans. Boniface Ramsey (Grand Rapids, MI: Eerdmans Publishing Co., 1995), 16.

23. Ratzinger, *The Spirit of the Liturgy*, 28.

24. Ibid., 39.

25. Ibid., 36, especially note 1.

26. Ibid., 36.

27. Ibid., 35–38.

28. Ibid., 28. Cardinal Ratzinger gets to the heart of the notion of sacrifice on p. 28 of this work. The recovery of sacrifice is one of the great contributions of his *The Spirit of the Liturgy*.

29. Cited in Synod XII, "Message to the People of God," 4.

30. The errors here are a Monophysitism (and perhaps Gnosticism) that exaggerates the spiritual and divine element of Christ to the detriment of the human; and, on the other extreme, a Nestorianism that so emphasizes Christ's humanity that his nature as Logos is obscured. The errors surrounding the Incarnation also devolve upon the nature of the Church and of her liturgy.

31. Ratzinger, *The Spirit of the Liturgy*, 47.

32. Ratzinger, *Introduction to Christianity*, trans. J. R. Foster (San Francisco: Ignatius Press, 1990), 275; see also Joseph Ratzinger, *Credo for Today: What Christians Believe* (San Francisco: Ignatius Press, 2009), 102.

33. Saint Augustine, *Sermo* 293, 3; PL 1328–1329.

34. Niceno-Constantinopolitan Creed, *Missale Romanum*, third typical edition.

35. CCC 460; Saint Athanasius, *De inc.* 54, 3: PG 25, 192B.

36. Ratzinger, *The Feast of Faith*, 25.

37. Preface 35, VII of the Sundays in Ordinary Time.

38. Ratzinger, *The Spirit of the Liturgy*, 28.

39. Saint Anselm: "For the Father did not compel him to suffer death, or even allow him to be slain, against his will, but of his own accord he endured death for the salvation of men . . . . It seems to me that you do not rightly understand the difference between what he did and suffered at the demand of obedience, and what he suffered, not demanded by obedience, but inflicted on him, because he kept his obedience perfect . . . God did not, therefore, compel Christ to die; but he suffered death of his own will, not yielding up his life as an act of obedience in maintaining holiness; for he held out so firmly in this obedience that he met death on account of it." (*Cur Deus Homo*, in *Opera Omnia*, ed. G. S. Schmitt, vol. 3, pp. 60–62, trans. S. N. Deane in *Basic Writings* [La Salle, Ill.: Open Court Publishing Co., 1965], pp. 191–94) in Louis Dupré, *Symbols of the Sacred* (Grand Rapids, MI: Eerdmans Publishing Co.), pp. 36–7, footnote 73.

40. Ratzinger, *The Spirit of the Liturgy*, 34.

41. Ratzinger, *The Spirit of the Liturgy*, 28.

42. Ratzinger, *The Spirit of the Liturgy*, 208.

43. Ratzinger, *God Is Near Us: The Eucharist, the Heart of Life,* ed. Stephan Otto Horn and Vinzenz Pfnür, trans. Henry Taylor (San Francisco: Ignatius Press, 2003), 49.

44. Ratzinger, "Is the Eucharist a Sacrifice?" *Concilium* 24 (1967) 77, cited in Richard Malone, "Eucharist: Sacrifice According to the Logos," in *Antiphon,* 13.I (2009), 80.

45. Ratzinger, *The Feast of Faith,* 37.

46. Ratzinger, *A New Song for the Lord: Faith in Christ and Liturgy Today,* trans. Martha M. Matesich (New York: The Crossroad Publishing Company, 1996), 57–176.

47. Ibid., *The Spirit of the Liturgy,* 58.

48. Ibid., *The Spirit of the Liturgy,* 58.

49. Ratzinger, *The Spirit of the Liturgy,* 173.

50. See Pius X and SC, 14.

51. Ratzinger, *Pilgrim Fellowship of Faith,* as found in "'Worship in accord with the Logos'—Inculturation, Liturgy, and Inculturation," by Rev. Robert A. Pesarchick, in *Antiphon* 13.1 (2009): 39.

52. Ratzinger, *The Feast of Faith,* 29–30.

Chapter 2

The Sacramental Nature of the Liturgy

The liturgy is fundamentally sacramental. In order to understand its language, we must understand the reality to which it points. In the Christian mystery, Christ, the Word of God, became our "Second Adam" to undo what had been done through the sin of the first Adam. When our common ancestor did not listen to God, did not wish to follow God's plan, and did not thirst for God, Christ took us to himself and listened to God,[1] followed his plan,[2] and made us thirsty again for him.[3] Christ carried out this work throughout his entire life, but most especially in the sacrifice of his Paschal Mystery.

From the time of Christ's return to the Father, it has been the task of his followers to imitate him in every aspect of their lives. As Christ undertook his fundamental mission to obey his Father's will in all things (thirsting for God, desiring to be one with him, saying "yes to the *reditus*"), so too do Christians strive to obey the Father's plan. We achieve this most effectively in the liturgy, the "source and summit" of a holy life, where the sacrificial work of Christ is made present to us so that we are able to share in it. Christ speaks his "yes" to the Father in and with the Church as she celebrates the liturgy. The liturgy is the way we join our voice to this "Mystical Voice" of his Body.

How do we actively participate in the work of Christ, practically speaking? We do so through sacraments:

> Christ indeed always associates the Church with himself in this great work wherein God is perfectly glorified and men are sanctified. The Church is his beloved Bride who calls to her Lord, and through him offers worship to the Eternal Father. [. . .] In the liturgy the sanctification of the man is *signified*

by signs perceptible to the senses, and is effected in a way which corresponds with each of these signs . . . . (SC, 7, emphasis added)

Christ's saving work is "signified" by signs; the salvation offered us through them is "effected" by these same signs. These efficacious signs are called "sacraments" by the Church. It is to them that we now turn our attention.

The Age of the Church: Christ Acting Sacramentally

In Lent 2004, *The Passion of the Christ* seized the attention of pious and impious moviegoers around the world. The film was produced by one of Hollywood's biggest names, and it featured a cast of accomplished actors and actresses. Particularly noteworthy was the fact that the actors spoke Aramaic, requiring English subtitles for the viewer. But the most astonishing feature that had both critics and audiences wild about *The Passion of the Christ* was its graphic character. The well-known film critic Roger Ebert wrote:

> The movie is 126 minutes long, and I would guess that at least 100 of those minutes, maybe more, are concerned specifically and graphically with the details of the torture and death of Jesus. This is the most violent film I have ever seen. [. . .] You must be prepared for whippings, flayings, beatings, the crunch of bones, the agony of screams, the cruelty of the sadistic centurions, the rivulets of blood that crisscross every inch of Jesus' body. Some will leave before the end. (For the full review, see http://rogerebert.suntimes.com/apps/pbcs.dll/article?AID=/20040224/REVIEWS/402240301/1023.)

The realistic and graphic nature of the film moved many in the theater to tears and sobs, so emotionally trying was the experience. For those who did not sympathize with the portrayal of Christ's Passion, there was still a strong reaction to it. It was even reported that when guilty criminals viewed the film, their consciences moved them to turn themselves in.[4]

As Mel Gibson's epic attempts to portray, Christ's suffering, death, Resurrection, and Ascension—his Paschal Mystery—is his priestly work in which he bridges the gap between the fallen world of sin and the heavenly world of the Father. The Paschal Mystery is Christ's thirst for the Father on our behalf, his "yes" to the divine plan, and his founding of the City of God where "love-transformed mankind" is fully alive. Christ's suffering and death—his Passion—is what is portrayed for us in *The Passion of the Christ*. It is likewise Christ's Passion and Paschal Mystery that are remembered at the Mass and in each of the Church's liturgies. We might even ask, How does the film *The Passion of the Christ* compare to the Mass, which is also "the Passion of the Christ"?

Apart from their common theme—Christ's Passion—the film and the Mass manifest the Passion through similar media. The film version of the Passion uses, like any film, actors and actresses to portray the events of Christ's life: James Caviezel takes the part of Jesus; Maia Morgenstern, that of the Virgin Mary; and Hristo Shopov plays Pontius Pilate. The Mass also has its participants who play particular roles: the priest, deacons, readers, musicians, and assembly. The movie has a certain setting, being filmed "on location" at Basilicata, Italy. Different sets were made as the environment for the action. In a similar way, the Mass is celebrated in a particular place, a church. Were the movie to be filmed or the Mass to be celebrated in surroundings foreign to each one's unique world, the unnecessary shift would distract from the reality. There are other similarities: both use music, "props," and actions; they employ certain "scripts" in particular languages. If James Caviezel or Hristo Shopov were to start "ad-libbing," Mel Gibson would surely yell, "Cut!" and another "take" would have to be made. Similarly, the Church's liturgical ministers speak in a definite way. Speaking other words produces a different reality, one other than *The Passion of the Christ*.

Yet there remain real differences between Mel Gibson's version of Christ's Passion in his film and the Church's celebration of Christ's Passion. Were there no differences, we might just as easily view the film presentation on Sunday mornings instead of the liturgical re-presentation. In short, the principal difference is this: the Mass' Passion is real, while the movie's *Passion* is not.

Despite the fact that the reviews and reactions to the movie included descriptions like "graphic," "realistic," and "authentic," the Passion of Christ that shone on the screen was not, in fact, so. This is not to diminish the power of the movie or the reactions it stirred; rather, the screen portrayal of Christ's work brought to people's minds images of a reality that exists in its substance elsewhere. It is not Gibson's directing skills, Caviezel's acting abilities, nor the challenges of the Italian landscape that are responsible for this shortcoming. The nature of film precludes such true and authentic realism.

Hollywood drama aside, the Mass is the *real* portrayal of Christ's saving Passion and his entire Paschal Mystery. The Church's ministers, texts, buildings, and appointments are not identical reproductions of the people, places, and events of the original. The priest does not dress like Jesus and the people of his day; he does not speak Aramaic; our churches do not resemble the upper room or Mount Calvary; our altars, chalices, and stained glass would not be found in an archeological treasure hunt of the first century. How can we claim the Church's "Passion of the Christ" to be superior to Hollywood's? Ours is *real*, the other is only *realistic*. The reality of each depends on the nature of the signs: while the film director is limited to the natural signs of his trade, the Church has inherited supernatural signs from Christ. As a consequence, when it comes to remembering the events of Christ's life, the Church's signs and symbols *work*; they are, in the language of the Catholic Tradition, *efficacious*, because Christ is present and working in them and in the Church.

Christ works through the sacraments! In light of chapter 1's Logical look at the liturgy, we could say that Christ continues to "speak" effectively in them. The *Catechism of the Catholic Church* puts it this way:

> The Church was made manifest to the world on the day of Pentecost by the outpouring of the Holy Spirit. The gift of the Spirit ushers in a new era in the "dispensation of the mystery" the age of the Church, during which Christ manifests, makes present, and communicates his work of salvation through the liturgy of his Church, "until he comes." In this age of the Church Christ now lives and acts in and with his Church, in a new way appropriate to this new age. He acts through the sacraments in what the common Tradition of the East and the West calls "the sacramental economy"; this is the communication (or "dispensation") of the fruits of Christ's Paschal mystery in the celebration of the Church's "sacramental" liturgy. (CCC, 1076)

The "age of the Church" mentioned here signifies the third and final period of salvation history, as well as the third and final manner in which Christ carries out his work. During the period of the Old Covenant, sometimes called the "time of the promises" (see CCC, 702), Christ, along with the Holy Spirit, worked *in a hidden way*, yet they are revealed in various theophanies: the pillar of fire (Exodus 13:21) and the glimpses given to Moses (Exodus 33:11; 20–23), for example. When it came time for God's promises to be fulfilled, Christ became incarnate by the power of the Holy Spirit and carried out his work *in the flesh*. Now, in this final age, "'seated at the right hand of the Father' and pouring out the Holy Spirit on his Body which is the Church, Christ now acts *through the sacraments* he instituted to communicate his grace" (CCC, 1084, emphasis added). Let us look more closely at this age of the Church and the place of the sacraments in it.

"Can there really be special holy places and holy times in the world of Christian faith? [. . .] Is the whole world not now his sanctuary? [. . .] Can there be any other holy time than the time for practicing love of neighbor, whenever and wherever the circumstances of our life demand it?"[5] Like the ages or periods before it, this final age of the Church has its own unique qualities. Pope John Paul II taught that the liturgy was a real encounter with the face of Christ: but if Christ has already won the victory over sin and death through his sacrifice to the Father, why are we not yet seeing him face to face, but still indistinctly and partially (see 1 Corinthians 13:12)?

The reason is due to the limitations of our existence during this time. While those celebrating the heavenly liturgy surround the throne of the Lamb and worship before him unceasingly, we participants in the earthly liturgy are not yet there. We are in a "peculiar kind of 'in-between,' a mixture of 'already and not yet.'"[6] More precisely, we are "in-between" the saving work of Christ and its heavenly fulfillment. Borrowing an image from Pope Gregory the Great, our age is like the early dawn, when the darkness of night is fading, but the radiance of the noonday sun is yet to come.[7] Our time is that of the *image*, when we are between the *shadows* of the Old Testament and the *reality* of heaven. In short: although Christ has already conquered death and now reigns in heaven, those of us on earth have *not yet* arrived. "This idea of the New Testament as the between-time, as image between shadow and reality, gives liturgical theology its specific form."[8]

Like this age which has a foot in both worlds (one on earth and one in heaven; one already victorious and the other not yet there; one in the realm of the shadows and another in that of reality), our sacramental worship will also be characterized by this "specific form." Christ works, the *Catechism* says of the age of the Church, "in a new way appropriate to this new age. He works through the sacraments" (CCC, 1076). Is Christ fully and really present to us in the sacraments? Yes. Is he present to us directly, face to face? Not entirely. The liturgy's sacraments are a reality wherein Christ is made present to us, although he is so through the media of signs and symbols. "The theology of the liturgy is in a special way 'symbolic theology,' a theology of symbols, which connects us to what is present but hidden. . . . We do indeed participate in the heavenly liturgy, but this participation is mediated to us through earthly signs."[9]

Our liturgical participation in Christ's work in the age of the Church is therefore a sacramental one. The sacrament, through its outward and sensible dimension, connects us with him who "is present but hidden." To worship in accord with the Logos and "logify my existence" is to participate in his work through sacraments. We do—and in fact we must—imitate Christ in our daily lives, but our sacramental participation in his work through the liturgy is the "source and summit" (SC, 14) of the Christian life in the world.

The liturgy, at its very heart, is a *sacramental* reality, and it must be seen to be so. It is true that it exists in a ceremonial ritual and is governed by rubrics, norms, and laws: but these laws do not constitute the essence of the liturgy. The liturgy likewise meets our desire to assemble with one another (we are, after all, social animals), but liturgy is not principally a communitarian undertaking. The liturgy is fundamentally sacramental, where "the sanctification of the man is signified by signs perceptible to the senses, and is effected in a way which corresponds with each of these signs . . . " (SC, 7). What, then, is a sacrament? Where do they come from? How do we actively participate in them? With a richer, more nuanced understanding, let us engage in the restored dialogue of the Logos that leads us to heaven.

Signs, Symbols, Sacraments, and Sacramentals

Classic catechesis teaches that sacraments are "outward signs," and the entire liturgy is woven together from them. Twentieth-century theologians call liturgical studies "'symbolic theology,' a theology of symbols."[10] Yet the terms *sign* and *symbol* can be used and understood in opposing ways.

In January of 2010 a magnitude 7.0 earthquake rocked the country of Haiti. Amid the suffering, heroism, and international aid, the following stories made the headlines:

"Obama Taps Former Presidents for Haiti Relief Role."

This story tells of President Barak Obama's selection of past presidents Bill Clinton and George W. Bush as fundraisers and facilitators of U.S. aid. At one point the story asks: "Will Obama seek [Bush's] advice or will he serve a mainly *symbolic* purpose?"[11]

"Destruction of Haiti's Political, Spiritual Infrastructure a Symbolic Blow."

The story unfolds: "In a country plagued by poverty and unrest, they [public buildings] stood for years as potent *symbols* of hope, history and nationalism. Today, the Port-au-Prince National Cathedral and presidential palace—along with the Parliament building, United Nations Haiti headquarters, and local churches—have either collapsed or been left in ruin, their *symbolism* turned into something tragic and macabre.[12]

In the first story, "symbolic" connotes empty, unreal, insincere, or fake. In another phrase we might often hear or say, it is "only symbolic." The second story uses the term in the opposite way. To describe Haiti's National Cathedral and its national government buildings as "symbolic" emphasizes their great meaning both within Haiti and outside of it. These physical structures truly represent the people; they are full of meaning, as if the country itself is somehow tied to them. It is surely not the story's intention to say these landmarks are empty, unreal, or meaningless.

In which of these two senses does the Church understand "symbol," especially as it relates to sacramental liturgy? When theologians tell us the liturgy is a "theology of symbols," what does this mean? How are we to understand the *Catechism of the Catholic Church's* teaching that "A sacramental celebration is woven from signs and symbols" (CCC, 1145)? These important questions require clear answers, since we ourselves commonly use the terms *sign* and *symbol* in different ways.

Generally speaking, a sign is some sensible thing that brings another, absent reality to mind. The Stop sign brings to mind the civil traffic law requiring us to stop our cars at a particular point prior to reaching the intersection. The first robin of the year signifies spring's approach, just as the geese flying south tell us of winter's coming. Certain "golden arches" make us think of hamburgers; Stars and Stripes atop the flagpole recall our United States; and tolling steeple bells tell us that Mass is about to begin. In each of these instances, there is some part that we encounter through our senses (part A) and another that is not sensible (part B). We note further that a sign can be both natural, as when the robin hearkens spring, or artificial (or conventional), as when a country decides that red, octagonal shapes bearing the letters S–T–O–P mean to bring the vehicle to a stop.

Symbols are a type of sign insofar as they convey unseen realities by means of sensible things. Yet symbols differ from signs in that the relationship between the two parts (the sensible form and the unseen reality) is never an arbitrary one.[13] In other words, a sign or signal may at times be contrived or artificial, where part A and part B are placed together by convention. There is nothing in the geometric nature of an octagon that communicates the command "stop," for example. But the symbol is more integral and necessary; part A and part B *belong* together. Smoke belongs with fire in the natural world. The seal of a notary public on documents is another example, yet one not of nature: the impression made on the paper belongs with the instrument used to impress the seal. There is here an intrinsic relation between the seal (which is the sign) and the signified (which is the authority and testimony of the notary). A "seal" is also used to signify the Bishop's authority in Confirmation; this time, in a sacramental way.

The Church's Creed is called "the Symbol of faith" because the words of the Creed are in no way accidental or arbitrary. While there is more than one form of Catholic creed or profession of faith (albeit a small number),[14] the words employed in them are in some way necessary to the expression of the Catholic faith. About the term *symbol* and its application to the Creed, the *Catechism* explains:

> The Greek word *symbolon* meant half of a broken object, for example, a seal presented as a token of recognition. The broken parts were placed together to verify the bearer's identity. The symbol of faith, then, is a sign of recognition and communion between believers. *Symbolon* also means a gathering, collection, or summary. A symbol of faith is a summary of the principal truths of the faith and therefore serves as the first and fundamental point of reference for catechesis. (CCC, 188)

The terminology here is not the important point; what is important is that, whichever term is employed—be it "sign" or "symbol"—the meaning each has for the Church is one of fullness, reality, and truth. In fact, that to which signs and symbols point is *the* fullness, reality, and truth: Christ himself.

To have an accurate understanding of Catholic sacraments and the Church's sacramental liturgy, we must therefore share her understanding of signs and symbols. When we say that liturgical theology is symbolic theology, we do not mean that such theology is meaningless and empty. We mean, rather, that in a liturgical celebration "we do indeed participate in the heavenly liturgy," and this participation is "mediated to us through earthly signs . . . ."[15] When the *Catechism* describes the liturgy as "woven from signs and symbols," it does not mean to imply that the liturgy is some kind of ineffectual charade that only conjures up the historical Christ to our memories. And when we are taught that a sacrament is "an efficacious sign of grace," we are not to interpret such a definition to mean that a sacrament is "only just a sign" and, as a consequence, it doesn't *really* offer grace to us.

Sacraments, then, *work*; they do what they symbolize and signify. Unlike Hollywood's *The Passion of the Christ*, the Church's Passion of the Christ is in actual fact made really, truly, and—in the case of the Eucharist, substantially—present before us. The Church's sacraments have many of the same characteristics as the signs and symbols we have been discussing. Like signs and symbols, sacraments convey an unseen and otherwise hidden reality through an external and sensible sign or symbol. The connection between the unseen reality and its symbolic expression is, like a sign or symbol in

Sacraments, then, *work;* they do what they symbolize and signify.

the truest sense, a natural and organic one. Yet the Church's sacraments and sacramental signs are not just another kind of sign, ones that have simply a "religious" character to them. Rather, Christ's presence and the grace of his Paschal Sacrifice distinguishes sacraments and sacramental signs from other symbols.

Christ's sacramental activity, however, is not solely that of the liturgy. It is not uncommon for the Church to refer to Christ himself as a sacrament, indeed, the most fundamental of sacraments. After Saint Paul's description of Christ as "the image of the invisible God, the firstborn of all creation" (Colossians 1:15), the *Catechism* recalls Saint Augustine: "For there is no other mystery of God except Christ" (CCC, 744). Saint Thomas Aquinas echoes the thought of the "ancient Doctors" when he tells us that "the human nature in Christ was 'a kind of organ of the divinity,' just as the body is held to be an organ of the soul."[16] Christ, the *sacramentum Dei*, becomes the instrument of the divine in his human nature. And in the words of Pope Saint Leo the Great, "What was visible in our Savior has passed over into his mysteries" (CCC, 1115). "Mystery," it should be noted, is a term for the sacramental reality or *res*: where the term *sacrament* emphasizes the external sign, the term *mystery* conveys its hidden reality (see CCC, 774). The liturgy's sacraments are founded upon Christ, the sacrament of the Father.

In addition to Christ himself being identified as a sacrament, the Church also is called a sacrament. This should not be surprising to us since the identity and mission of the Church is that of Christ. Whatever belongs to him must also be found as a characteristic of the Church. In its *Constitution on the Sacred Liturgy*, the Second Vatican Council recalls Saint Augustine's typological explanation of the origins of the Church from Christ's side: "For it was from the side of Christ as he slept the sleep of death upon the cross that there came forth 'the wondrous sacrament of the whole Church'" (SC, 5). Just as Eve (our mother in the order of nature) was drawn from the side of the sleeping Adam, so now the Church (our mother in the order of grace) is formed from the side of the Second Adam as he slept on the cross. The same Council opens its *Dogmatic Constitution on the Church* (*Lumen gentium*), again, likening the Church to a sacrament: "Since the Church is in Christ like a sacrament or as a sign and instrument both of a very closely knit union with God and of the unity of the whole human race, it desires now to unfold more fully to the faithful of the Church and to the whole world its own inner nature and universal mission" (LG, 1).[17] Even members within the Church are likened to sacraments. "Thus the risen Christ, by giving the Holy Spirit to the apostles, entrusted to them his power of sanctifying: they became sacramental signs of Christ" (CCC, 1087). Following the apostles, "the ordained minister is, as it were, an 'icon' of Christ the priest" (CCC, 1142).

In what way are Christ, the Church, and her ministers "sacraments"? They are, like the seven sacraments we are familiar with, outward signs of inward realities. The Incarnate Christ makes the Father present: "Whoever has seen me has seen the Father" (John 14:9). Like Christ, the visible Church manifests her invisible reality to the world:

> It is of the essence of the Church that she be both human and divine, visible and yet invisibly equipped, eager to act and yet intent on contemplation, present in this world and yet not at home in it; and she is all these things in such wise that in her the human is directed and subordinated to the divine, the visible likewise to the invisible, action to contemplation, and this present world to that city yet to come, which we seek." (SC, 2; also LG, 8)

Ordained ministers (indeed, all of the baptized), in virtue of the sacramental character that conforms them to Christ, are empowered to act like Christ, who is priest, prophet, and king, for the salvation of the world and the glory of God.

Understanding how the Church uses the term *sacrament* helps ground our own knowledge of the sacramental liturgy and our actual participation in it. The twentieth-century liturgical movement and the Magisterium that supported it sought to make our engagement in the sacraments dynamic, meaningful, and participatory rather than a kind of "mechanical transaction." In Peter Shaffer's play *Amadeus*, the character Antonio Salieri epitomizes this mechanical attitude toward grace. He kneels before a portrait of God, commissioned by tradesmen—made in their likeness. Looking into the eyes of the smoky fresco, he deals with the God of Bargains: "You give me so—I'll give you so! No more. No less!"[18] But sacraments are neither bartering nor business deals. They are encounters with the Person of Christ and the occasion for our maturation into his likeness, which is in the end our "logification." In the sacraments "divine life is dispensed to us" (CCC, 1131), but this grace is the life of God which makes man himself "fully alive." To situate "the seven sacraments" within an understanding of Christ as sacrament helps to make such a point. Pope John Paul called the sacrament of the Eucharist "the outstanding moment of encounter with the living Christ" (*Ecclesia in America*, 35), "the deepest and most effective answer to this yearning for the encounter with God" (SS, 12). Reception of the Eucharist gives grace, and this grace is precisely the life of Jesus Christ, the Second Person of the Trinity, in whose image we are remade.

Recalling that the Church herself is sacramental also benefits our understanding of the sacraments. Not only do the sacraments "actualize" Christ, making him "contemporaneous" with us,[19] they also animate the Church. The Church is most herself, most visibly "Church," when she celebrates the sacramental liturgy. If one wishes to see the Church, it will be during her celebration of the liturgy, most especially the Mass, her "preeminent manifestation" (SC, 41). The sacraments also belong to the Church — they are hers — in the sense that "she is the sacrament of Christ's saving action at work in her through the mission of the Holy Spirit" (CCC, 1118). In short, the sacraments allow us to encounter the living Christ, Head of his Mystical Body, the Church.

The Church "has discerned over the centuries that among liturgical celebrations there are seven that are, in the strict sense of the term, sacraments instituted by the Lord" (CCC, 1117). Classic catechisms define a sacrament as "an outward sign, instituted by Christ, to give grace."[20] The *Catechism of the Catholic Church* elaborates this definition, calling a sacrament "an efficacious sign of grace, instituted by Christ and entrusted to the Church, by which divine life is dispensed to us through the work of the Holy Spirit" (CCC, Glossary).

Like signs and symbols, sacraments have a sensible dimension. The sacrament of Confirmation, for example, includes the words "Be sealed with the gift of the Holy Spirit" with the laying on of the hands by the Bishop and the action of anointing with sacred chrism. The larger ritual celebration includes music, other ministers and members of the faithful; it takes place in a church, and it usually takes place in a season of some liturgical meaning, such as Easter. These sensible elements (what the Scholastics called the *sacramenta tantum* ["signs only"]) are an essential part of the sacrament, and when they are altered or removed, so too is the sacramental reality. When the Eucharistic wine turns to vinegar, for example, the reality of Christ's blood is no longer present.[21]

Sacraments also, following signs and symbols, have an internal and otherwise imperceptible reality. Called the *res tantum* ("reality only"), this unseen reality for each of the sacraments is the grace of Christ, the source of which is his Paschal Mystery. In this "age of the Church," this time of "in-between-ness," after the "already" but before the "not-yet," these two dimensions of the sacrament exist together. The Church's seven sacraments are both sign *and* reality: they are *sacramentum et res*. If we return to our earlier explanation of shadow–image–reality, we can say that the time of the promises (the Old Testament), the shadow, was the time of the *sacramentum tantum*, the sign only. In heaven, where all reality is "face to face" (see 1 Corinthians 13:12; 1 John 3:2), we will live in the *res tantum*, the *ultimate* reality of God. Today, the time of the image, is the time of both *sacramentum et res*: the sign *and* the reality. We live in the time of the sacraments, the time of the *et* (and), the bridge where our encounter with the living God is *in* and *through* the Church's sacraments. It is true that the sacraments are not the only ways for us to encounter Christ and become cooperators in his work (we encounter him in the scriptures, the saints, and the poor), but they are the best ways for us to do so. Nor has God restricted himself to acting solely in the sacraments. The sacraments remain, though, "the deepest and most effective answer to this yearning for the encounter with God" (SS, 12), the place par excellence to meet God this side of heaven.

Before leaving the topic of sacraments, it is necessary to look at sacramentals. A sacramental, such as a blessing or consecration, is "a sacred sign which bears a certain resemblance to the sacraments, and by means of which spiritual effects are signified and obtained through the prayers of the Church" (CCC, Glossary). Sacramentals "resemble" sacraments according to their nature as signs, where unseen realities are presented to us by means of sensible expression. The reality, or *res,* of the sacramental is also the same, namely the grace of Christ, even though the Church will distinguish between the "sacramental grace" of the sacraments and the "actual graces" offered through the sacramentals. Where sacramentals differ from sacraments is in their institution: sacraments are "instituted by Christ," while sacramentals are instituted by the Church (see CCC, 1667). The sacramentals also carry out their work in a manner different from that of the sacraments. Because of their institution by Christ and his continued presence in the sacrament, sacraments work *ex opere operato*, "by the very fact of the action's being performed" (CCC, 1128). That is, when the signs of the sacrament are validly performed, the commensurate grace becomes a reality. The sacramentals, on the other hand, do not work in this way. The graces that they confer are brought about through the workings of the Church and, to a certain extent, the cooperation of the recipient (see CCC, 1670). The efficacy of Ash Wednesday's mark on the forehead, for example, derives from the intercession of the Church and my own active participation with her in receiving and wearing the cross of ashes.

Lastly, following a look at sacramentals, we should look at the liturgy as a whole as sacramental. There are many signs and symbols used in the liturgy that are meant to bring us to Christ and the "yes" of his Paschal Sacrifice, things that are neither, strictly speaking, "sacraments" nor "sacramentals." In fact, most of the signs that we encounter are either "extensions" of the sacrament *per se*, or are elements of another liturgical celebration, such as the Liturgy of the Hours. In the end, the entire liturgy, from beginning to end, is "woven from signs and symbols" (CCC, 1145).

The *Catechism of the Catholic Church* presents the question, How is the liturgy celebrated? It gives a variety of answers: the liturgy uses signs and symbols (CCC, 1145–1152); words and actions (CCC, 1153–1155); singing and music (CCC, 1156–1158); holy images (CCC, 1159–1162); sacred times, including the seasons, weeks, days, and hours (CCC, 1163–1178); and sacred places (CCC, 1179–1186). Each of these elements combines in a "rite" or "ritual" which is used in liturgical celebration. Joseph Ratzinger provides a similar definition of ritual: "the practical arrangements made by the community, in time and space, for the basic type of worship received from God in faith."[22] The Rite of Baptism, for example, is woven from signs and symbols: oil of the catechumens and sacred chrism; candles, white garments, and font; words such as "I baptize you in the name of the Father, and of the Son, and of the Holy Spirit"; the gestures and actions of pouring, anointing, and lighting; song, such as at the litany of the saints; ministers, normally a priest or deacon, lectors, and servers, as well as an assembly, godparents, parents, and, lest we forget, the one to be baptized; sacred times such as Sundays or possibly during the Easter season; and sacred places such as a baptistry or font. All of these sacramental signs and symbols are knitted together to manifest the Person of Christ and to allow us humans to encounter him and to participate in his saving work.

In this age of the Church, signs, symbols, sacraments, and sacramentals are the primary means by which we encounter Christ and join him in his sacrificial act of divinization, of saying "yes" to God's economy, and of passing-over to the redeemed world of the Father. In short: *liturgical signs (sacramenta) mean things (res)*, and in particular they mean Christ himself. We began this section with examples of two headlines drawn from the press, and we saw that the word *symbolic* can be understood in opposite ways. It can either refer to something meaningless and empty, or it can bring to us what is real, full, and authentic. For the Church, the liturgy's signs, symbols, sacraments, and sacramentals are truly, really, and actually full of Christ. To engage in the liturgy's signs, symbols, and sacraments is to encounter the living God, Christ, seated now at the right hand of the Father in heaven. It is only within this context that the various signs and symbols of the liturgy make sense. In this light, vestments suddenly radiate value, since they are signs of Christ. The entrance to a church building ushers one into the Mystical Body of Christ. Singing now truly makes "our voices one with the angels and saints." And reciting the words of our liturgical rites resounds with *the* Word, the Logos, in his sacrificial "*fiat*" to the Father.

The Meaning and Origin of Sacramental Signs

In the natural world in which we live, signs mean things. In the supernatural world, in the world of faith, supernatural signs, called sacraments, mean Christ himself. But how is it that sacraments *mean Christ*, point to him, and actually present him to us in the liturgy?

We saw previously that signs can acquire their meaning by convention or mutual agreement: red flashing lights mean stop, cakes covered with lit candles signify birthdays, golden arches point us to lunch, and checkered flags indicate the end of the race. They are called conventional signs (or artificial) because they are created by groups, and they have an artificial and often arbitrary quality about them. The act of stopping, for instance, could be signified in any number of ways, and in some other countries it is. Birthdays don't need cakes to be celebrated, McDonald's could just have easily chosen another trademark sign, and the conclusion of races could be announced by horns, buzzers, and lights as at hockey and basketball games. Because each sign was invented by a group, it can also be changed by that group or another in the future.

Symbols are a second type of sign. They differ from conventional and artificial signs in that the external expression shares an organic, intimate, and somewhat necessary relation to that which is signified. In chapter 1 we learned that the term *symbol* is used for this kind of sign, because the literal meaning of *symbol* is "to throw" (*-balleo,* in Greek) "together" (*sym-*) into a whole. The two "halves" of a symbol or *authentic* sign share an intrinsic rather than arbitrary connection. Their relation develops "organically" (see SC, 23) from sources other than human imagination and artifice. The example used earlier of the notary's seal is this kind of sign: the embossment on the page fits together with the stamp, and only with one particular stamp. The sacramental signs and symbols employed by the Church are of these types of signs. The reality of Christ's body belongs with the sacramental sign of bread, and it does so in an integral way. His eucharistic body cannot be present to us by any other symbol.

A liturgical ritual, as we saw above, is the ordering and use of signs and symbols, such as objects, words, actions, gestures, postures, ministers, assembly, singing and music, sacred times, art and architecture. Each of these is symbolic—which is to say sacramental—of Christ or some aspect of him. If these were merely artificial signs, they could be manipulated and changed at will to convey the desired meaning. The ministers of the Church—whether on a parish worship committee, the United States Bishops' Committee on Divine Worship, or even the Pope himself—could determine the meanings of the various signs and how the realities of our faith would be expressed. "Violet will symbolize joy in our Church." "Polka music is the best musical sign among our group." "The Lord's Day will now be observed on Wednesday in this country." "Standing will now replace kneeling as an expression of prayerful humility." Since the liturgy's signs and symbols are organic, the meaning is not assigned to them, but emerges from within. Even the Pope himself is the servant of the liturgy and must respect what has come down to him through the course of history.[23] This is why the *General Instruction of the Roman Missal* insists that not even a priest (*sacerdos*) has the authority to change the liturgy on his own (GIRM, 93).

The elements of the liturgy's celebrations are symbolic in the truest sense and are not inventions of ecclesiastic or pastoral experts. If the meaning does not come from us, from where do liturgical signs derive their meaning? The *Catechism of the Catholic Church* responds: "A sacramental celebration is woven from signs and symbols. In keeping with the divine pedagogy of salvation, their meaning is *rooted* in the work of creation and in human culture, specified by the events of the Old Covenant and fully revealed in the person and work of Christ" (CCC, 1145, emphasis added). The Church's sacraments "purify and integrate all the richness of the signs and symbols of the cosmos and of social life . . . , fulfill the types and figures of the old covenant, signify and make actively present the salvation wrought by Christ, and prefigure and anticipate the glory of heaven" (CCC, 1152). Six different sources of sacramental meaning thus emerge: 1) nature and creation, 2) human culture and social life, 3) the signs and events of the Old Covenant, 4) the person and work of Jesus himself, 5) the realities of heaven, and 6) the integration of each of these sources in her sacramental liturgy and its development through the centuries. These sources are the genesis of the rites as we celebrate them today. Let's look at each source more closely.

Signs from Nature and Creation

The relationship between nature and grace has never been easy to comprehend, as two fifth-century ecumenical councils and their final determinations made clear. The Council of Ephesus in 431 found the Syrian-born Patriarch of Constantinople, named Nestorius, the subject of a quarrel. Nestorius, in his defense of Christ against the Arians and many of the other false teachers at the time, championed the humanity of Christ to such an extent that it was unclear whether he believed Christ to be a single Person (the Second Person of the Holy Trinity) or two persons, one human and one divine. Added to this was his teaching that Mary was not the Mother of God (which is called *Theotokos)* but only the mother of the *human person* of Christ. Confronting Nestorius on this point was the Patriarch of Alexandria, Saint Cyril. Unsympathetic to Antiochene (Syrian) theology generally, Cyril disagreed with Nestorius's teaching on Christ. He taught (and the Council agreed) that Christ was not two persons but one, the divine Son of the Father, the Second Person of the Trinity. Ephesus was thus an apparent victory for the "supernatural" over the natural.

It was only twenty years later, at the Council of Chalcedon, when a second heresy emerged, this time championing the divinity of Christ to the detriment of his humanity—the opposite error of Nestorius. While Nestorius believed he was fighting for the integrity of the humanity of Christ, Eutyches and others known as Monophysites ("one" [*mono*] "nature" [*physis*]) taught that at the Incarnation the human nature assumed by the Second Person of the Trinity was transformed in such a way that it left its humanity behind.

In other words, where the Church believed Christ to be one Person in two complete natures, the Monophysites thought Christ to be one Person in one divinized nature, a sort of composite of human nature and divine nature. In 451 Pope Saint Leo the Great confirmed the condemnations made by the Council of Chalcedon in his famous tome: "We teach that one and the same Christ, the Lord, the only begotten Son consists of two natures, without confusion, without change, without separation, without division."[24] Chalcedon thus seemed a counterpoint to Ephesus, an evident triumph of those promoting the "natural" element.

The reformers of the sixteenth century, especially Calvin and Zwingli, held different views still. Where the Monophysites and others thought salvation to be an elevation and divinization out of this world and into the next, one that transforms human nature into another supernatural reality, many of the Protestant Reformers held that it was not possible for human nature to be perfected and divinized. On the contrary, the natural world and man's own nature were not capable of God's perfecting grace. On the topic of original sin, the *Catechism* explains the point: "The first Protestant reformers . . . taught that original sin has radically perverted man and destroyed his freedom; they identified the sin inherited by each man with the tendency to evil (*concupiscentia*) which would be insurmountable" (CCC, 406–407; see also CCC, 1046–1047). Since fallen man cannot cooperate with grace, redemption cloaks man's sinfulness but leaves him wounded and fallen. Nature is simply not compatible with grace.

In the thought of the Catholic Church, the relationship between nature and grace, between the natural world and the supernatural world, is more harmonious than in the thought of the Nestorians, Monophysites, or the early Protestant Reformers. In the formulation of the Scholastics, "Grace builds upon nature." Nature is compatible with grace and is to be perfected, in its entirety, by grace. Cardinal Ratzinger and Saint Augustine both make this point, positing salvation as love-transformed mankind abiding in the City of God. Here, man is not left in his fallen state, but neither is he transformed into another reality altogether. By extension, the natural and created world is able to serve as means for us to encounter God (see CCC, 1047). What can be known about God is evident because God reveals himself. As Saint Paul says, "Ever since the creation of the world, his invisible attributes of eternal power and divinity have been able to be understood and perceived in what he has made" (Romans 1:19–20). The natural and supernatural, creation and grace, coexist for the Catholic.

Because creation has this sacramental character about it, elements from nature can and are used in the Church's liturgy. "God speaks to man through the visible creation. The material cosmos is so presented to man's intelligence that he can read there traces of its Creator. Light and darkness, wind and fire, water and earth, the tree and its fruit speak of God and symbolize both his greatness and his nearness" (CCC, 1147). The supernatural meaning of the sacraments is, after the saying of the Scholastics, "built upon" the meaning of the signs in nature and creation, the Church "purifying and integrating" their richness in her rituals today.

Signs from Human Culture and Social Life

As the fifth-century ecumenical councils of Ephesus and Chalcedon sought to make clear, the Incarnate Christ is both fully human and fully divine. The Church, like her spouse, founder, and Head, is also human and divine: "It is of the essence of the Church that she be both human and divine, visible and yet invisibly equipped, eager to act and yet intent on contemplation, present in this world and yet not at home in it" (SC, 2; also LG, 8). The sacraments and sacramental celebrations are, like Christ and his Church, also human and divine, natural and supernatural, uniting the city of man and the City of God.

Inculturation is the term that expresses the union of the human and the divine in the Christian life and the Church's liturgy. In its *Constitution on the Sacred Liturgy*, the Second Vatican Council directed that "Provisions . . . be made, when revising the liturgical books, for legitimate variations and adaptations to different groups, regions, and peoples, especially in mission lands, provided that the substantial unity of the Roman Rite is preserved;

> It is as important that human elements be a part of the sacramental liturgy . . .

and this should be borne in mind when drawing up the rites and devising rubrics" (SC, 38). The model for all inculturation, as we might now expect, is the Incarnate Christ, who "became man so that man might become God."[25] There is a "double movement" in the process of inculturation based upon Christ's own Incarnation. Inculturation is "the incarnation of the Gospel in autonomous cultures and at the same time the introduction of these cultures into the life of the Church . . . , an intimate transformation of the authentic cultural values by their integration into Christianity and the implantation of Christianity into different human cultures" (VL, 4).

It is as important that human elements be a part of the sacramental liturgy as it was for the human element to become a part of Christ. It is not accidental that the liturgy contains a human dimension as well as a divine: it is *essential* that it does so. The liturgy is not only human, but *humanizing*. It was a theme of the Council's *Constitution on the Church in the Modern World* that Jesus not only reveals God to man, but "fully reveals man to man himself" (GS, 22). The actions of "washing and anointing, breaking bread and sharing the cup can express the sanctifying presence of God and man's gratitude toward his Creator" (CCC, 1148). In the liturgy these elements of our human nature lived together find expression, supply meaning, and become "fully alive" in Christ.

Man's natural religious quest and the components of his natural religious rites are also "presupposed, integrated, and sanctified" in the Church's liturgy. A central theme in the history of man is his search for communion with God. "The [figure of the] Praying Boy," says G. K. Chesterton, "may be said to express a need rather than to satisfy a need. It is by a normal and necessary action that his hands are lifted; but it is no less a parable that his hands are empty . . . ."[26] It is natural for men and women of every time and place to seek the supernatural.

Prayer and worship are not simply actions of individual men and women. Since we are naturally social animals, piety belongs collectively to human nature. Religious rites and the symbols these rites contain are aimed at the worship of God (or the gods). By offering sacrifice, they seek to reconcile the breach that separates the human from the divine.[27] "The great religions of mankind witness, often impressively, to this cosmic and symbolic meaning of religious rites" (CCC, 1149). Not only do social and cultural life contribute to the meaning of the sacraments, but aspects of the human religious search also offer a layer of meaning. These components form a part of the natural foundation upon which grace is built. Incorporated by the Church in her liturgy, these signs and symbols, like man and all of creation, are "destined to be transformed . . . , sharing their glorification in the risen Jesus Christ" (see CCC, 1046–7).

Signs from the Old Testament

Saint Augustine calls the Easter Vigil the "Mother of all Vigils."[28] This Vigil and the Triduum liturgies (from the Mass of the Lord's Supper through Easter Sunday) form the center of the liturgical year.[29] Here the Church makes her annual remembrance (*anamnesis*) of Christ's saving work, marks her birth from the side of Christ, and allows the faithful to unite themselves to Christ's Paschal Mystery. A significant part of the Vigil is the Liturgy of the Word, which recalls these events, showing over the course of many readings how God's economy of salvation is fulfilled in Christ. Nine readings survey salvation history. The *pericope* (passage) from the book of Exodus recounts Israel's liberation through the Red Sea. Perhaps more than any other Old Testament passage, this dramatic account of Israel's escape from Egypt through the waters of the sea and the Passover sacrifice that preceded it are *types* or *prefigurements* of the Passover of Christ.

We have access to the deep meaning of the texts of the Mass through the use of typology, which is the way persons, images, and events of our faith have been prefigured in the Old Testament. The Church distinguishes between two senses found in the scriptures, the literal and the spiritual. The literal is "the meaning conveyed by the words of Scripture and discovered by exegesis, following the rules of sound interpretation" (CCC, 116). For example, when Christ says, "I am the vine, you are the branches," he does not mean that he is made up of plant cells. That would be a literalistic interpretation. His saying means that he is the source of our strength so that we can act in his name: "without me you can do nothing" (John 15:5). "Thanks to the unity of God's plan," says the *Catechism*, "not only the text of Scripture but also the realities and events about which it speaks can be signs" (CCC, 117).

There are three categories of the spiritual sense: the moral, the anagogical, and the allegorical. The moral sense[30] shows us the way to right action in the world (CCC, 117). The scriptures are written "for our instruction." The Lord tells us, "You have heard that it was said, 'An eye for an eye and a tooth for a tooth.' But I say to you, offer no resistance to one who is evil. When someone strikes you on (your) right cheek, turn the other one to him as well" (Matthew 5:38–39).

The anagogical sense, which in Greek means "leading, up" sees "realities and events in terms of their eternal significance" and how these lead us toward heaven (CCC, 117). The parable of the five wise and five foolish virgins teaches us to be prepared at all times for Christ's coming: "Stay awake, for you know neither the day nor the hour" (Matthew 25:13). The prayers of Judas Maccabeus for the dead (see 2 Maccabees 12:46) demonstrate the responsibility that the living have for the deceased, those who are being led to the beatific vision.

The allegorical[31] is the third of scripture's spiritual senses. It is of particular importance for liturgical symbolism and essential for a Catholic understanding of the Sacred Liturgy. People and events point to Christ, his Church, and the sacraments. Melchizedek, the "king of peace," as priest, offered bread and wine. He is "without father, mother, or ancestry, without beginning of days or end of life" (Hebrews 7:3). Melchizedek prefigures Christ in these ways. Christ himself is the fulfillment of each of the characteristics found in Melchizedek of old. Christ is the figure; Melchizedek, the *pre*-figurement. Christ is the *proto*-type; Melchizedek is type of Christ. Christ is the reality; Melchizedek is the *fore*-shadow of that reality. Similarly, the hoar frost on the ground in the desert of Sin (Exodus 16:13) is the prefigurement of the dew of the Holy Spirit that descends on our altars during the Eucharistic Prayer; the manna in the desert (Exodus 16:15) is a prefigurement of the Eucharist; the gathering of the Chosen People at Sinai (Exodus 19:1) is a foreshadowing of the Church to come; and the crossing of the Red Sea (Exodus 14:22) is a type of passing through the waters that anticipates the true baptism of the Church. Consequently, when the Church uses the word *water* in the liturgy, we do not understand H_2O, a chemical formula. On the contrary, the *meaning* of the term from the Church's perspective draws on all of water's prefigurements (or types) in the Old Testament: the water of creation, the waters of the flood, the waters of the Red Sea, the water at Meribah. Water in the Christian world is an image, a symbol of a deeper reality. This is how our language itself is sacramental. We will discuss this more in chapter 3.

Signs Taken Up by Christ

The Old Testament offers much about the Mystery of Christ and his Passover, but of all the sources from which the Church's sacraments derive their meaning, it is the Person and work of Christ that is the most important. In virtue of his authority as Son of God, Christ gives meaning to the signs of creation, culture, and the Old Covenant. "He gives new meaning to the deeds and signs of the Old Covenant, above all to the Exodus and the Passover, for he himself is the meaning of all these signs" (CCC, 1151).

What, for example, is the significance and meaning of the "first-born lamb" in the faith and in the Church's liturgy? *Naturally* speaking, the new-born lamb is a sign of purity, meekness, and new life. *Human culture*, especially nomadic and rural culture, adds another layer of meaning, that of the rebirth of all creation, since the lambing season usually takes place in the spring of the year. Nomadic tribes prior to the exodus from Egypt also were accustomed to slaughtering one of their lambs and offering it to the gods as a sign of thanksgiving for the beginning of the spring's growing season. The Old Covenant saw a great deal of lambs: Abel offered a lamb and was, after a fashion, made an offering as well; Abraham offered a ram in place of his only son, Isaac; the captive Israelites likewise slaughtered a year-old and unblemished lamb whose blood was then placed upon the door posts and lintel of their homes so that the Lord would pass over their homes and spare their sons (see Exodus 12). Upon this foundation, John the Baptist points to Jesus, saying: "Behold, the Lamb of God, who takes away the sin of the world" (John 1:29). The Church incorporates this declaration in the Eucharistic Liturgy: *Ecce, Agnus Dei* (Behold, the Lamb of God).

Two complementary observations are important. The first is that without even making reference to Christ, the symbolic meaning of the lamb is rich due simply to natural, human, and Old Testament sources. The meaning of the lamb precedes Christ. It is not "in keeping with the divine pedagogy of salvation" (CCC, 1145) that God should simply say that "the lamb will from henceforth be a symbol of Christ." On the contrary, the meaning of the lamb is "rooted in the work of creation and in human culture [and] specified by the events of the Old Covenant" (ibid.). The second point is that the significance of the lamb (innocence, new life, thanksgiving, salvation, freedom, etc.) would be incomplete without Christ himself. The lamb is "fully revealed in the person and work of Christ" (ibid.), for "he himself is the meaning of all these signs" (CCC, 1151). Where other sources give a general and at times unspecified meaning, Christ gives to every sacramental sign its ultimate and authoritative meaning.

Signs of Heaven

In addition to the sources mentioned thus far, liturgical signs, symbols, and sacraments often derive meaning from heaven's own realities. As we have seen previously, the Christ who works through the sacraments is now "seated at the right hand of the Father" in heaven (CCC, 1084). The earthly Church to which we belong is at the same time "the Church enriched with heavenly things" (LG, 8). Likewise, in this age of the Church, the sacrament itself is not only a material sign *but also* a supernatural reality: *sacramentum et res.* Recall that when the *Catechism* asks who celebrates the liturgy (1136 and following), it answers first that the principal celebrants, after the Persons of the Trinity, are all those abiding and "recapitulated" in Christ. "It is in this eternal liturgy, that the Spirit and the Church enable us to participate whenever we celebrate the mystery of salvation in the sacraments" (CCC, 1139). Just as the things of created and human nature have a place in the sacraments, so too do the things of heaven: the *natural* foundation is the basis for the *supernatural* life of grace.

But how do we know what heaven looks like? We are, after all, "not yet" there. As creatures, we are familiar with the created world; we exist within a culture, even when that culture is difficult to define. We are able to read about the events of the Old Covenant and the life of Christ in the scriptures. But of heaven, "eye has not seen, and ear has not heard" (1 Corinthians 2:9). Or so it would seem.

Exiled on the island of Patmos, John was "caught up in the spirit" on the Lord's Day to a great vision of the heavens (see Revelation 1:9–10), and the Church has seen heaven itself in the descriptions he has given us. What does John see? Among other things, he sees a Lamb that appears to have been slain (5:6), and before it are four living beings and twenty-four elders worshipping and singing (5:8–14). In addition, he hears the same living creatures proclaim "Holy, holy, holy is the Lord God almighty" (4:8), as well as the Song of Moses: "I will sing to the Lord, for he is gloriously triumphant; horse and chariot he has cast into the sea" (15:1 and following). He also sees a throne before which burned "seven flaming torches" (4:5, also 1:12) and incense (5:8, 8:3). The Heavenly City had streets of "pure gold" and walls of jasper (21:18). Among the heavenly citizens are angels (5:11, 8:2), elders (4:4, 7:11), the four living creatures (4:6, 7:11), "white-robed" martyrs (7:14), a "woman clothed with the sun" (12:1), and "a great multitude which no one could count" (7:9). We encounter a great deal of these in our own liturgies: incense, lamp or candle stands, white-robed ministers, the *Sanctus*, gold chalices and ciboria, stained glass, and depictions of Mary, the angels, and the other heavenly host.

In addition to the particular images of heaven used as sacramental signs, the Church herself is a sign of the heavenly gathering. Signs and symbols of the Old Covenant prefigured Christ and the fulfillment of the

Father's plan in time, and so the signs and symbols of the age of the Church look forward to completion in heaven. Heaven is a liturgy, the center of which is Christ the Lamb, seated on a throne, and ministered to by the assembly of the heavenly host, those who sing, offer incense, and pray. Our own liturgical gatherings, in addition to fulfilling the sign of the Israelites gathered at Mount Sinai, anticipate the heavenly liturgy. The Bishop is conformed to Christ's priesthood in such a way that he is the image of Christ among us to the fullest extent: he uses seven candles at Mass, he uses Jesus' own words to greet us: "Peace be with you," and he carries a shepherd's staff like the Good Shepherd. Based upon the Bishop's conformity to the heavenly Christ, the Second Vatican Council then says that "all should hold in great esteem the liturgical life of the diocese centered around the bishop, especially in his cathedral church; they must be convinced that the pre-eminent manifestation of the Church consists in the full, active participation of all God's holy people in these liturgical celebrations, especially in the same Eucharist, in a single prayer, at one altar, at which there presides the bishop surrounded by his college of priests and by his ministers" (SC, 41).

Liturgical signs are consequently heavenly signs: they take their meaning from the heavenly realities shown us in the scriptures, and they anticipate heaven by allowing us to participate in it along with the celebrants of that eternal liturgy.

Sacramental Signs of the Church

The Church's sacramental signs grow from a variety of sources, "taking root" in the rich soil of nature and grace. And although Christ is a single Person, the Church his one Body, and human nature shared by all, the incarnate nature of the faith will express the divine truth in manifold ways. "The [Paschal] mystery celebrated in the liturgy is one, but the forms of its celebration are diverse" (CCC, 1200). While there are fundamental values shared among all peoples, as well as common religious hierophanies (sacred revelations), the varying cultures of different regions will incarnate the mystery of Christ in ways peculiar to themselves. Most of us are familiar almost exclusively with the Roman Rite, but the Latin or Western Church also contains the Ambrosian Rite (celebrated in Milan, Italy) and Mozarabic Rite (celebrated in Toledo, Spain).[32] The Eastern Catholic Churches share a number of rites, among them the Syrian, Maronite, Malankar, Chaldean, Syro-Malabar, Coptic, Ethiopian, Byzantine, and Armenian. Each of these rites celebrates the one Mystery of Christ, and the meaning of their sacramental signs comes from the same sources. The Mystery of Christ, however, "is so unfathomably rich that it cannot be exhausted by its expression in any single liturgical tradition" (CCC, 1201). This truth, coupled with the natural diversity among peoples, leads to a broad yet complementary liturgical expression (CCC, 1201).

Just as rites are different from one another according to place, variations within individual rites occur over time. Latin Catholics of the Third Millennium celebrate a Roman Rite essentially the same as Christians in the first centuries. There are, nevertheless, sacramental elements that have changed over the centuries. As the *Constitution on the Sacred Liturgy* explains, "the liturgy is made up of immutable elements divinely instituted, and of elements subject to change. These [latter] not only may, but ought to be changed with the passage of time if they have suffered from the intrusion of anything out of harmony with the inner nature of the liturgy or have become unsuited to it" (SC, 21).

Not only should foreign and discordant elements be removed from the liturgy, but positive influences of progress and culture ought, as seen above, to enhance the liturgy of the Church. We do not, for example, worship in houses any longer as was the case when the early Christians had no public buildings. In the sacraments proper, significant clarifications and changes can be seen in the history of the rites of Penance (from so-called "canonical" to "tariff") and the Ordination of Priests (from the handing over of the elements to the laying on of hands). Even today we enjoy "two expressions" of one rite: the extraordinary form according to the Missal of Blessed John XXIII from 1962 and the ordinary form of the Missal according to Paul VI (1969) and, in its third edition, John Paul II (2000). Like most liturgical signs and symbols, a great deal of the Mass' language has also undergone changes through the centuries. Our words at public prayer have a history, having been passed down to us from our fathers and mothers, sisters and brothers in the faith. This inheritance is now our own, and by this historical treasure of words we encounter the eternal Word, Christ.

Conclusion

Earlier in this chapter we made a distinction between arbitrary signs (those determined conventionally and springing from human invention) and "symbolic signs" that grow from various sources beyond the simple agreement of

minds and which consequently possess a relation to the signified or symbolized that is not arbitrary but natural, necessary, and needed. Sacramental signs
and symbols are decidedly *not* invented. Whether they are objects, words,
actions, singing, music, ministers, assembly, times, art, or architecture, sacramental signs have roots, they grow from a multi-layered composite of rich
organic soil, and grow into "God's masterpieces" (CCC, 1091) in the liturgy.

To dig in the soil of sacramental signs and symbols to see their roots is
a "mystagogical" endeavor. *Mystagogy* is a Greek term that means "to lead"
(from the root *agogue*; see the "anagogical" sense of scripture above) into the
"mystery" (from *mystes*, that which is secret or hidden). Mystagogical seeing
or "mystagogical catechesis" is a *leading* from the sensible sign or symbol into
the *mystery* contained within: it is a going from the *sacramentum* into the
res. John Paul II explains: "The best way to enter into the mystery of salvation made present in the sacred 'signs' remains that of following faithfully
the unfolding of the liturgical year. Pastors should be committed to that
'mystagogical' catechesis so dear to the Fathers of the Church, by which the
faithful are helped to understand the meaning of the liturgy's words and
actions, to pass from its signs to the mystery which they contain, and to enter
into that mystery in every aspect of their lives" (*Mane nobiscum Domine*, 17).
Practically, a mystagogical catechesis looks at the various symbols of the
liturgical rite (objects, actions, words, ministers, time, music, art, and architecture), examines them "in keeping with the divine pedagogy" according to
their genetics, and sees how Christ is present and working in them. When
this happens, our own active participation in the liturgy and sacraments can
become "full, conscious, and active." Experiencing Christ in this way—for it
is not simply an intellectual endeavor—is the source of holiness, the key to
the Christian life, and means to worship God rightly.

On these foundations, then, let us now look to the sacramental words
of liturgy and hear how Christ himself continues to speak his "Mystical
Voice" in and with his "Mystical Body."

Endnotes

1. Proverbs 1:8: "Hear, my son, your father's instruction, and reject not your mother's teaching."

2. Mark 2:14: "As he passed by, he saw Levi, son of Alphaeus, sitting at the customs post.
He said to him, 'Follow me.' And he got up and followed him."

3. Psalm 42:2: "As the deer longs for streams of water, so my soul longs for you, O God."
This is a principal image of the twentieth-century liturgical movement.

4. Carl Limbacher, "'The Passion' Prompts Robber to Surrender, Couple to Batter," *Newsmax*, 2004–MAR–18. Posted at: http://209.157.64.200/.

5. Joseph Ratzinger, *The Spirit of the Liturgy,* trans. John Saward (San Francisco: Ignatius Press, 2000), 53.

6. Ratzinger, *The Spirit of the Liturgy*, 54.

7. Ibid.

8. Ibid.

9. Ibid., 60.

10. Ibid., 60.

11. Todd J. Gillman, Dallas Morning News, January 16, 2010. See http://www.dallasnews.com/sharedcontent/dws/news/nation/stories/011610dnnatobamahaiti.84131219.html.

12. Misty Harris, Canwest News Service, January 14, 2010. See http://www.nationalpost.com/news/story.html?id=2442064.

13. See, for example, Karl Rahner, "The Theology of the Symbol," in *Theological Investigations*, vol. IV, pp. 221–52.

14. For example: Niceno-Constantinopolitan Creed, Apostles' Creed, Athanasian Creed.

15. Ratzinger, *The Spirit of the Liturgy*, 60.

16. Thomas Aquinas, trans., Charles J. O'Neil, *Summa Contra Gentiles: Book IV, Salvation* (Notre Dame, IN: University of Notre Dame Press, 1975), 193–97, (article 41).

17. "Cum autem Ecclesia sit in Christo veluti sacramentum seu signum et instrumentum intimae cum Deo unionis totiusque generis humani unitatis, naturam missionemque suam universalem, praecedentium Conciliorum argumento instans, pressius fidelibus suis et mundo universo declarare intendit."

18. Peter Shaffer, *Amadeus: A Play by Peter Schaffer* (New York: Harper Perennial, 2001), 10.

19. Ratzinger, *The Spirit of the Liturgy*, 7.

20. *Baltimore Catechism*, Revised Edition, (New York: Catholic Book Publishing Company, 1999), question 304.

21. See *Summa Theologica* III.77.4.

22. Ratzinger, *The Spirit of the Liturgy*, 160.

23. Ratzinger, *The Spirit of the Liturgy*, 166.

24. Clement Raab, OFM. *The Twenty Ecumenical Councils of the Catholic Church* (Westminster, Maryland: The Newman Press, 1959), 30–1.

25. The notion of "divinization" is reflected both in the New Testament and in the writings of the Fathers of the Church. See CCC, 460, 1129, 1265, 1812, 1988, 1999.

26. G. K. Chesterton, *The Everlasting Man* (San Francisco: Ignatius, 1993), 113. See also CCC, 843.

27. Ratzinger, *The Spirit of the Liturgy*, 27, 35.

28. "Mother of All Vigils" (Augustine, Sermon 219: PL 38, 1088).

29. Cf. Proclamation of the Date of Easter on Epiphany, Sacramentary supplement.

30. This is also called the tropological.

31. Also known as typological.

32. There also exist forms of the Roman Rite proper to some religious orders (e.g., Dominican and Benedictine); "two forms of one Roman Rite," the ordinary and extraordinary forms; as well as an "Anglican-use" rite for Anglicans who have come into full communion with the Catholic Church.

Chapter 3

The Use of Words in the Church's Liturgy

As we have seen, the liturgy is "woven" of signs and symbols, all of which point to Christ himself and make him present to us. The manner by which they signify is not arbitrary or determined by a committee of experts. Much larger than any one person or group, time or place, sacramental signs and symbols grow organically; their roots extend deeply into a many-layered soil. This is the fertile ground of culture, the Old Covenant, the person and work of Christ, and the realities of heaven. These signs live in the Church, and as the Church herself is the living Body of Christ, so too do her sacraments live through the centuries of the Mystical Body's earthly pilgrimage.

"[Christ] is the meaning of all these signs" (CCC, 1152). Even though certain liturgical signs and symbols are more closely associated with sacraments per se, being either the matter (water, oil, wine, bread) or the form of them (words of the rite), each liturgical element, either in itself or as a part of the larger rite, symbolizes and signifies Christ. As the Lord Jesus once spoke of "the temple of his body" (John 2:21), so now the church building symbolizes his Mystical Body: "visible churches are not simply gathering places but signify and make visible the Church living in this place, the dwelling of God with men reconciled and united in Christ" (CCC, 1180). The vesture of the liturgy is likewise sacramental in that it points to Christ. Saint Paul's exhortation to "put on the new self" (Ephesians 4:24, Colossians 3:10) becomes symbolized by the liturgy's vestments: "The liturgical vesture has a meaning that goes beyond that of external garments. It is an anticipation of the new clothing, the risen Body of Jesus Christ, that new reality which awaits us."[1] The Paschal candle is Christ, the pillar of fire, leading the people of the New Covenant to our Promised Land; the ordained minister is priest in the person of Christ the Head; and sacred music that sings with Christ's voice is "that hymn which is sung throughout all ages in the halls of heaven" (SC, 83). Liturgical language for its part sacramentalizes Christ, for it is that Mystical Voice spoken and sung by the Mystical Body to the Father. In a way unlike any other liturgical sign, there is a special affinity between the *sacramenta* of words and the *res* who is Christ, precisely because this Son of God identifies himself as *Word*. The Logos, the Word, is inseparable from Christ's divine identity.

How do the Church's human, meager words mean *the* divine, eternal Word? How do we encounter Christ in the words of the Mass? This chapter begins to examine the sacramental meaning of texts in the mystagogical manner outlined in chapter 2. As we deepen our appreciation for the sacramentality of liturgical language, we uncover its roots in nature and creation, in human society and culture, in the dialogue of God and the people of the Old Covenant. Then we examine the value of linguistic expression in the Incarnation of the Word and in the language of heaven. We will also explore how the Mystical Body of Christ receives these words and gives them voice to speak to Christ, her Spouse, and with Christ to the Father.

Words Are Sacramental Signs of Christ

The story of the movie *Babette's Feast*[2] captures in a vivid way the meaning of sacramental signs. A French woman exiled in Denmark is welcomed by two pious sisters of an austere Christian sect. Babette lives with these elderly women, participating in their life and works of charity. When Babette receives an announcement that she has won the French lottery, she implores the sisters to allow her to prepare a genuine French dinner in honor of their deceased father on the centennial of his birth. The first part of the story is slow, as if to help us appreciate the weight of life and the tedious nature of human existence. But the dynamism of the second part is animated by the preparation and celebration of the festival. Babette's feast is a dinner that includes sacrifice, memorial, banquet, and test. In the end it echoes the Eucharist, in that the physical food yields to spiritual nourishment. (This dinner is clearly not about taking in calories.) Having spent all her winnings and energy on the extraordinary celebration, Babette declares, an artist is never poor!

While Babette acts behind the scene in the kitchen, another character, General Lowenhielm, presides at table. He fulfills his role as one who uses spoken language to name the symbols and to indicate the reality to which they point. As the exquisite courses are presented, he recognizes, names, and manifests his deep appreciation of each. The other guests at the table observe his careful attention to the meal (he knows how to dine) and begin to imitate his example. While some take champagne to be "a kind of lemonade," his appreciation leads him to conclude that it is Veuve Cliquot. He can even name the vintage!

In *Babette's Feast* we can recognize the following:

- a Catholic and sacramental reality;
- the feast involves not only food and drink, but candles, fine china, crystal, cloth, dress, and language;
- the general speaks the language of the feast and teaches the other guests the same;
- in short, a feast has its own "language" generally, a component of which is language per se. Language is meaningful and sacramental.

On the natural level, *Babette's Feast* has a great deal in common with the Wedding Feast of the Lamb and its sacramental presentation in the Mass. Like Babette's feast, the Feast of the Lamb has a language, which is communicated not only through words, but by gestures and objects. What's more, it is the nature of the feast that determines the nature of the language. Not just any *sacramenta*, in the terminology of the Scholastics, can express the *res*. The "new age of the Church," as we have seen, is a time of "in-between" heaven and earth, one where the reality is mediated by the sacrament. Like all sacramental signs and symbols, the language of the Church is full of meaning, pointing to Christ, making him present in our midst.

Let's look at a few examples to see language's essential role in the liturgy. The Rite of Marriage uses a variety of sacramental elements: rings, man and woman, minister of the Church, vows, songs, and flowers. Each of these ritual components—the signs—is efficacious in its own way. In the end they symbolize the marriage of Christ to his Church and, by symbolizing, actually bring together the man and woman as sacramental signs of this reality. While some of these elements are not essential to the rite (the bride does not have to wear a white gown, nor does the couple need rings), other parts (what we have come to call the matter and form) are indispensable. The priest or deacon poses the question: "John, do you take Mary for your lawful wife, to have and to hold, from this day forward, for better, for worse, for richer, for poorer, in sickness and in health, until death do you part?" If John says:

"I do . . . not," or even, "I might," the reality, which is Christ sacrificing himself for the sake of his Bride, the Church, will not be present. Another reality altogether (and perhaps, for John, an unpleasant one) will be manifest. The words sacramentalize the reality, and without the proper words, a different reality is present.

The Trinitarian formula for Baptism offers another example. When the Congregation for the Doctrine of the Faith made clear that the "baptismal formula must be an adequate expression of Trinitarian faith," and that "approximate formulae are unacceptable," it not only reinforced a dogmatic declaration, but also provided a safeguard for the sacramental use of language.[3] To say a different formula (such as "I baptize you in the name of the Creator, and of the Redeemer, and of the Sanctifier" or "I baptize you in the name of the Creator, and of the Liberator, and of the Sustainer") is to symbolize or signify another reality. It does not denote membership in the Trinity. Since one of the realities of the sacrament of Baptism is membership in the divine life of the Trinity, the sacramental signs must express (and efficaciously cause) this reality. "The different effects of Baptism are signified by the perceptible elements of the sacramental rite" (CCC, 1262). Once again, words sacramentalize the reality. Without the proper words, the reality intended by the Church is jeopardized.

These two examples of the use of words in sacramental expression belong to what is called the form of the sacrament. These words lead us to an encounter with Christ. Does the same principle—that linguistic signs cause spiritual realities—apply to sacramental signs that are not strictly speaking part of the sacramental form? Do the other words of the liturgy lead to encounter with Christ? The answer is found in the fact that they "bear a certain resemblance to the sacraments" (CCC, Glossary). Let us illustrate the point by considering how the *General Instruction of the Roman Missal* understands the greeting of priest and people at the beginning of Mass. "When the Entrance Chant is concluded, the Priest stands at the chair and, together with the whole gathering, signs himself with the Sign of the Cross" (GIRM, 50). There are a number of sacramental signs here that combine for the sake of manifesting the nature of the Church. The priest stands at the chair, and not at the ambo or altar or in the choir loft, because the chair is a sign of the priest's conformity to Christ the Head of his Church. In other words, when the priest stands in the person of Christ the Head *in reality*, he also stands at the head of the church *sacramentally*.

The Sign of the Cross is also significant. The priest does not make just any gesture, such as waving to the people, for only one gesture is appropriate here. If the reality of the sacramental liturgy is the gathering of the Mystical Body of Christ made possible through his Paschal Sacrifice, then the sacramental sign most expressive of this reality is the Sign of the Cross upon which Christ offered the perfect sacrifice. By virtue of word and gesture, the assembly wraps itself in the saving work of the Blessed Trinity.

More important for the purposes of language is the next element of the same paragraph from the *General Instruction*. "Then by means of the Greeting he *signifies* the presence of the Lord to the assembled community. By this greeting and the people's response, the mystery of the Church gathered together is made manifest" (GIRM, 50, emphasis added). The words of the Greeting and response are: Priest: "The

> . . . sacramental language signifies sacramental realities, and speaking poorly, symbolizes poorly.

Lord be with you." People: "And with your spirit." Compare this sacramental greeting to a secular one, such as "Hello, everyone." While we don't consider such greeting in anyway offensive, it is nevertheless out of place. Even a religious greeting such as "Merry Christmas" or "Happy Easter" might as easily be heard at the grocery store. A lecturer might begin his talk with "Good Morning" to signal the beginning of the lecture and to establish a friendly atmosphere. The reality of the Mass is that the Bride of Christ, born from his pierced side on the cross, is called together and gathered under the headship of Christ upon whom the Spirit rests. This reality is correspondingly signified by the priest standing *in persona Christi capitis* at the chair, making the Sign of the Cross, and wedding the Mystical Body of Christ with this initial dialogue. To greet with words inconsistent with this invisible reality is to skew the image of the gathered Church.

In short, sacramental language signifies sacramental realities, and speaking poorly, symbolizes poorly. Unclear language disfigures, shadows, and obscures the authentic reality of the sacramental celebration, which is ultimately Christ.[4]

Both the careless and the witty in sacramental celebrations are consequently detrimental to the active participation of the people in them. "The word 'part-icipation' refers to a principal action in which every one has a 'part.'

And so if we want to discover the kind of doing that active participation involves, we need, first of all, to determine what this central *actio* is in which all the members of the community are supposed to participate."[5] The central action of the Mass, as we have seen in chapter 1, is the sacrificial offering of the Son to the Father in the Spirit, now presented under the sacramental signs of the liturgy: the mediating symbol connects the *laos* (people) with the *ergon* (work) of Christ. Participation in a liturgy (a *laos-ergon*, a work done in the name of the people) is accordingly sacramental. "Disfiguring" the liturgy's reality by inarticulate signs and symbols deprives the laity of its own right and duty to active participation.

The Church regulates the liturgy in order to guarantee right sacramentality for her members. The liturgy is fundamentally the right way to relate to God (*ortho-doxa*). In the time between the victory of Christ's cross and the consummation of that victory in heaven, our relationship with God is mediated by sacramental symbols. The sacramental liturgy presents the work of Christ to the Church, and in so doing enables her members to participate actively in it. The liturgical language used by the Church likewise presents Christ and his work to us and allows us to become cooperators with him. As for her sacramental signs and symbols, the Church relies on many sources to cultivate a dialect that is suitable to her reality. Like General Lowenhielm at Babette's feast, the Church serves as model and mentor to form us in her language, so that, with her, we may talk in Christ to the Father:

> The language of our Mother becomes ours; we learn to speak it along with her, so that, gradually, her words on our lips become our words. We are given an anticipatory share in the Church's perennial dialogue of love with him who desired to be one flesh with her, and this gift is transformed into the gift of speech. And it is in the gift of speech, and not until then, that I am really restored to my true self; only thus am I given back to God, handed over by him to all my fellow men; only thus am I free.[6]

Origins of Liturgical Language

There is an intrinsic logic to the liturgy. It is Logical: it is reunion of the human and divine mediated by a Person who is the Word. "A sacramental celebration is a meeting of God's children with their Father, in Christ and the Holy Spirit; this meeting takes the form of a dialogue . . . " (CCC, 1153). Etymologically, *dialogue* means "to speak across," and is composed of the Greek roots *logos*, meaning "word" or "speech," and *dia*, meaning "through."

A dialogue is, in short, a speaking across, one to another. A monologue, on the other hand, signifies a lone speaker. In the life of faith, and in the celebration of the liturgy, the dialogue is between God and man: God speaks his good word to us, and we return our word to God. The *Catechism* points out that "from the beginning until the end of time the whole of God's work is a blessing" (CCC, 1079). In Greek, *word* is called *logos*, and with the prefix *eu-*, meaning "good," we can say that God's good word—that is, his Son—is *the eulogy,* or blessing. Latin similarly reveals the substance of God's economy: God speaks his good word, his *bene-dictio*, and we return the benediction, or blessing, to God. Engaging in God's plan requires our listening and response. We listen to the Word, and we respond by joining our words to his. As a living member of his Body, Christ the Logos teaches us how to hear and how to speak.

In the supernatural world of grace, our human faculties lead us to a mystagogical encounter with Christ. With our physical eyes we see bread, and yet with our mystagogical sight we see the body, blood, soul, and divinity of Christ. With our bodily ears we hear the choir, and yet on account of our mystagogical hearing we listen to the choir of angels. With our mouths we speak to God, yet with our mystagogical voices we join the Mystical Voice in praise of God. The mystagogical encounter begins with what is perceptible and leads us deeper into the invisible reality, which is Christ. In order to listen and speak with the Church we must acquire supernatural faculties, so that we can be led (*agogue*) into the mystery (*mystes*). We can acquire this supernatural perception by examining the genetics of liturgical language: creation, culture, Old Covenant, Christ, and heaven.

Language and Creation

The echo of Genesis in the opening of John's Gospel account is not accidental. The same Word that opens the Gospel opens creation. "In the beginning, when God created the heavens and the earth, the earth was a formless wasteland, and darkness covered the abyss, while a mighty wind swept over the waters. Then God *said*, 'Let there be light,' and there was light" (Genesis 1:1–3). The Word that God *speaks* is none other than his Son, the Logos, the Second Person of the Trinity and the Father's own perfect image. It is this voice "which entered the scene at the very beginning of creation, when it tore through the silence of nothingness."[7] The Word and the Spirit (the "mighty wind sweeping over the waters") are the "divine artisans"[8] and, in the words of Saint Ireneaus, the Father's "creating hands" (see CCC 292, 703).

From this point forward the scriptures recount God's creating voice: "By the Lord's word the heavens were made; by the breath of his mouth, all their host. For he spoke, and it came to be, commanded, and it stood in place" (Psalm 33:6, 9). Saint Paul, accordingly, says to the Romans that God "calls into being what does not exist" (Romans 4:17). Creation's "good word" is also returned to the Father in a "dialogue of love":

> A "first 'cosmic' revelation is found which makes creation similar to an immense page opened up before all of humanity, in which a message from the Creator can be read: 'The heavens declare the glory of God, the vault of heaven proclaims his handiwork, day unto day makes known his message; night unto night hands on the knowledge. There is no speech or language where their voice is not heard. Their message goes out into all the earth'" (Psalm 19:2–5).[9]

The Word of God is therefore the center of creation, for "all things were created through him and for him. He is before all things, and in him all things hold together" (Colossians 1:16–17). The Logos mediates the communion and communication between God and creation. He is the creative Word from which all things come; he is also the reciprocal song of praise ascending to the Father from all of his creation. He is, in short, *the* dialogue (the "speaking across") by which the cosmos is "held together" in itself and united under its Creator in harmony.

God not only creates by his Word, he reveals to Adam (and in him to every human being as the perennial Adam) how he is supposed to live in the world: "You are free to eat from any of the trees of the garden except the tree of knowledge of good and bad. From that tree you shall not eat; the moment you eat from it you are surely doomed to die" (Genesis 2:16–17). Salvation and divinization come from listening to God's Word and following his economy of salvation, while listening to another voice leads to annihilation. Disobedience, of course, is what Adam had chosen. Cosmos turns to chaos, harmony turns to discord, and the original union with God is dissolved. Such is the consequence of breaking the dialogue with God by ignoring his voice.

Much later in time, at the threshold of a new creation, God again speaks his Word. The evangelist John links the first creation with the new by formulating the "conclusive and normative scriptural creation account."[10] The Gospel muses: "In the beginning was the Word, and the Word was with God, and the Word was God. He was in the beginning with God. All things came to be through him, and without him nothing came to be" (1:1–3). The definitive creation account reported by Saint John, while restoring and even surpassing the first creation described in Genesis, is prefigured by two other creations, each of which comes about by the articulation of a word.

In the covenant established between God and Israel on Mount Sinai, God instructs Moses on the construction of the tabernacle which would house the Ark of the Covenant. Three similarities between the creation of the cosmos and the creation of the covenant's tabernacle can be noted. First, the Hebrew term *bara* is used to designate establishment of both: "it denotes the process of the world's creation, the separation of the elements, through which the cosmos emerges out of chaos," and "it denotes the fundamental process of salvation history, that is, the election and separation of pure from impure, and therefore the inauguration of the history of God's dealings with men."[11] Second, the foundation of the tabernacle takes place by God's command. Just as God's creative voice brings forth the cosmos ("Then God said"), so now does his voice inaugurate the tabernacle, which anticipates the new creation in Christ: "And the Lord said to Moses . . . " (Exodus 25–31). Finally, work is spread over seven days and concludes with "a kind of vision of the Sabbath."[12] "So Moses finished the work. Then the cloud covered the tent of meeting, and the glory of the Lord filled the tabernacle" (Exodus 40:33). The creative and life-giving word of God is central in both cases.

The later and definitive creation account also hinges upon the response to God's word to Mary. The Blessed Virgin Mary "most perfectly embodies the obedience of faith" (CCC, 148), for she receives the word of God delivered by Gabriel and, even without comprehending fully the meaning of his words, gives her assent. At the dawn of this new creation, Mary's *fiat* ("let it be done") harkens back to the *fiat* of the first creation: *fiat lux*, "let there be light." Her reception of the word incarnates the Word of God in her womb.

Creation and nature are a primary source of meaning for the language of faith, especially as it comes to life in the Church's liturgy. God's word means life, light, and creation; it means communion with God and divinization when following his word; and following the Fall, it means salvation in a new creation. Each of these meanings is apparent in our liturgical language today.

Language and Human Culture

In the United States, an incoming president is required to recite the following at his inauguration: "I do solemnly swear that I will faithfully execute the

Office of President of the United States, and will to the best of my ability, preserve, protect and defend the Constitution of the United States" (U.S. Constitution, Article II, Section I, Clause 8). At the 2009 inauguration of Barak Obama, the Oath of Office was administered by Supreme Court Chief Justice John Roberts, as Constitutional protocol dictates. But instead of the word order prescribed by the Constitution ("that I will *faithfully* execute the Office of the President of the United States"), Chief Justice Roberts delivered the words in this way: "that I will execute the Office of President of the United States *faithfully*." A single word was misplaced. What seemed to be a minor technicality turned out to be significant enough that President Obama and Chief Justice Roberts met again the next day to re-administer the oath "out of an abundance of caution." "We believe that the oath of office was administered effectively," a statement from the White House said, "and that the President was sworn in appropriately yesterday. But the oath appears in the Constitution itself."[13]

What's in a word? A great deal, apparently. But of course we all know this, and not only because of cultural influences, religious prescriptions, or personal preferences. Words are meaningful—are significant—based on our own human nature. Language is at the core of the human person. As Catholic novelist Walker Percy notes, "it seems more accurate to call man not *Homo sapiens*—because man's folly is at least as characteristic as his wisdom—but *Homo symbolificus*, man the symbol-mongerer, or *Homo loquens*, man the talker."[14] Theologian Hans Urs von Balthasar points out that language is not incidental to human beings. "To speak is not an epiphenomenon of human nature. It is an integral part of our being, and even of being as such. The recent philosophers who take the phenomenon of language as their starting-point are actually taking the most direct route to an understanding of man and of being."[15] In short, man talks: it's a part of what he does and, consequently, who he is.

We do not, however, speak the same way on every occasion and to every person. The language of the doctor differs from that of the computer technician and from that of the second-grade teacher. In each of these instances, a person speaks: to the patient, to the computer, and to the child. But the elements in each type of speech (the vocabulary, the arrangement of words [syntax], and the presentation) vary according to the intended hearer. The doctor may inform his assisting nurse that the patient suffers from "myocardial ischaemia" for which they need to perform a "percutaneous coronary intervention." To the patient he might say the same thing, but he would, in most cases, be forced to say also that the patient's lack of blood (ischaemia) to the heart (myocardial) will necessitate an angioplasty (percutaneous coronary intervention). Similarly, the computer technician speaks in a certain way to his computer. To perform the regular "defragmentation" of his machine, he can't simply tell it "in plain English" what to do. Rather, he must say, through his keyboard: "defrag.exe_c:." In fact, he must speak in this way, for it is the only language of the computer world. The second-grade teacher has her own in-class manner of speaking, suited to the second-grade ability: slower, simpler, and more concise. When this same teacher meets with parents for parent–teacher conferences, her classroom language is replaced with more sophisticated usage. This variation in human language is called a language's "register," and it is a natural trait of human communication. We convey meaning in different registers, depending on our audience: the computer, the cat, our boss, our child, the commuter who just cut us off in traffic, our beloved, our own selves, and our God.

This linguistic register can help us understand the language we use in worship. When the priest greets us on the street, we respond with "Hi, Father"; but when he greets us in the liturgy as the image of Christ, the Head of his Church, we respond with "And with your spirit." Similarly, when we make a request of another person, the language of the request is commensurate with the person to whom we ask and the importance of the favor. While at the dinner table it is appropriate to ask a friend to "please, pass the salt," in the context of the Mass the dictates of the register demand something more: "In humble prayer we ask you, almighty God: / command that these gifts be borne / by the hands of your holy Angel / to your altar on high / in the sight of your divine majesty, . . . " (*Supplice*, Roman Canon). The clerk at the grocery store can rightly ask us to "have a nice day," but the cleric at Mass more appropriately tells us, the Mystical Body, to "Go and announce the Gospel of the Lord."

Among the various registers that exist, we recognize further that there is an excellence proper to each. Some people have a gift for speaking to teenagers, others are skilled computer programmers, and others have an ability to captivate an audience; but excellence in one does not guarantee proficiency in another. Great public orations, for example, survive through the years, serving as models for present-day speeches and teaching today's students the qualities of public discourse. Lincoln's Gettysburg Address, even with some of its phraseology being foreign to many ears today ("Four score and seven years ago . . ."), lives on as one of our nation's great speeches. Apart from the substance of the speech, it lives at the high end of its linguistic register. The qualities of word choice, figures of speech, rhythm, and construction of phrases, when taken together, create an expression that signifies in a most excellent way the contents of the message.

The same qualities of natural language appear in the supernatural language of the liturgy. The "Four score and seven years ago" of the Gettysburg Address could just as easily—but less remarkably—have been rendered "eighty-seven years ago," just as "Holy, Holy, Holy Lord God of hosts" might be more efficiently conveyed by "*Most* Holy Lord God of Hosts."

Because in his natural element man is a "languaged creature" (revealing his mind through language and also being formed by it), so too in the supernatural realm man speaks and is spoken to.[16] To speak to God is not an optional way to relate to him, but one dictated by human nature. At the same time, man's speech to God will be of a particular register, for speaking with God, especially publicly, is a conversation unlike any other, and it will be governed by those characteristics of the greatest of human speeches that express the noblest of human aspirations.

> . . . speaking with God, especially publicly, is a conversation unlike any other . . .

Language and the Old Testament

As we saw in chapter 1, the story of the Old Covenant is the story of the conversation, or dialogue, between God and men. God creates Adam and all of the cosmos with his Word. In harmony with the Creator in paradise, Adam hears how to live and what to avoid. Not listening to the Word of God becomes his sin. His deafness to the voice of God results in saying "no" to the *reditus*; "no" to his ultimate divinization. In Adam's "no" to God and "yes" to himself, the dia-*logue* once established is broken, and Adam's wish for a mono-*logue* is realized. Despite this, both God and man still seek to converse with each other and to reestablish communion: "The Bible is thus the story of God's struggle with human beings to make himself understandable to them over the course of time; but it is also the story of their struggle to seize hold of God over the course of time."[17]

Left to their own devices, Adam's descendants are not only unwilling, but also incapable of reestablishing communion with God. Language is a unitive force, for it allows a communion to form—for good or for evil—and action to follow. Abraham was prepared to listen to the voice of God. He is called a model of the obedience of faith because he submits "freely to the word that has been heard," not because it is necessarily understandable, agreeable, or reasonable, but "because its truth is guaranteed by God, who is Truth itself" (CCC, 144). When God tells Abraham to travel to a strange land for his inheritance, he listens. When God tells him that his aged and barren wife will give him a son, he listens. And when God tells him to offer his son back to God in a sacrifice, he listens (see CCC, 145). Because his ears are attuned to God's voice, Abraham will be the father of many nations. Unlike those building the tower of Babel, who do so to make a name for themselves (Genesis 11:1–14), it is God who makes a name for Abraham, formerly Abram.

The dialogue continues. The just hear God. God *hears* the cries of his captive people in Egypt, and he *calls* them out of the land of slavery to a land "flowing with milk and honey" (Exodus 3:7). The Chosen People are called together at Mt. Sinai. An important pattern establishes itself at this gathering. First, the people are called together by God: "So Moses went and summoned the elders of the people" (Exodus 19:7). Second, God speaks, through Moses, his revelation of the covenant's conditions to the people: "Then God delivered all these commandments: 'I, the Lord, am your God, who brought you out of the land of Egypt, that place of slavery. You shall not have other gods besides me . . .'" (Exodus 20). Third, the people give their response to the word of God just spoken to them: "When Moses came to the people and related all the words and ordinances of the Lord, they all answered with one voice, 'We will do everything that the Lord has told us . . . . all that the Lord has said, we will heed and do'" (Exodus 24:3, 7). Lastly, the agreement is sealed with a sacrifice:

> . . . rising early the next day, [Moses] erected at the foot of the mountain an altar and twelve pillars for the twelve tribes of Israel. Then, having sent certain young men of the Israelites to offer holocausts and sacrifice young bulls as peace offerings to the LORD, Moses took half of the blood and put it in large bowls; the other half he splashed on the altar. (Exodus 24:4–6)

This gathering, called the Qahal Yahweh, or *ekklesia* (from the roots *kalein*, "to call," and *ek*, "out"), is characterized by these same four features throughout the Old Covenant:[18] God calls the people together, to speak his word to them, to which they may give their assent, and then to ratify the New

Covenant with a sacrifice. Notice, though, that the first and necessary step, and that which gives the name to the entire gathering, is the calling together by God, *ecclesia,* the original Greek designation for *church.*

The larger *ekklesia* became the foundation also for the individual prayers of the Israelites. Just as the corporate gathering began with a calling together and listening, the individual Jew's daily prayers would also recall, in summary form, the calling of the Lord and his command: *Shema, Israel!*

> Hear, O Israel! The LORD is our God, the Lord alone! Therefore, you shall love the LORD, your God, with all your heart, and with all your soul, and with all your strength. Take to heart these words which I enjoin on you today. Drill them into your children. Speak of them at home and abroad, whether you are busy or at rest. (Deuteronomy 6:4–7)

In short, the Mosaic covenant continues to strengthen the dialogue between God and man. God speaks, and man must learn to listen and respond in kind. "The whole Bible is dialogue: on the one side, revelation, God's words and deeds, and on the other side, man's response in accepting the word of God and allowing himself to be led by God. To delete prayer and dialogue, genuine two-way dialogue, is to delete the whole Bible."[19]

The prophets of the Old Testament have a central role in re-forming God's Chosen People and teaching them how to listen. God leads those who are "deaf though they have ears" to a new beginning, a new creation (see Isaiah 43:8, 19). Throughout this period it is the voice of the prophets calling out to prepare for the "sacred invasion" of the Word and his reconquest of the world back to himself.[20] "Listen to my voice" (John 10:27) and be obedient (1 Samuel 15:22): salvation comes by following God's path, God's economy, God's design—and not our own. The prophets are, in essence, teaching us to hear the voice of God, to receive it with docility, and to respond rightly.

This prophetic message is fulfilled in Christ and continues to resonate today in the Church. The Church's liturgy consequently recalls these words not only when she proclaims the scriptures, but when she incorporates them into her Mass texts as well. In chapter 6 we will see how Eucharistic Prayer III weaves together images from the prophets Malachi, Isaiah, and Jeremiah. As prophetic language spoke to the Old Testament *ecclesia,* so now is it incorporated within the new *ecclesia,* the new Body of Christ, becoming her own Mystical Voice spoken with Christ, her Head, in the Spirit, to the Father.

Old Testament language, by way of summary, provides another significant source of meaning for the Church's liturgical language today. The

Old Covenant brings God and his wayward children into closer communion with one another. The Torah's sacrifices, the commandments on the moral life, and the voice of God spoken through the prophets are key. After the Fall, man cannot listen properly to God, nor can he speak adequately with God. But God *hears* his people's cries, *calls* them together before him, *tells* them how they might return to him, and *speaks* through the prophets of the Logos who will establish the everlasting covenant. The divine pedagogy toward the Chosen People is now in many ways our own: as the first ecclesial gathering was a shadow of the definitive *ecclesia*, so also did Israel's dialogue with God find fulfillment in the Logos and his eternal "hymn which is sung throughout all ages in the halls of heaven" (SC, 93).

Language and Christ

The Incarnation of the Son of God, the Logos, announces the end of the Old Covenant. It inaugurates the fulfillment of the promise. "But when the fullness of time had come, God sent his Son, born of a woman, born under the law, to ransom those under the law, so that we might receive adoption" (Galatians 4:4–5). Now is the time for God's Logos to receive a sufficient hearing. The Father speaks his creative Word once more.

Like Abraham before her, Mary says "yes" to God, even when his word is unclear to her. Regarding the divine promise of a child, both Abraham and Mary believe God, even though it seems impossible from the human perspective. "The Virgin Mary," the *Catechism* teaches, "most perfectly embodies the obedience of faith" (CCC, 148). More precise words could not have been chosen, for her *fiat* to God's request quite literally embodies in her womb that very Logos. Mary's receptivity to God's word is the fruit of centuries of preparation, the high point of God's redemptive plan to restore all things in Christ. While God's people turned away from him (when they said "no" to the *reditus*), Mary's "yes" allows the Logos to become flesh, to dwell among us, and, with us and for us, to say "yes" to God's plan.

John the Baptist is also attuned to Christ's voice. When still in the womb, John "leaps for joy" at the sound of Mary's greeting and the presence of the Lord. Later, John testifies to the authenticity of the Logos, saying, "The one who has the bride is the bridegroom; the best man, who stands *and listens for him*, rejoices greatly at the bridegroom's voice" (John 3:29). Along with Mary, John the Baptist is prepared to receive the Word of God and to speak that same Word to the house of Israel. In John the Baptist, "the Holy

Spirit concludes his speaking through the prophets" (CCC, 719). His is the final cry in the wilderness, heralding the "last word" of the Father: "In giving us his Son . . . , he spoke everything to us at once in his sole Word—and he has no more to say . . . because what he spoke before to the prophets in parts, he has now spoken all at once by giving us the All Who is His Son."[21]

In the Incarnate Logos, God's speech takes on a different tone. Before the Incarnation, when God spoke, it was in a disembodied way. As Moses describes the voice of God on Mt. Horeb, "the Lord spoke to you from the midst of the fire. You heard the sound of the words, but saw no form; there was only a voice" (Deuteronomy 4:12). On the other hand, when God speaks through the mouths of the prophets, it is only indirectly, for these prophets relayed what God had first revealed to them. But with Christ, the literal voice of God becomes human, and he now speaks directly as a man, face to face. Whereas in the past God spoke "to our ancestors through the prophets . . . , in these last days, he spoke to us through a Son" (Hebrews 1:1–2).

The new Mediator, Jesus the Logos, speaks clearly for the Father, not only because he is one with the Father, but because his identity is not merely a description: he is *the* Word. The dialogue of communion has now become quite literally a Logos who speaks across the divide between God and humanity and bridges their separation. While the words between human beings pass away, the Word between God and his people abides, for the Logos of the dialogue is a Person. Jesus' unique standing as true representative of both God and man allows him to speak with authority. He is *authorized* to speak on behalf of God to men because he is God; likewise, he is authorized to speak for men to God, since he is at the same time fully human. Jesus Christ, the *Logos incarnatus*, represents perfectly and completely both sides of the dialogue, for he is a Person—a Word—who shares the nature of each. Saint Ephraim the Syrian goes so far as to speak of a "double incarnation"[22] of the Son of God. Not only does God become restrained by the limitations of our flesh, but he likewise takes on the limitations of our language. The infinite and all-creating Word condescends to the constraints of his very creation.

Christ's role as perfect mediator—that is, as perfect priest—is seen in the conclusion of the principal orations of the Church's liturgy. The Roman's term for priest was *pontifex*, literally, "bridge-builder," since he mediated between the gods on the one hand and human beings on the other. A vestige of this term exists in the Church today, of course, in one of the titles of the Pope, the supreme bridge-builder: *Pontifex maximus*. The priest offers prayers, sacrifices, and petitions to God on behalf of the people, while bestowing grace, forgiveness, and divine promise on behalf of God. Since Christ is both God and man and works on behalf of both, our prayers reflect this function. At times we conclude our prayers with "*We ask* this through Christ our Lord," indicating his role as our human representative before God. Other times we say, "*Grant* this through Christ our Lord," signifying Christ's divinity and source of our answered prayers. The Latin text, however, concludes in a way different from both of these: *Per Christum Dominum nostrum*, literally, "Through Christ our Lord." In other words, it does not limit the interpretation of Christ's intercessory role, but "has us look in both directions simultaneously, to see that Christ's mediation works in two ways."[23]

Apart from Jesus' identity with the Word of God, his historical words give precise and definitive meaning to the words used by the Church today. At the heart of the Eucharistic Prayer are Jesus' own words: "Take this, all of you, and eat of it, for this is my body, which will be given up for you." And while we do and should pray to God in words arising from our own aspirations, we pray together "at the Savior's command and formed by divine teaching." The Church says the Creed together with Christ, the Head of the Mystical Body. As this "organically structured priestly communion" is precisely that—a communion—the Church speaks not as a collection of voices but as a single voice belonging to a single Body: "I believe in one God . . . " (see LA, 65).

Other biblical events surrounding Christ also inform our liturgical language, for the liturgy today is every bit as real an encounter with Christ as those happening in Palestine centuries ago. At the birth of Christ, the angels appeared to the shepherds, singing, "Glory to God in the highest and on earth peace to those on whom his favor rests" (Luke 2:14), and we take the example of their words for ourselves in the *Gloria* sung on Sundays and solemnities. John the Baptist called his contemporaries to "Behold, the Lamb of God" (John 1:29), and the priest does the same now: "Behold the Lamb of God, behold him who takes away the sins of the world." The good centurion in Saint Luke's Gospel account requests that Jesus heal his dying servant, without traveling to his house, adding, "Lord, do not trouble yourself, for I am not worthy to have you enter under my roof. . . . But say the word and let my servant be healed" (Luke 7:6–7). Our preparation for Jesus' entry under our own "roof" at communion takes its meaning from this encounter with Christ: "Lord, I am not worthy that you should enter under my roof, but only say the word and my soul shall be healed."

It is Christ himself, the Word of God in the flesh, who gives liturgical language its definitive meaning. He is the voice of God and the voice of man, and he is therefore the standard that all of our language seeks to imitate. "I urge you brothers," Saint Paul says, "by the mercies of God, to offer your bodies as a living sacrifice, holy and pleasing to God, your spiritual worship" (Romans 12:1). This "spiritual worship," or *logikē latreía*, is taken by Pope Benedict to mean "worship in accord with the Logos."[24] Christians are meant to sing in accord with the Logos, to build churches in accord with the Logos, to measure time in accord with the Logos, and especially to speak in accord with the Logos. To learn this "logification"[25] is to speak with the voice of Christ. Our language, consequently, takes its principle point of reference from the words of the Word found in scripture. The dialogues of Jesus with the men and women of his age are examples of the ongoing dialogue taking place today in his Mystical Body, where the Mystical Voice unites heaven and earth.

Language of Heaven

At the Tower of Babel, men sought to make a name for themselves, but instead became confused and separated from one another. In heaven, the angels and saints sing of the name of God, and do so gathered in harmonious order around the throne of the Lamb. How do we know what heaven looks like or, more to the point, sounds like? The prophet Isaiah tells us of his vision: "I saw the Lord seated on a high and lofty throne, with the train of his garment filling the temple. Seraphim were stationed above; each of them had six wings: with two they veiled their faces, with two they veiled their feet, and with two they hovered aloft. 'Holy, holy, holy is the Lord of hosts!' they cried one to the other. 'All the earth is filled with his glory!'" (6:1–3).

It is essential for us to understand, as much as we humanly can, the nature of heaven, for it is in heaven's eternal liturgy that we participate when we gather for the sacramental liturgy of the Church on earth. Heaven's celebration is primary and normative; its inhabitants stand directly before the Lamb and sing his praises. Our liturgy, in time, mediates the heavenly reality through sacramental signs. These signs, the Second Vatican Council tells us, not only express these eternal truths, but foster an affinity toward them in us. In other words, the eternal and heavenly character of the sacraments shows us what heaven is like, and while they do, they form us to be suitable citizens of the City of God.

While Saint John in his Revelation discovers an unimaginable diversity (hierarchies of angels, white-robed martyrs, horsemen and winged creatures), there exists simultaneously a harmony and order. Heaven does not appear as a place of chaos, discord, and caprice, and the heavenly host does not fill the City with gossip and cacophony. They cry out, sing, and exclaim the Lamb's praise with one harmonious voice.

The Church is a single entity, yet she exists in heaven and on earth. Her liturgy, likewise, is a single celebration that takes place in heaven and on earth. Her liturgical praise—her Mystical Voice—sings of God's glory, fills the halls of heaven, while at the same time it resounds in churches of stone and glass. "And so, with the Angels and all the Saints we declare [God's] glory, as with one voice we acclaim: Holy, Holy, Holy Lord God of hosts. / Heaven and earth are full of your glory" (Preface Acclamation, Eucharistic Prayer II). Our singing not only unites men and women with the heavenly band, but we—as priests of creation—"give voice to every creature under heaven" when we join our voices to the Mystical Voice of the Church (Preface, Eucharistic Prayer IV).

To speak and sing in this way requires formation and training: like Saint Paul's athlete training for a competition, we prepare for the liturgy in order to win the crown of glory (see 1 Corinthians 9: 24–27). This is what our tradition calls *askesis*. The demands of any language include a certain degree of practice, whether of the child learning his native tongue ("I *finished-ed* my dinner!") or an adult wishing to learn a second language. Our liturgical language also requires *askesis* based on the realities of heaven: "The body must be trained, so to speak, for the resurrection."[26] C. S. Lewis's *The Great Divorce* describes "a fantastic bus ride from hell to heaven—a round trip for some but not for others." In his dream-story, busloads of ghost-like men and women arrive in heaven, only to find that the grass is so sharp, the rain drops so solid, and the sounds of nature are so clear and loud that only the "solid people" can tolerate them. For the earth-like phantasms, these heavenly realities are so immensely real that they are uncomfortable and require a great deal of acclimation. Only with time will their feet not suffer from the real grass, their skin not welt under the rain drops, and their ears not deafen at the heaven's true sounds. Without proper training, the liturgy will be either too heavy to bear or too real to comprehend.

John Henry Cardinal Newman (on whose tombstone is written, "Out of the shadows and phantasms into the Truth") is another who speaks to heaven's reality and our subsequent need for *askesis* to live comfortably in it.

Instead of seeking liturgical novelties, he preaches, we must begin to conform ourselves to heaven's new way of life as found in the sacramental liturgy:

> Now is it not plain that those who are thus tired, and wearied, and made impatient by our sacred services below, would most certainly get tired and wearied with heaven above? Because there the Cherubim and Seraphim "rest not day and night," saying, "Holy, holy, holy, Lord God Almighty." Such as this, too, will be the way of the Saints in glory, for we are told that there will be a great voice of much people saying, Alleluia; and again they said Alleluia; and the four-and-twenty elders said Alleluia; and a voice of many waters and of mighty thunderings said Alleluia. Such, too, was our Lord's way, when in His agony He three times repeated the same words, "Thy will, not Mine, be done." It is the delight of all holy beings, who stand around the Throne, to use one and the same form of worship; they are not tired, it is ever new pleasure to them to say the words anew. They are never tired; but surely all those persons would be soon tired of hearing them, instead of taking part in their glorious chant, who are wearied of Church now, and seek for something more attractive and rousing.[27]

Our liturgical language, then, not only expresses heavenly and eternal truths, but shapes us and prepares us to abide with these truths for all eternity. For this reason, a great deal of our sacramental language takes its meaning from the heavenly context. The *Sanctus*, as has been noted, comes to us from the heavenly visions of Isaiah and John. The victorious in heaven sing in the Song of the Lamb that "you alone are holy" (Revelation 15:4), and in the *Gloria* we echo them, singing, "For you alone are the Holy One, / you alone are the Lord . . . ." Those who have suffered for Christ now live joyously in heaven, where God "will wipe every tear from their eyes, and there shall be no more death or mourning, wailing or pain" (Revelation 21:4). We pray accordingly for ourselves and our dead, that we may enter heaven where "we hope to enjoy for ever the fullness of your glory, / when you will wipe away every tear from our eyes" (Eucharistic Prayer III). Saint John not only recounts his senses of heaven, but transcribes exactly what he is told: "the angel said to me, 'Write this: Blessed are those who have been called to the wedding feast of the Lamb.' And he said to me, 'These words are true; they come from God'" (Revelation 19:9). The Church's voice, speaking in heaven

Heaven provides our sacramental language with yet another layer of meaning.

and on earth, says consistently: "Behold the Lamb of God. / [. . .] Blessed are those called to the supper of the Lamb."

Heaven provides our sacramental language with yet another layer of meaning. The words proclaimed in the earthly liturgy come in many cases from the mouths of the Church's surest members, those recapitulated in Christ, those who are permanently and eternally under his headship. The victorious know how to listen, how to speak, and how to sing. Their lives have been *logified*, reformed "according to the Logos," and part of their *askesis* has been the acquisition of the tongue of Mother Church. With the Lamb at the center (Revelation 5:6), the angels and saints of the City of God sing the Mystical Voice truly, clearly, and eternally. The sacramental language employed by the earthly Church seeks to capture, to the degree possible in this age, the qualities and characteristics of this heavenly norm.

Language of the Church

There's a phrase in the English language that denotes a small or meaningless difference: "not an iota's worth." "It doesn't make an iota's worth of difference whether Republicans or Democrats win; all politicians are the same," for example. The iota is the ninth letter of the Greek alphabet and is usually rendered as the letter "i" in English. It's odd that the expression surrounding this letter means what it does, for this lone little letter, seemingly so insignificant, was the source of a great controversy in the early Church. In 325, the Council of Nicaea was called to settle a dispute between the camps of Arius on the one hand, and Saint Athanasius on the other. The Arian position (here greatly simplified) was essentially that Jesus was not God; that he was, at best, only "like in being to God." In Greek, this term is rendered *homoiousios*, from "like" or "similar," *homoi*, and "being," *ousios*. The Catholic position, put forward by Saint Athanasius and others, held that Jesus is in fact God; that he is the "same in being to God," or *homoousios*, from "same," *homo*, and *ousios*, "being" or "essence." What's the difference? This one little letter—the Greek *iota*—makes all the difference between Jesus being a creature or Jesus being God.

The Council of Nicaea, by confirming that Jesus is *homoousios*, resulted in great and often violent division, depending in large part on the leanings of the territorial ruler. Saint Athanasius himself was exiled more than once for supporting the Catholic position.

That Jesus is *homoousios* (or, in Latin, consubstantial) with the Father is a truth guarded energetically by the Church. She teaches it clearly (or as clearly as is possible for such a mystery), includes its truth in the Creeds of her liturgy, and safeguards it in her manner of speaking. Pope Paul VI, when explaining the Church's use of the term *transubstantiation* with regard to the Eucharistic mystery, invokes Nicaea's formulation of *homoousios* in what he calls a "rule of language." He says:

> Once the integrity of the faith has been safeguarded, then it is time to guard the proper way of expressing it, lest our careless use of words give rise, God forbid, to false opinions regarding faith in the most sublime things . . . and so the rule of language which the Church has established through the long labor of centuries, with the help of the Holy Spirit, and which she has confirmed with the authority of the Councils, and which has more than once been the watchword and banner of orthodox faith, is to be religiously preserved, and no one may presume to change it at his own pleasure or under the pretext of new knowledge. Who would ever tolerate that the dogmatic formulas used by the ecumenical councils for the mysteries of the Holy Trinity and the Incarnation be judged as no longer appropriate for men of our times, and let others be rashly substituted for them? (MF, 23–24)

The Magisterium speaks often today about the law of believing (*lex credendi*) and the law of celebrating (*lex orandi*): to these we might add another, after the words of Paul VI, a law of speaking (*lex dicendi* or *lex loquentis*). In these expressions, the Church articulates the laws of her own constitution; namely, that she prays what she believes and believes what she prays, without, we might add, an iota's worth of difference. The Church also says what she means, and she means to say Logos, Christ.

Through the centuries, "with the help of the Holy Spirit, and . . . confirmed with the authority of the Councils," the Church has developed a language of her own, one particularly suited to her own reality and the truths she wishes to confess. This should not surprise us, for, as we discovered above, every institution and human endeavor has a *lingua franca* of its own. The language of the police scanner differs from that of the cocktail party which differs from the State of the Union address. The language of the Mystical Body, and especially the language of her prayer, is built upon the vocabulary and grammar of nature, human culture, the Old Covenant, Christ's own words, and heaven. Her language incorporates these various strata, and from them she developed organically a manner of speaking all her own, one rich in meaning and content.

The liturgical language spoken by the Church is one of many elements that combine in a ritual celebration, yet it has a unique standing among other ritual elements (e.g., art, time, objects, etc.). Called the "form" of the sacraments proper, language articulates and specifies the supernatural meaning of the material used in the rite. To say, "I baptize you in the name of the Father, and of the Son, and of the Holy Spirit" means that the poured water effectively symbolizes death to the old self and rebirth into Christ and the Trinitarian family. As we have seen, to say,

> ... the Church has developed a language of her own, one particularly suited to her own reality...

"I baptize you in the name of the Creator, the Redeemer, and the Sanctifier" means something else and causes something else. When the *lex dicendi* is not consonant with the *lex credendi* or the *lex orandi*, the speech is meaningless, or at least without its divine meaning, which is Christ.

Summary

The Mystical Body of Christ is most actualized, most truly herself, when united with Christ her Head in his eternal offering of himself to his Father. In the liturgical wedding feast of Christ with his Bride, all things unite in a single Voice (which is the Voice of the Logos and is the Logos) in a resounding "yes" to the Father, his plan, and his thirst for our divinization. This theo-*logical* reality (or *res*) is sacramentalized in a particular way in the Church's language.

As a true symbol, sacramental language has an organic affinity to the reality of the Logos it seeks to manifest. Like most liturgical signs or symbols, the meaning of language is rooted in the rich and multilayered soil of creation, culture, Old Covenant, Christ, and heaven. Then, over the centuries and according to local values, her language develops and speaks to and from God's people.

Liturgical language is unique to the reality of the Mystical Body. While it can and does influence secular language, sacramental language is intended, like Christ, to elevate, transform, and divinize the things of the earth. Like the language used in other areas of human life that may be foreign to us (medicine, law, technology), the language of the liturgy requires formation, an *askesis*, to speak it and hear it rightly and clearly. Such linguistic asceticism is in some ways a microcosm of our larger Christian goal. We are called to identify with Christ, thinking, loving, and acting as he would and for the reasons he would. To conform ourselves to Christ is to become a saint

Liturgical language is unique to the reality of the Mystical Body.

or, in the phrase of Cardinal Ratzinger, to "logify our existence," thinking, loving, and living in accord with the Logos. Our language seeks the same goal, to be speech in accord with the Logos. We are formed by our language to speak the language of Christ, the language of his Bride, and the language of heaven.

To speak in accord with the Logos is therefore to worship in accord with the Logos and become divinized in accord with the Logos: it is *logikē latreía* (spiritual worship) (Romans 12:1). How do we learn this language? Much like the learning of our native and natural language, we are led to speak the supernatural language of heaven by experience. But to help us and form us along the way, our ears and our voices attune themselves by means of a sacramental mystagogy. Mystagogy is a "leading (*agogue*) into the mystery (*mystes*)," by which "the faithful are helped to understand the meaning of the liturgy's words and actions, to pass from its signs to the mystery which they contain" (MND, 17). A sacrament is both sign and reality, *sacramentum et res*. We see, hear, taste, and otherwise sense the external sign of the sacrament, but we need "mystagogical senses" to detect the reality that lies within the external sign. We see bread, but must be led to see the reality of Christ's body within it. We hear the choir, but if we have learned to hear mystagogically, we hear the "Holy, Holy, Holy" of the angels and saints in heaven. We smell incense, but should be led to smell the "bowls filled with incense" at the Wedding Feast of the Lamb in heaven (Revelation 5:8). So, too, with our language: hearing and speaking sacramental language leads us to hear and speak on another plane altogether.

One of the roots of the word *liturgy* is *ergon*, which means "work." Now that we have worked to build a proper foundation (Part I), let's next look at or listen more directly at the sacramental language of *The Roman Missal*.

Endnotes

1. Joseph Ratzinger, *The Spirit of the Liturgy,* trans. John Saward (San Francisco: Ignatius Press, 2000), 219.

2. Based on a short story by Isak Dinesen, "Babette's Feast," in *Anecdotes of Destiny and Ehrengard* (New York: Vintage Books, 1993).

3. On February 1, 2008.

4. See *Vicesiumus quintus annus,* 13; *Ecclesia de Eucharistia* (EE), 10; and *Spiritus et Sponsa* (SS), 15, respectively.

5. Ratzinger, *The Spirit of the Liturgy,* 171.

6. Ratzinger, *The Feast of Faith: Approaches to a Theology of the Liturgy,* trans. Graham Harrison (San Francisco: Ignatius Press, 1986), 29–30.

7. "The Message to the People of God, XII Ordinary General Assembly of the Synod of Bishops" October 5–24.

8. See Ratzinger, *The Spirit of the Liturgy,* 153–4; CCC, 1091.

9. These reflections on the Word's place in creation are those of the XII Ordinary General Assembly of Bishops, "Message to the People of God," October 24, 2008, 1.

10. Ratzinger, *In the Beginning: A Catholic Understanding of the Story of Creation and the Fall,* trans. Boniface Ramsey (Grand Rapids, MI: Eerdmans Publishing Co., 1995), 15.

11. Ratzinger, *The Spirit of the Liturgy,* 27.

12. Ibid.

13. Details of this story are found in "Obama Sworn In Again, With Right Words," by Michael D. Shear, *Washington Post,* on Thursday, January 22, 2009. See http://www.washingtonpost.com/wp–dyn/content/article/2009/01/21/AR2009012103685.html.

14. Walker Percy, *Sign Posts in a Strange Land* (New York: Noonday, 1992), 120.

15. Hans Urs von Balthasar, "God has spoken in human language," in *The Liturgy and the Word of God* (Collegeville, MN: Liturgical Press, 1959), 43.

16. Percy, *Signposts in a Strange Land,* 122.

17. Ratzinger, *In the Beginning,* 9.

18. See the dedication of Solomon's Temple in 1 Kings 8; the renewal of the covenant under King Josiah in 2 Kings 23; the restoration of the Temple cult in 2 Kings 29; and the rediscovery of the Torah following the Babylonian exile in Nehemiah 8. The latter reading from Nehemiah, incidentally, is a required text at the Rite for the Dedication of a Church.

19. Ratzinger, *The Feast of Faith,* 16.

20. The expression is Louis Bouyer's. See Louis Boyer, *Rite and Man* (South Bend, IN: University of Notre Dame Press, 1963), 115.

21. John of the Cross, in CCC, 65.

22. See Sebastian Brock, *The Luminous Eye: The Spiritual World Vision of Saint Ephrem* (Kalamazoo, MI: Cistercian Publications, revised edition, 1992).

23. Archbishop Allen Vigneron, "The Art of Pastoral Translation at the Service of Communion," Keynote Address at the Gateway Liturgical Conference, St. Louis, MO, November 7–8, 2008. See www.adoremus.org/0209Vigneron.html.

24. Ratzinger, *A New Song for the Lord: Faith in Christ and Liturgy Today,* trans. Martha M. Matesich (New York: The Crossroad Publishing Company, 1996), 57–176.

25. See Ratzinger, *The Spirit of the Liturgy,* 46, 58.

26. Ratzinger, *The Spirit of the Liturgy*, 176.

27. John Henry Newman, *Parochial and Plain Sermons,* Vol. 8 (Whitefish, MT: Kessinger Publishing, 2008), Sermon 1.

PART II

THE LANGUAGE OF THE ROMAN MISSAL

Behold, I stand at the door and knock. If anyone hears my voice
and opens the door, then I will enter his house and dine with him,
and he with me. I will give the victor the right to sit with me on my throne,
as I myself first won the victory and sit with my Father on his throne.
Whoever has ears ought to hear what the Spirit says to the churches.

Revelation 3:20–22

In a well-known work of popular religious art, Christ Jesus is standing
at the threshold of a house, knocking on its door. As the keen observer
notes, the door of the house has no outside handle or doorknob: it
can only be opened from within. Part I of this book seeks, by analogy,
to help us to hear the voice of the Christ who stands before us at the
Mass, waiting for us to open the doors of our hearts to him.

With Christ in our heart we can be "victorious." To be a victor
and sit with Christ on his throne we must first have ears to hear. Our
initial task, therefore, is to acquire the supernatural ears to hear the
voice of God prayed today by his Mystical Body. We do this by recalling the essentially sacramental nature of the liturgy; namely, that the
liturgy's ultimate reality (Christ and the grace of his Paschal Mystery) is

made available to us in the Church's sacramental signs. Each of the liturgy's sacramental signs is rooted in the scriptures, Christ, heaven, and culture. To see them in these contexts aids our liturgical encounter with Christ.

We sought to sharpen our "sacramental hearing" in Part I as we examined the origins of the Mass' language. The lexicon of the Mass, while in some ways consonant with other human languages, is in other ways proper to the divine dialogue. Because the voice of the Church at prayer speaks to God, the tenor of the Church's language has been formed by scripture, Tradition, and the Mass' history. The Church's Mystical Voice, expressed for us in her Mass texts, now goes on to form us. We hear Christ in the words of the Mass, and in hearing him we become like him, "logified."

With our ears now attuned to the supernatural, we turn next to the very words of *The Roman Missal*. In her *Constitution on the Sacred Liturgy* and subsequent documents, the Church gives numerous principles that direct the choice of liturgical texts and also their translation into various modern languages. In chapter 4 we trace the current translation principles through the post-conciliar popes back to their sources in the *Constitution*. Chapters 5 through 7 then demonstrate how these principles have helped cultivate the sacred language of the different parts of the Mass. Finally, to help the Church's prayers take root in our hearts, chapter 8 offers further direction on how to form ourselves and others to hear clearly the voice of the Logos in the Mass.

"Behold, I stand at the door and knock. If anyone hears my voice and opens the door, then I will enter his house and dine with him, and he with me" (Revelation 3:20). The Mass is the heavenly banquet, at which we dine with the whole Church, the Bride of Christ. To hear the voice and receive it with docility is nothing other than to partake of the eternal banquet in the present age of the Church. Part I has built a foundation; Part II invites the Word into our house.

Chapter 4

Vatican II and the Third Edition of *The Roman Missal*

Every Catholic liturgy, in every Catholic rite, continues the obedient "yes" of the Logos by the Holy Spirit's power in the Church's sacramental signs, so that men and women of every age might become holy by participating in Christ's saving work. The Catholic Church's individual rites (e.g., Coptic, Byzantine, and Latin) celebrate this one supernatural reality in diverse ways, according to the varying theological and cultural emphases and the sacramental rituals that express them. The Roman Rite of the Latin Church, for example, shares common ground with all Catholic rites, yet reflects the particular character of the culture in which the one Mystery of Christ has taken root. In its restoration of the Sacred Liturgy, the Second Vatican Council calls the Latin Church back to these roots, so that modern adaptations can be more fruitful for the Roman Rite's participants. The Council's *Constitution on the Sacred Liturgy* encourages "legitimate variations" to local cultures, while emphasizing the needed integrity of the traditional Roman Rite. Language itself, as a constituent part of the liturgy and of culture, is also allowed to adapt itself to the needs of the people, and the *Constitution* provides general yet fundamental norms for introducing the vernacular language into the Roman Rite.

It was the responsibility of the post-conciliar Church to elaborate and implement the Council's norms on liturgical vernacular. No less than forty Papal and Vatican documents on language preceded Pope John Paul II's election.[1] His own lengthy papacy applied the general norms of the *Constitution* more precisely. The apostolic letter on the 25th anniversary of the Liturgy Constitution (*Vicesimus quintus annus*, 1988) reviewed the process of vernacularization and called for a deepening of the translations. The Dicastery documents on inculturation, *Varietates legitimae* (1994), and translations,

Liturgiam authenticam (2001) give still clearer articulation to the Second Vatican Council's call, and the *Ratio translationis* for the English language (2007) lays out the precise application of the *Constitution's* norms for *The Roman Missal*. In short, the bridge between the *Constitution on the Sacred Liturgy* and the third edition of *The Roman Missal* in English is carefully built, organically developed, and consistently planned. The common thread connecting the Second Vatican Council to the third *Roman Missal* in English is the next topic of our examination.

Sacrosanctum Concilium, the Constitution on the Sacred Liturgy

As he prepared the Church for the third Christian millennium, Pope John Paul II reviewed the twentieth century and the developments in the Church's life. He examined many aspects of ecclesial and cultural activity (e.g., the universal call to holiness, ecumenism, and the sacramental encounter with Christ) in light of the teaching of the Second Vatican Council. He described the Council as that *"great grace bestowed on the Church in the twentieth century"* and the "sure compass by which to take our bearings in the century now beginning" (*Novo millennio ineunte*, 57).

The first of Vatican II's documents, *Sacrosanctum concilium*, was promulgated by Pope Paul VI on December 4, 1963. Setting the tone for the Ecumenical Council itself and for each of its subsequent documents, the *Constitution on the Sacred Liturgy* opens:

> This sacred Council [*sacrosanctum concilium*] has several aims in view: it desires to impart an ever increasing vigor to the Christian life of the faithful; to adapt more suitably to the needs of our own times those institutions which are subject to change; to foster whatever can promote union among all who believe in Christ; to strengthen whatever can help to call the whole of mankind into the household of the Church. (SC, 1)

To "invigorate," "adapt," "unify," and "strengthen" the Church and her members, the Council says, begins with that component of the Church's life which dwells at the heart of the Mystical Body—the liturgy. An oft-quoted phrase of Saint Prosper of Aquitaine, a disciple of Saint Augustine, also gives some primacy to the liturgy: "let the law of prayer establish the law of belief" (*Legem credendi lex statuat supplicandi;* see CCC, 1124). In this light, the Council "sees particularly cogent reasons for undertaking the reform and promotion of the liturgy" (SC, 1).

Building on the labors of the liturgical movement in Europe and the United States, and inspired by the initial reforms of twentieth-century popes, particularly Pius X and Pius XII, the *Constitution* puts forward in a clear and definitive way the true nature of the liturgy and its significance for the ongoing life of the Church and her members. The liturgical principles defined in the *Constitution* are the fruits of the liturgical movement and the Magisterium: the manifold presence of Christ in the liturgy (SC, 7); the centrality of his word (SC, 24) and the sacrifice of the Paschal Mystery (SC, 6, 47, 61); the nature of the Church as Mystical Body (SC, 2, 41) and her cooperation with Christ her Head (SC, 7) in his praise of the Father (SC, 83); and the participation by the members of the Body (SC, 14, 30) in this work through the sacraments (SC, 7). Already found in the Church's tradition, each of these realities is promoted in a definitive way by the Council and her liturgical *Constitution*, and they continue to guide the liturgy's celebration and deepen our participation in it today.

We see the liturgy as the Church herself understands it, thanks to the *Constitution on the Sacred Liturgy*. Likewise, to view a particular aspect of it properly (such as language) we must examine it according to these same principles of *Sacrosanctum concilium*. Part I of this book examined these principles: 1) the Paschal Sacrifice of the Logos, in which he proclaims his unreserved "yes" to the Father; 2) the union of the Mystical Body with her Head in the re-presentation of that sacrifice in the Eucharist; and 3) the "logification" of the faithful through their rational participation in the sacraments. There are other liturgical principles of the *Constitution* that also speak directly to the matter of liturgical language, especially as it exists in contemporary ritual texts. A review of these principles will help demonstrate how *Varietates legitimae* and *Liturgiam authenticam* (the documents on inculturation and translation, respectively) "invigorate, adapt, unify, and strengthen" the Church's liturgy as the Council desired.

Unity

One of the foremost liturgical principles, especially in the Western Church,[2] is unity. We recall the Council's opening line, which states four principle aims, including "to foster whatever can promote union among all who believe in Christ" (SC, 1). Liturgical celebrations, the *Constitution* continues, " . . . are not private functions, but are celebrations of the Church, which is the 'sacrament of unity,' namely, the holy people united and ordered under their bishops" (SC, 26). Because Christ's Bride, the Mystical Body, is *one*, the liturgy which symbolizes the Church possesses a oneness and unity. In the genius of Vatican II, original insights from the early Church were retrieved and recast for our new time. The Council reflects the thought of Saint Ignatius of Antioch in his letter to the Magnesians:

> . . . I exhort you to strive to do all things in harmony with God: the bishop is to preside in the place of God, while the presbyters are to function as the council of the Apostles, and the deacons, who are most dear to me, are entrusted with the ministry of Jesus Christ. [. . .] Let there be nothing among you tending to divide you, but be united with the bishop and those who preside — serving at once as a pattern and as a lesson of incorruptibility. [. . . N]either must you undertake anything without the bishop and the presbyters; nor must you attempt to convince yourselves that anything you do on your own account is acceptable. No; at your meetings there must be one prayer, one supplication, one mind, one hope in love, in joy that is flawless, that is Jesus Christ who stands supreme.[3]

The clearest manifestation of the Church includes the bishop at the altar of his cathedral. When surrounded by his priests, ministers, and all the faithful actively participating in the same Eucharistic sacrifice, the mystery of the Church is sacramentally present before us (SC, 41).[4] In order that the unity of the Church may be ritually manifested, there should not be

As the Church is a living and dynamic Body, so also is her sacramental expression.

a "notable difference" between rites in adjoining territories. The *General Instruction of the Roman Missal* (2000), integrating the principle of unity into its norms on the celebration of the Mass, concludes its instructions thus: "And so, the Roman Missal, though in a diversity of languages and with some variety of customs, must in the future be safeguarded an instrument and an outstanding sign of the integrity and unity of the Roman Rite" (GIRM, 399). Finally, in allowing a broader use of the Missal of Blessed John XXIII, Pope Benedict has gone to great pains to explain that today's use of the *Roman Missals* of 1962 and 2000 do not constitute two rites, but "a twofold use of one and the same rite" (Accompanying letter to *Summorum Pontificum*).

Unity, however, does not mean uniformity, for there are differences within a single rite, and legitimate variations exist according to different groups and regions. The *Roman Missal* has been legitimately adapted to children, for example. These official changes, however, should not be equated with some particular, fundamentally idiosyncratic adaptations that have been deemed inappropriate.[5] Nevertheless, legitimate differences between and within rites serve to manifest the diversity of the single Church, as well as provide for a fuller participation by those to whom the one rite is adapted. While the Mystery of Christ cannot be fully captured by any one of the Church's liturgical traditions (see CCC, 1201), a substantial unity within each rite signifies the one household of the Church (SC, 1), called together by God, in order to listen to the voice of his Son and through the Spirit become one with him in his redemptive sacrifice to the Father. Even human households strive to balance diverse interests within their own unity: the children's many activities, for example, are matched against the common family meal. As long as equilibrium exists, the activities of family members enrich the household, but if family unity is sacrificed in their pursuit, the household often disintegrates.

Traditional Restoration

As the Church is a living and dynamic Body, so also is her sacramental expression. The ritual forms are accessible to men and women of every age, yet have grown "organically from forms already existing" (SC, 23). Rooted in Christ and the Apostolic Church, the Church's celebration connects all times and places to the historical work of the Incarnate Logos. For although there are parts of the liturgy that can and do change over time, other elements have been instituted by Christ himself and are immutable, and the Church does not have the authority to adapt them to particular groups (SC, 21). The one, holy, and Catholic Church is also *apostolic*, so she has desired over time to keep rooted in the Apostolic Church. Echoing Pope Saint Pius V's words upon promulgating the Tridentine Missal in 1570 (*Quo Primum*), the *Constitution on the Sacred Liturgy* prescribed that certain elements of the Mass that have been obscured through the years "are now to be restored to the vigor which they had in the days of the holy Fathers" (SC, 50). And while the liturgy *Constitution* is directed primarily at the Roman Rite, many of its principles and norms are applicable to the Eastern rites. The Church desires that all rites, if revised, take into account their own liturgical and ecclesial traditions (SC, 4).

The purpose of revising or restoring in accord with sound tradition is not born of nostalgia nor for the sake of "being traditional." Rather, the *Constitution* speaks of traditional restoration for the same reasons outlined in its paragraph one: to invigorate, adapt, unify, and strengthen. For the Church to *adapt* successfully, she keeps her bearings and roots herself in *tradition*. By keeping her footing in a traditional restoration, rites will "be given new vigor to meet the circumstances and needs of modern times" (SC, 4) and their participants "may more certainly derive an abundance of graces from the sacred liturgy" (SC, 21).

Modern Adaptation

The Bride of Christ was taken from the side of the Second Adam as he slept in death upon the cross, and she is now the mother of a supernatural race of a new creation (SC, 5). But the roots of the Tree of Life extend beyond the cross, through the prefigurements of the Old Covenant and before creation itself to the Trinity's own plan for humanity and creation (see CCC, 758–66). Even though in some ways the Church predates creation itself (CCC, 760), the Mystical Body, which is the living Christ, is animated by the Holy Spirit. This Mystical Body lives in all ages and in all ages adapts herself, where possible, to the exigencies of the period so that men and women of all times can hear clearly the voice of God, the Logos, calling them together (see SC, 1). So in addition to the Council's call for a *traditional restoration* is the need for a simultaneous *modern adaptation*.

The *Constitution's* call for adaptation is made alongside her desire to maintain tradition. "Provisions shall also be made, when revising the liturgical books, for legitimate variations and adaptations to different groups, regions, and peoples, especially in mission lands, provided that the substantial unity of the Roman Rite is preserved; and this should be borne in mind when drawing up the rites and devising rubrics" (SC, 36). In other words, an adaptation not rooted in tradition risks losing ritual ties to the apostles and even to Christ. Pre-adolescent children constitute one such group to whom the Roman Rite has been adapted, and the Lectionary and Eucharistic Prayers used at Masses with children are meant to foster their participation in the one Roman Rite. Perhaps more significantly in this regard is the adaptation of the Roman Rite to the diverse cultures of the world. Now called "inculturation," the one Roman Rite "incarnates" itself into a culture, and in so doing enriches itself while transforming the culture at hand. The eleventh and twelfth centuries witnessed such an exchange: the rite benefited immensely from the Aristotelian philosophy received from the Mozarabic culture, while the culture profited from Catholic universities, as at Paris, which educated the larger continent. It is for local Bishops' Conferences, with the authority of the Holy See, to determine the particulars of inculturation and adaptation (SC, 22, 40) after the norms currently laid out in *Varietates legitimae*, about which more will be said below.

Vernacular Language

Liturgical language is one concrete application of the Council's desire to renew the rites according to the principles of traditional practice and modern needs. The *Constitution* directs as follows in number 36:

1. Particular law remaining in force, the use of the Latin language is to be preserved in the Latin rites.

2. But since the use of the mother tongue, whether in the Mass, the administration of the sacraments, or other parts of the liturgy, frequently may be of great advantage to the people, the limits of its employment may be extended. This will apply in the first place to the readings and directives, and to some of the prayers and chants, according to the regulations on this matter to be laid down separately in subsequent chapters [i.e., numbers 54 and 63].

3. These norms being observed, it is for the competent territorial ecclesiastical authority mentioned in Art. 22, 2, to decide whether, and to what extent, the vernacular language is to be used; their decrees are to be approved, that is, confirmed, by the Apostolic See. And, whenever it seems to be called for, this authority is to consult with bishops of neighboring regions which have the same language.

4. Translations from the Latin text into the mother tongue intended for use in the liturgy must be approved by the competent territorial ecclesiastical authority mentioned above.

As our current liturgies attest, allowing for the use of the vernacular is, on the whole, one of the *Constitution's* most well-received ideas. With the approval of the Holy See, the conferences have determined that the vernacular's use be extended widely to include not only readings and particular orations and chants, but also to nearly every text of the liturgy. As number 36 clearly states, and as later documents confirm, the use of Latin is to be preserved. While the document is relatively silent about the details of vernacular translations, it notes that local Bishops' Conferences have the task of developing the ritual translations, and the Holy See has the responsibility of confirming them. This collaboration expresses further the unity of the Latin

Church and also assures that translations accurately reflect the reality of the liturgy.

All liturgical texts, whether in Latin or the vernacular, are founded principally upon the Sacred Scriptures. The scriptures are not only read during the liturgy and explained in the homily, but they also inspire the chants, songs, prayer, and other ritual texts of the Church (SC, 24, 121). The Latin psalms of the Divine Office, furthermore, are to reflect the Christian style of Latin and not the style of classical authors such as Cicero and Virgil (SC, 91).

In the years following the promulgation of *Sacrosanctum concilium*, bishops, scholars, translators, and the Holy See did immense work to provide translations according to the Council's principles. The 1969 Instruction *Comme le prévoit* provided initial guidelines in rendering the first vernacular editions of the Mass. (Translations of at least certain parts of the Mass had been published since the end of the nineteenth century, but these resources had not been designed to be *spoken* during the liturgy; they were there to assist the comprehension of the faithful.) More than thirty years' experience of actual vernacular liturgy informs the 2001 instruction *Liturgiam authenticam*. This more extensive and sophisticated document collects the wisdom of the earlier efforts and formulates succinct instructions for applying the Council's norms in this regard.

Shining with Noble Simplicity

The product of a ritual revision according to both traditional practice and modern needs is a rite "shining" with noble simplicity ("*Ritus nobili simplicitate fulgeant*," SC, 34) in which the faithful are able to participate to their full potential. "In the liturgy, the sanctification of the man is signified by signs perceptible to the senses, and is effected in a way which corresponds with each of these signs" (SC, 7). The earthly liturgy, in other words, is sacramental: Christ's saving work, his obedient "yes" to the Father, is now carried out with his Body, the Church, in her sacramental liturgy. Our union with the Trinity takes place through Christ, his Church, and her sacraments. The full, conscious, and active participation of the people in the sacraments and sacramental liturgy is "the aim to be considered before all else" (SC, 14). To facilitate actual participation, the sacramental signs and symbols used (including the language) ought to be easily understood by the faithful, so that in them and through them the reality of the Logos' saving work can be seen and engaged (SC, 59). The rites as a whole "should be distinguished by a noble simplicity; [. . .] they should be within the people's powers of comprehension, and normally should not require much explanation" (SC, 34).

"Noble simplicity" itself, however, is not a simple idea. *Noble* means "illustrious," "outstanding," or "respectable."[6] Those things worthy of our knowing are great and glorious, magnificent and renowned: in a word, *noble*. The *Constitution* points out that liturgical rites should "be distinguished" by noble simplicity (*nobili simplicitate*). Here, too, a look at the term translated as *distinguished* is enlightening. The original Latin text uses the word *fulgeant*, meaning "let them flash" or "lighten." (*Fulgor* is Latin for a "flash of lightning.") The *editio typica tertia* of *The Roman Missal* uses this term in several places and translates it not as "distinguished" but as "shining" and "radiant." For example, consider the Prayer after Communion for December 17:

> Nourished by these divine gifts, almighty God,
> we ask you to grant our desire:
> that, aflame with your Spirit,
> we may shine (*fulgeamus*) like bright torches
> before your Christ when he comes.

On Tuesday of the First Week of Lent, it appears again in the Collect and is translated as "radiant":

> Look upon your family, Lord,
> that, through the chastening effects of bodily discipline,
> our minds may be radiant (*fulgeat*) in your presence
> with the strength of our yearning for you.

Rites that are "distinguished by noble simplicity" (*ritus nobili simplicitate fulgeant*) should flash with illuminating straightforwardness. The point of this etymological examination of the Latin text is to illustrate that the rites of the Church are to be illuminating and glorious like the realities they seek to convey. In this age of the Church, the sacramental rites mediate the person and work of Christ, sharing both divine and human natures. God is perfectly one, is perfectly simple: there is no division in God. And so, while rites radiating divine simplicity and clarity do justice to God, rites that are accessible to his people foster participation in Logical worship, which is the people's right and duty by virtue of Baptism. Language is a key ritual component and therefore a means by which the Church's members participate (SC, 30).

Summary

The Second Vatican Council's documents are for the twentieth-century Church a high point in her ongoing renewal and are for us the "sure compass by which to take our bearings" in the twenty-first century. The guiding principles outlined in *Sacrosanctum concilium* have directed the Church's liturgy since the Council and will continue to do so for years to come. There are a number of principles that are especially relevant to our topic of ritual language and its vernacular expression. These principles inform and enlighten the process of liturgical translation and ritual celebration:

1. The liturgy is celebrated for the glory of God and the sanctification of his people (SC, 5, 7, 10).

2. The liturgy is a work of the Holy Trinity: Father, Son, and Holy Spirit (SC, 5).

3. Christ the Logos carried out his work principally by the Paschal Mystery: his suffering, death, Resurrection, and Ascension (SC, 5).

4. The risen Lord founded his Church upon the apostles (SC, 6).

5. As her Head, Christ the Priest has joined the Mystical Body to himself in carrying on his work of salvation (SC, 7–8).

6. The dialogue between God and his people is ongoing through the scriptures, chants, and prayers (SC, 33, 35).

7. The liturgy and sacraments of the Church signify and cause the sanctification won by Christ (SC, 7).

8. By fully, actively, and consciously participating in the sacraments, men and women enter the Church and become cooperators in God's glorification and their own sanctification (SC, 14).

9. The sacramental signs of the rite are rooted in salvation history, yet some elements of them may be adapted to modern needs (SC, 21, 38).

10. Ritual language is one element that may be adapted to modern circumstances through translations into the vernacular, but the Latin language remains normative for the Roman Rite (SC, 36, 54, 63).

Vicesimus Quintus Annus and *Spiritus et Sponsa*

Twenty-five years (*vicesimus quintus annus*) after the promulgation of *Sacrosanctum concilium*, Pope John Paul II (himself a vote-casting Bishop of the *Constitution*), wrote a document recalling the *Constitution's* principles, analyzing their results, and promoting their ongoing implementation. The apostolic letter *Vicesimus quintus annus*, on the 25th anniversary of the *Constitution on the Sacred Liturgy*, encourages the Church's members to "deepen" their grasp of the liturgy according to the revised rites (VQ, 14), "bringing to maturity" the "fruitful seeds which the Fathers of the Ecumenical Council, nourished by the word of God, cast upon good soil" (VQ, 2). Keeping to the organic metaphor, he concludes: "The seed was sown; it has known the rigors of winter, but the seed has sprouted, and become a tree. It is a matter of the organic growth of a tree becoming ever stronger the deeper it sinks its roots into the soil of tradition" (VQ, 23). In fact, the Holy Father makes a clear distinction between the strictly "liturgical reform" of the Council and the post-conciliar work of the Church since then: the reform is complete[7]— what is now required is a "maturation," a "deepening," and a "strengthening" of liturgical understanding and praxis (VQ, 2, 14, 23). *Vicesimus quintus annus* is especially relevant for our understanding of the Mass' current texts. This papal document helps direct the *Constitution's* translation principles to their definitive form in *Liturgiam authenticam*. The English-language texts of *The Roman Missal* are the logical product of the *Constitution on the Sacred Liturgy,* and the letter on the 25th anniversary begins to make this clear.

Of the numerous principles given by the Council in its *Constitution*, the Pope highlights three that are the bedrock upon which the "liturgical edifice" (VQ, 3) rises: the re-enactment of the Paschal Mystery, the proclamation of the Word of God, and the liturgical manifestation of the Church. First, the Paschal Sacrifice of Christ is the center around which the other sacraments, the liturgical life of the Church, and the liturgical year revolves. The Paschal Mystery is the heart of the Church, and her members "must understand that truly 'each time we offer this memorial sacrifice the work of our redemption is accomplished'" (VQ, 6). Second, Christ speaks to us in his word proclaimed in scriptures at the liturgy. This is where the faithful discover him (VQ, 8). Despite this renewed potential for the scriptural encounter with Christ, John Paul cautions that true renewal demands fidelity to scripture's authentic meaning, "especially when the scriptures are translated into different languages . . ." (ibid.). Other liturgical words, such as those found in hymns, chants, instructions, and the homily, although not necessarily scriptural, must "harmonize" with the scriptural word: "words of men must be at the service of the word of God without obscuring it" (VQ, 10). Third, in the liturgical sacrifice, the Church "epiphanizes" her own reality: she is one, holy, catholic, and apostolic (VQ, 9).

We can recast these three principles from *Vicesimus quintus annus,* using the concepts explained in Part I of this book. First, the Incarnate Logos and his Paschal Mystery is the center of the Church's liturgical life. Second, the Logos speaks to us in the liturgical proclamation of the Word of God. Third, in the liturgical *Sacrifice* of the *Word,* the Church manifests herself as a Mystical Body who is one, holy, catholic, and apostolic. Christ's Body, the Church, is most fully alive when animated by the Holy Spirit in the Logical praise of the Father.

These fundamental ideas, rooted in conciliar teaching, express themselves in more practical norms and guidelines for "the pastoral promotion of the liturgy" (VQ, 10). *Pastoral* comes to us by way of the Latin *pascere,* "to lead to pasture" or "to food," and hence involves both nourishment as well as hungry mouths who need it. In nature, the shepherd leads his hungry sheep to green pastures; supernaturally, the pastor leads his flock to spiritual food. But unlike natural food, which is changed into the body consuming it, the supernatural food of faith (the *Logos incarnatus*) transforms and divinizes us "to mature manhood, to the extent of the full stature of Christ" (Ephesians 4:13; see also SCar, 70). Consequently, the pastoral "food" of the liturgy which is consumed by the faithful "will always be the prime objective of liturgical and pastoral care" (VQ, 10). In short, pastoral action is concerned not only with the faithful, but also with the faith which nourishes them.

One *pastoral* application of the liturgical reform accomplished after Vatican II is found in the translation of Latin rite books. The liturgy, which is our Mother's "school of prayer" (VQ, 10), forms us to listen to and to speak with her. Like a good teacher, the Church employs not only the Latin of the Roman Rite, but also the vernacular of the people in her sacramental language "so that every individual can understand and proclaim in his or her mother tongue the wonders of God" (ibid.). To put it differently, our own "mother tongue" harmonizes with the "Mother's tongue" in that "hymn which is sung throughout all ages in the halls of heaven" (SC, 83).

The "great balance" required between the Church's faith and the culture's character (here the Latin and the vernacular) is not easily obtained (VQ, 23). One of the positive results of the Council's reform is the "immense effort undertaken throughout the world to provide the Christian people with translations of the Bible, the *Missal* and other liturgical books . . ." (VQ, 12). The quick adaptation to the vernacular, though, was a difficult one, especially in its desire to maintain the unity of the Roman Rite now existing in various languages (VQ, 16). And despite the "incarnation" of the rite into the local culture, the Pope laments that some "have received the new books with a certain indifference, or without trying to understand the reasons for the changes . . ." (VQ, 11).

With the purpose of calling the Church to a deeper appreciation of the reformed liturgy, *Vicesimus quintus annus* reiterates the *Constitution's* principles and evaluates their implementation, including how the Roman Rite has been adapted linguistically. While pastoral progress has been successful in adapting to the vernacular, translations from the Latin original to the mother tongue of the people in a given culture need (like the liturgy as a whole) to mature, deepen, and strengthen. After recounting the initial translation work of the Bishops' Conferences, the Holy Father says pointedly:

> But now the time has come to reflect upon certain difficulties that have subsequently emerged, to remedy certain defects or inaccuracies, to complete partial translations, to compose or approve chants to be used in the Liturgy, to ensure respect for the texts approved and lastly to publish liturgical books in a form that both testifies to the stability achieved and is worthy of the mysteries being celebrated. (VQ, 20)

The challenges of liturgical translation are many. In the years following the twenty-fifth anniversary of *Sacrosanctum concilium*, the Holy See would promulgate two other instructions to assist Bishops' Conferences in their "weighty responsibility" (VQ, 20) of completing the task of translation. *Varietates legitimate* [VL] (1994) on inculturation, and *Liturgiam authenticam* [LA] (2001) on translations will be examined in the next sections. But first let us look at another apostolic letter which celebrates and evaluates the achievement of *Sacrosanctum concilium*, this time forty years after its promulgation by the Council.

Spiritus et Sponsa (2003) reexamines liturgical practice and looks ahead to a deepening of liturgical renewal. Regarding translations, the document urges us to evaluate our progress based on the values of the revised rituals themselves: "The Council's renewal of the Liturgy is expressed most clearly in the publication of *liturgical books*. After a preliminary period in which the renewed texts were little by little incorporated into the liturgical celebrations, a deeper knowledge of their riches and potential has become essential" (SS, 7). What "is needed is a *pastoral care of the Liturgy* that is totally faithful to the new *ordines* [rituals]" (SS, 8), which would promote the transformative engagement with the liturgy. This reminder expresses yet again the relationship between the renewal of the Council and the maturation that was to follow. On the one hand, the promulgation of the revised rituals most fully represents the fruits of the Council; on the other hand, the way in which the Church understands and celebrates the reformed rites manifests our maturation and assimilation of the theological truths.

We can again apply our "logical" approach to *Spiritus et Sponsa*. The document illustrates the Logos-character of the liturgy: "The Spirit and the Bride say 'Come.' And let him who hears say, 'Come.' . . . What, indeed, is the Liturgy other than the voice of the Holy Spirit and of the Bride, holy Church, crying in unison to the Lord Jesus: 'Come.'" (SS, 1). *With* the Logos the Church proclaims her "yes" to the divine plan for her heavenly fulfillment, and *to* the Logos she, the Bride, replies. In the Mystical Body's calling and hearing, the Church cooperates with the Logos and the Spirit and so enters with them into the eternal dialogue of love in the Trinity (see chapter 1 of this book).

So that the Mystical Voice resonates with the eternal dialogue, her liturgical and sacramental language must resonate, as clearly as possible, with the liturgy's unseen realities: "A faith alive in charity, adoration, praise of the Father, and silent contemplation" (VQ, 10). To direct this effort, the Church gives us *Varietates legitimae* and *Liturgiam authenticam*. It is to these instructions that we now turn.

Varietates Legitimae and Liturgiam Authenticam

Varietates legitimae is the "Fourth Instruction for the Right Application of the Conciliar Constitution on the Liturgy." It was published on March 29, 1994, by the Congregation for Divine Worship and the Discipline of the Sacraments. As a response to John Paul II's call on the twenty-fifth anniversary of the *Constitution* to "make the liturgy take root in different cultures"(VL, 2), *Varietates legitimae* addresses paragraphs 37–40 of *Sacrosanctum concilium*, which provide for the adaptation of the Roman Rite to various cultures.

Several post-conciliar instructions[8] on the implementation of liturgical reform were necessary since *Sacrosanctum concilium* only provides theological grounding, principles, and general norms for liturgical reform. For example, on the topic of liturgical translations, *Liturgicae instaurationes* (1970), advises that it "would be better not to hurry the work of translation. With the help of many experts, not only theologians and liturgists, but also writers and poets, the vernacular liturgical texts will be works of real literary merit and of enduring quality, whose harmony of style and expression will reflect the deeper riches of their content" (11). The United States Bishops, however, had *already* approved a translation of the Order of Mass, which was confirmed by the Holy See. This same translation of the Order of Mass, with a few modifications over the course of the subsequent decades, was used in America until the promulgation of the English language version of the *editio typica tertia* of *The Roman Missal*.

The *Constitution's* norms on inculturation needed to be more clearly defined. *Varietates legitimae* notes that "certain principles expressed in general terms in those articles [SC 37–40] are explained more precisely" (VL, 3)in this Fourth Instruction. The procedure to be followed is also delineated, "so that in the future this will be considered the only correct procedure" (VL, 3). *Varietates legitimae* says in specific terms what *Sacrosanctum concilium* could say only in a general way. *Varietates legitimae* becomes the definitive interpretation of the Council's norms on adaptation. Going from general to specific, we'll look next at (1) *inculturation* generally, (2) *liturgical* inculturation particularly, and (3) the liturgical inculturation of *language* specifically.

What in *Sacrosanctum concilium* is called "adaptation" to different cultures, the Fourth Instruction now calls "inculturation." Adaptation, the Instruction says, reflects missionary terminology and therefore "could lead one to think of modifications of a somewhat transitory and external nature" (VL, 4). On the contrary, *inculturation indicates an inherent transformation of a culture into the supernatural sphere.* Following the example of the dogma of the Incarnation (in which God, the Logos, takes on human flesh so that humans might become divine), inculturation signifies a "double movement" where "the Church makes the Gospel incarnate in different cultures and at the same time introduces peoples, together with their cultures, into her own community" (VL, 4). As the Incarnation of Christ has the aim of leading us to heaven, so also the two-way street of inculturation leads to the encounter and contemplation of the divine realty. In other words, the process of inculturation does not transform the faith (or in this case, the liturgy) to reflect the culture's values, but divinizes the culture according to the faith. Its aim is to "penetrate all cultures" (VL, 22) and divinize them. God became human for a purpose: to divinize humanity, make us God-like, allowing us a voice in the dialogue of the Trinity. This dynamic engagement is similar in the liturgy. The Church has, in fact, her own culture. It is one founded upon the call of God, and is now on pilgrimage toward heaven, our true homeland (VL, 22). The supernatural culture of the Church is authentic and abiding, and the natural culture of human beings on earth looks to the eternal

Jerusalem as its destiny. Saint Augustine reminds us that the earthly culture of the city of man is but a shadow of the heavenly culture of the City of God.

Specifically, *liturgical* inculturation must keep three points in mind, drawn from the teaching of Vatican II and articulated by the Instruction. Note how *Varietates legitimae* cites *Sacrosanctum concilium* as its source because it continually ties this "deepening" to the *Constitution* itself. First, (1) the goal of liturgical inculturation serves the goal of inculturation generally, which is the divinization or logification of creation. From this perspective, *Varietates legitimae* reminds us of the sacramental nature of the liturgy: that unseen realities are made present in sacred signs, and that in these signs the faithful are called to participate. Bearing in mind inculturation's double movement, the revised rites must "express more clearly" that which is signified, namely, Christ, while at the same time allowing the Church's members the opportunity "to understand them with ease and to take part in the rites fully, actively and as befits a community" (VL, 35, citing SC, 21). Second, (2) the work of inculturation is attentive to the "substantial unity" of the Roman Rite as it exists in the Church's typical editions of the liturgical books (VL, 36, citing SC, 37–40). Inculturation is not directed to these normative texts per se but to their adaptation to a particular culture. The product of modern inculturation, in other words, is not a new edition of the *Missal* but the normative Roman Rite clothed with local customs. Speaking, for instance, on *The Roman Missal* celebrated in the Congo, Cardinal Ratzinger described the celebration as "the Roman rite 'in the Zairean mode,' . . . clad in Congolese garments."[9] Finally, (3) the process of inculturation is carried out under the authority of the Church: by Bishops, Conferences of Bishops, and the Holy See (VL, 37, citing SC, 22). Toward the end of the document, the procedure itself is outlined, beginning with the preparations of adaptations and translations, the vote by the Conferences of Bishops, the approval by the Apostolic See, and the promulgation of the adaptations (VL, 62). What the Second Vatican Council proposed for the process of adaptation in a general way is given precise application in the Fourth Instruction.

On the inculturation of liturgical language itself, *Varietates legitimae* promotes the unity between the vernacular language of a people and the liturgical language of the Church. Ideally, a people understands the symbols of a rite when its native language is used. As a culture's first evangelization often attests, it is through the medium of the local language that the Gospel begins to take root. It is "by the mother language, which conveys the mentality and the culture of a people, that one can reach the soul, mold it in the

Christian spirit and allow it to share more deeply in the prayer of the Church" (VL, 28). At the same time, the double movement of linguistic inculturation holds fast to the Church's sacramental language as developed over the centuries and is rooted in many organic layers. "Liturgical language," the Instruction says, "has its own special characteristics: It is deeply impregnated by the Bible; certain words in current Latin use (*memoria, sacramentum*) took on a new meaning in the Christian faith" (VL, 53). Succinctly put, following the model of the Incarnation, the inculturation of liturgical language involves the mutual exchange of vocabulary, syntax, and modes of expression. By speaking according to the mother tongue of the people, the Church takes to herself even more voices in her unending song of praise. At the same time, by learning the Mother's tongue,[10] the mystery of the Logos resounds more clearly in the world so that the people can participate fully, consciously, and actively in that same hymn of praise to the Father.

Varietates legitimae directs the Council's desire for adaptation by including other aspects of the liturgical celebration, from vestments and postures, to music and devotions. And while the Fourth Instruction gives more precise articulation and clearer direction about translations than had previously existed, the challenges of translating liturgical texts continued to require more direction. A Fifth Instruction, this one devoted entirely to liturgical translations, was issued seven years later.

Meaning "authentic liturgy," *Liturgiam authenticam* (2001) places in its opening paragraph the tenuous unity of the meeting of cultures in the process of liturgical inculturation:

> The Second Vatican Council strongly desired to preserve with care the authentic Liturgy, which flows forth from the Church's living and most ancient spiritual tradition, and to adapt it with pastoral wisdom to the genius of the various peoples so that the faithful might find in their full, conscious, and active participation in the sacred actions—especially the celebration of the Sacraments—an abundant source of graces and a means for their own continual formation in the Christian mystery. (LA, 1)

The work of inculturation involves the Church's "authentic Liturgy" on the one hand, and the "genius of the various peoples" on the other; it requires a great deal of "pastoral wisdom" directing their union. *Liturgiam authenticam* applies this movement of liturgical inculturation (found first in SC, 38, and later developed according to *Varietates legitimae*) to language for the sake of developing a "liturgical vernacular" for use in the Roman Rite in different languages.

The foundational principles for linguistic inculturation are first given in SC, 36: "Particular law remaining in force, the use of the Latin language is to be preserved in the Latin rites. But since the use of the mother tongue, whether in the Mass, the administration of the sacraments, or other parts of the liturgy, frequently may be of great advantage to the people, the limits of its employment may be extended . . . [according to] the competent territorial ecclesiastical authority." Like the general principles for inculturation, the *Constitution's* broad guidelines for vernacularization also needed more precise definition with the passage of years since the Council. Written in light of more than thirty years of practical vernacular experience, ongoing Magisterial guidance, and numerous occasions for collaboration and consultation between local bishops and Vatican Dicasteries, *Liturgiam authenticam* puts forward a matured formulation of principles and specifies "more clearly certain norms that have already been published, taking into account a number of questions and circumstances that have arisen in our own day" (LA, 7). These norms, the introductory paragraphs go on to say, are at times illustrated by tendencies in past translations that ought to be avoided in the future (ibid.).

A second tool for liturgical translation is the *Ratio translationis*, or "rationale for the translation," which applies the directives of the Fifth Instruction in greater detail to a specific language. Called for by *Liturgiam authenticam* itself (see LA, 9), the *Ratio translationis* for the English-speaking world provides "a basic guide in the English language for the Bishops and the experts they call to assist them in the pastorally crucial, technically difficult and time-consuming task of preparing English-language translations of the liturgical books" (RT, Foreword). *Ratio translationis* is authored principally by the Vox Clara Committee, which is composed of bishops from English-speaking countries and was formed by the Congregation for Divine Worship and the Discipline of the Sacraments in 2003 to "assist it in finding ways of ensuring a timely and sure-handed implementation of the [Fifth] Instruction in the English-speaking world" (ibid.). Following consultation with English-speaking bishops and the International Commission on English in the Liturgy (ICEL), the Vox Clara Committee submitted a draft of the *Ratio translationis* to the Congregation which promulgated the document as its own in 2007.

The theological basis for the inculturation of language is the dialogue of love between God and humanity, restored by Christ's Paschal Mystery and carried out now by Christ's Mystical Body. United to Christ the Word, the single voice of the Church resonates in the halls of heaven in the eternal praise of God (RT, 1–3). This theological reality, which is a Logical reality, is, for us on earth, also a sacramental one, where the Church's Mystical Voice is *sensibly* heard in the proclaimed and sung texts of the liturgical rite. The numerous rites of the Church, grown as they have from the soils of diverse cultures, incorporate a number of human languages: the Syriac of the Maronite rite, the Ge'ez of the Ethiopian rite, and the Greek of the Divine Liturgy, to name a few. As Christ's natural body was united to the Second Person of the Trinity and divinized with him, so now the natural language of human cultures is incorporated into his Mystical Body and harmonizes with the Church's own Mystical Voice of praise. Recall that, patterned on the Incarnation of Christ, linguistic inculturation (what the *Ratio* calls the development of a "liturgi-

The theological basis for the inculturation of language is the dialogue of love between God and humanity...

cal vernacular") is a double movement, where the language of the Church's rites implants itself in the local culture and forms it according to Christ the Word, while at the same time taking the cultural language to herself and expanding her unique prayer. How these cultures meet (the Church's and the strictly human) and how their languages unite with and enrich one another is the task of *Liturgiam authenticam* and its *Ratio translationis*.

The engagement of ecclesial language and vernacular language in the inculturated rites of the Church is hard fought, for both retain their own autonomy, yet undergo a transformation in the process. We have been insisting on the union of natural and supernatural language in the Church's Mystical Voice at prayer, and noting its similarity to the hypostatic union of the natural and supernatural in the Incarnation.[11] As errors preceded the Church's eventual formulation of orthodox belief in the Incarnate Word (one divine Person in two complete natures) so, too, are we at risk of being distracted by errors when we try to inculturate her liturgical words "according to the Logos." To put it differently, the tendency to a sort of "linguistic Monophysitism"[12] can downplay the "genius of the various peoples" (LA, 1) as at one time it discarded the human nature of the Incarnate Christ. On the other hand, a kind of "linguistic Nestorianism"[13] can tend to cause a rupture in liturgical expression, the way the Nestorian heresy tended toward positing two separate Christs. We have to caution against a language that is either exclusively "too human" or "too divine."

The "pastoral wisdom" (LA, 1) directing liturgical inculturation is cognizant of the Church's supernatural culture and the various natural cultures of man. Ultimately the Church strives for the enrichment of the former and the divinization of the latter. A culture is the product of the values and history of a people or group as actualized in lived experience.[14] What, by way of example, is "American Culture"? America—in virtue of its European roots, the people and events of its founding, and its subsequent history—values liberty, independence, freedom, self-sufficiency, individualism, generosity, optimism, the "little guy," the underdog, hard work, and equality, among much else. Our heroes are those who personify all of these values, such as George Washington,[15] Jackie Robinson, and the Lone Ranger. Young Americans are encouraged to "pull themselves up by their own bootstraps" and to "go west." Each of these *values* is then put into *action* in the lives of Americans. Parents teach their children to become responsible and independent, the United States economy encourages and rewards individual success, and schools promote scientific inquiry. The country as a whole ritualizes these values in its annual observances of Presidents' Day, Memorial Day, the Fourth of July, Labor Day, and Thanksgiving. Ritualizing our American values then cultivates citizens who embody the same values: the flags, parades, the stories, and the fireworks of the Fourth of July should make one to be "more American." The "cultivated" American—that is, one who lives according to American values—thinks with an American mind, dreams with an American hope, acts with an American spirit, and, more to the discussion at hand, understands the language of American culture. The Fourth of July is Independence Day for Americans and carries with it the signing of the Declaration of Independence, the American Revolution, and all those values that are bound to the national story. For the French, the Fourth of July is only "*4 juillet.*"

> Inculturation is the union of two cultures—ecclesial and human—and the wedding of their own sets of values, history, and ritual enactment.

The Church also has a culture, which means she is founded upon certain values and history, and that these are ritualized and put into practice throughout her history and are incarnate in her linguistic expression. The Mystical Body is "born of a plan in the Father's heart" (CCC, 759). It is the purpose of creation (CCC, 760); it is prefigured in the time of the promises, born from the side of Christ sleeping upon the cross, and now is called together by God as his Son's Body. Into this Body men and women are incorporated to praise God and sanctify themselves. Her values are those of Jesus, her founder, and the saints who imitate him: faith, hope, charity. She esteems poverty, chastity, obedience, prudence, justice, temperance, and fortitude. These Christian virtues are held universally by the Church and are instilled in her members by her preaching (her prophetic office), prayer (her priestly office), and her works of charity (her kingly office). Yet in each place where the faith first took root (with Peter in Rome, Mark in Africa, Thomas in India, Paul in Greece) the one faith has grown according to the local culture and has taken to itself the values of that culture, transforming them according to her own. In the Latin west, the truths of faith incarnated themselves according to the character of western Europe, as expressed and influenced by ancient Rome itself. Romans, like Americans, carried out their lives in rites and activities that were founded upon particular beliefs, values, and history. As the faith took root and grew in Roman soil, it united with the values of the Roman world and cultivated (the root of which is "cult") an incarnate expression of the Christian faith that has come to us today. One aspect of this culture is its language, which is characterized by "a coherent system of words and patterns of speech, consecrated by the books of Sacred Scripture and by ecclesial tradition, especially the writings of the Fathers of the Church" (RT, 49). The cultic language of the Roman Rite, like every other aspect of the rite, is founded upon the "Sacred Scriptures" which recounts her history and describes her values, and upon the Latin "ecclesial tradition," especially as it was formed by the Fathers of the Church.

A culture is the product of a group's values and history as ritualized in life. Inculturation is the union of *two* cultures—ecclesial and human—and the wedding of their own sets of values, history, and ritual enactment. In the thought of *Liturgiam authenticam*, linguistic inculturation and vernacular liturgical expression emerge from the values, history, and their ritual actualization in ecclesial and human culture. The Fifth Instruction thus incorporates the fundamental values of the Christian faith with the desire to respond to the evangelical mandate. In her prayer, the Church's theology becomes incarnate; she says what she believes and values. The Latin expression of the Roman Rite preserves how she enacts and ritualizes this scriptural belief according to Roman and Western culture. When this liturgical expression meets the English language, it must embody the human culture that is the vehicle for its communication. Let us now turn to *Liturgiam authenti-cam's* principles, organizing them in three categories: 1) principles based on theology, 2) principles flowing from the Roman Rite, and 3) principles based on the character of the English language.

Principles Based on Theology

Liturgical Vernacular Expresses Divine Truths

The Church founds her culture (which derives from her cult or worship) on divine truths. If we return to the story of Exodus and listen to the delibera-tions between Moses and Pharaoh, we hear in the exchange how to worship God rightly (Exodus 8–10). God gives his command ("Go three days in the wilderness to worship me") and Pharaoh constantly qualifies the command ("only the men go," "stay in this land," and "leave the flocks behind"). The lesson here is that *God himself* reveals how to worship; it is not we who create right-worship. We receive it from outside ourselves; it is handed on to us. Our liturgical language reflects this early lesson:

> The words of the Sacred Scriptures, as well as the other words spoken in liturgical celebrations, especially in the celebration of the sacraments, are not intended primarily to be a sort of mirror of the interior dispositions of the faithful; rather, they express truths that transcend the limits of time and space.(LA, 19)

As the document indicates, liturgical language is essentially Trinitarian (see also RT, 4). Doxologies ("Glory be to the Father, and to the Son, and to the Holy Spirit") are found in the entrance and communion chants when sung, as well as in many Catholic hymns. The *Kyrie's* "Lord, have mercy, Christ, have mercy, Lord, have mercy" (whether said three times or nine) expresses the mystery of the Faith in the Trinity. The *Gloria* invokes the divine triad when it praises God the "almighty Father," God the "Son of the Father," and God the "Holy Spirit." Furthermore, the Church confesses in the Creed belief "in one God, the Father almighty," and "in one Lord Jesus Christ," and "in the Holy Spirit." The orations of the Roman Rite have always, in one form or other, implored the Persons of the Trinity: "Through our Lord Jesus Christ, your Son, who lives and reigns with you in the unity of the Holy Spirit, one God, for ever and ever." Sacramentally, the reality (*res*) of the liturgy (which, we noted earlier, is Christ's sacrificial and redemptive "yes" to the Father made with the Church by the power of the Holy Spirit) is spoken by the sacramental words of the liturgy (the *sacramenta*). The Church says *sacramentally* that which happens in *reality*: we speak *in words* to the

Father, through the Son, in the Holy Spirit (see RT, 4) because through *the Word* we communicate with the Father through the power of the Holy Spirit.

In addition to its appeal to the Trinity, liturgical language is also eschatological, speaking with the Bride to her Bridegroom at the heavenly Wedding Feast of the Lamb. Our sacramental language takes as its model those who see the Lamb face to face, no longer "as in a mirror" (1 Corinthians 13:12). Because the heavenly angels and saints abide in the City of God and thrive in its culture, we seek to imitate their language. The heavenly hosts sing Holy, holy, holy, and it is "with the Angels and Saints" that we strive to harmonize. We sing the *Gloria* in the way we do because the angels themselves reveal it. "Whether the source of the prayer is biblical, patristic, conciliar or other, this important eschatological quality always informs the content to the prayer insofar as the Liturgy unites the voice of the Church both in heaven and earth" (RT, 5). We pray, as a result, "that with the Blessed Virgin Mary, Mother of God, with the blessed Apostles, and all the Saints who have pleased you throughout the ages, we may merit to be co-heirs to eternal life, and may praise and glorify you through your Son, Jesus Christ" (Eucharistic Prayer II). We seek to speak "heaven," which is the "vernacular" language of the Mystical Body.

The source of liturgical language, both in its inspiration and often in its actual wording, is the Sacred Scriptures. The Church's liturgy carries out the restored dialogue of love through the Logos himself. Accordingly, the scriptures have a central role in the liturgy, for in them "God speaks continually with the Spouse of his beloved Son" (LA, 19). "There is, in fact, almost no text in the celebration of the Mass which is not drawn either directly from the Bible . . . or which does not take its inspiration from themes found in the Bible . . ." (RT, 38). To illustrate this, we turn to Saint Paul. In the letter to the Ephesians he explains to the Gentile converts that they are united now with Jewish converts: "So then you are no longer strangers and sojourners, but you are fellow citizens with the holy ones and members of the household of God, *built upon the foundation of the apostles and prophets, with Christ Jesus himself as the capstone*" (Ephesians 2:19–20, emphasis added). The Preface of the *Ritual Mass for the Dedication of a Church and Altar* uses Saint Paul's own words: "You also established the Church as a holy city, / *built upon the foundation of the Apostles, / with Christ Jesus himself the chief cornerstone*: a city to be built of chosen stones, / given life by the Spirit and bonded by charity . . ."

A further source for liturgical texts, and thus a tool for liturgical translation, is the teaching of the Fathers of the Church. Often a scriptural passage becomes a liturgical text by way of the Fathers. Through the Vulgate translation of Saint Jerome's Bible, for example, the scriptural texts incorporated into the liturgy bear his own mark and the character of the Patristic age (RT, 19). The credal expression "consubstantial with the Father" is itself an articulation of the Fathers at the Council of Nicaea in 325. The theology of the Patristic period is, as the example of "consubstantial" attests, often closely connected with precise vocabulary and syntax, and translations therefore should take into account not only the substance of the doctrine but the manner by which it has come to be expressed. In this way, the liturgical language of the Roman Rite in the vernacular will correspond with the "norm of the Fathers" as desired by the *Constitution on the Sacred Liturgy* (see SC, 50; RT, 7).

Liturgical Vernacular Is Doctrinally Precise

An "authentic liturgy" is one that sacramentalizes truly and accurately the realities of faith. We saw in chapter 3 that even a seemingly insignificant letter (the Greek *iota*) made an essential difference in the meaning of a word and the reality it symbolized. We also noted that the Church has clarified the authentic meaning of its baptismal formula: "in the name of the Father, and of the Son, and of the Holy Spirit."[16] As these instances demonstrate, all liturgical texts, whether those belonging to sacramental formulae or to simple instructions, must be theologically and doctrinally precise (LA, 25):

> The liturgical texts' character as a very powerful instrument for instilling in the lives of the Christian faithful the elements of faith and Christian morality, is to be maintained in the translations with the utmost solicitude. The translation, furthermore, must always be in accord with sound doctrine. (LA, 26)

Translations should not suffer from "an overly servile adherence to prevailing modes of expression" (LA, 27). Political slogans, commercial advertising, and other "passing fashions" are to be avoided. The goal of liturgical translation is not to be trendy, but to provide reliable access to the Catholic Tradition. Even current academic style manuals are not consulted in liturgical translation (LA, 32). Also, the original quality of nouns and pronouns that are employed to represent the larger human race (such as *anthropos* in Greek or *homo* in Latin) is to be found in the translated text. For example, when the Creed says that Jesus was "incarnate of the Virgin Mary and became man," *man* signifies the universality of the human race in a way that "person" or "human being" does not (see RT, 128). Similarly, pronouns for God are masculine and those for the Church are feminine. In the Church's view, this is neither political nor social commentary. The gender of liturgical language signifies not ideology or even human gender per se, but *theology*. It means to acknowledge how God has chosen to reveal himself to us and, in some way, who he is in himself. Even if the current culture's mode of speaking does not employ masculine and feminine language, the Church now, as at other times throughout history, "must freely decide upon the system of language that will serve her doctrinal mission most effectively, and should not be subject to externally imposed linguistic norms that are detrimental to that mission" (LA, 30).

Because of the doctrinal requirements of liturgical texts, *Liturgiam authenticam* recommends coordination between the vernacular missal and the vernacular versions of the *Catechism of the Catholic Church* in selecting vocabulary, especially of theologically significant words (LA, 50a). Traditional orthodox translations found in devotional exercises should also be respected when translating the liturgical text. We think of the familiar translation of the Our Father or the Hail Mary (RT, 107). To illustrate this principle, we can point to the Gospel readings heard at Mass. The account of the Lord's Prayer (Matthew 6:9–13) reflects the words as used popularly and not necessarily the most current scriptural translation.

A system of language, vocabulary, and speech patterns that have been cultivated over the centuries to express precisely the truths of divine faith ought to be maintained (LA, 30, 49, 50). We recall in this regard the "fixed rule of language" invoked by Pope Paul VI when discussing the term *transubstantiation* (MF, 23–24). Along with the "law of belief" and the "law of celebrating" is found a kind of "law of speaking," which employs a particular vocabulary and language singularly suitable for any particular mystery of faith. It has taken the Church centuries to fine tune her language in light of theological truths, and translations must respect the original vocabulary and manner of speaking in the process.

Liturgical Vernacular Is Based on the Typical Editions of the Ritual Books

As Pope John Paul II stressed during his pontificate, especially in apostolic letters on the twenty-fifth and fortieth anniversaries of the *Constitution on the Sacred Liturgy*, the Church today finds herself with a responsibility different from the one she had in 1963: her work is no longer that of reforming but of deepening (VQ, 14; SS, 6). For this reason, the Church's principal task is no longer revising rites and creating new books but learning to appreciate the reformed rites and celebrate them faithfully (SS, 7–8). We recall that in the reform of the liturgy "both texts and rites should be drawn up so that they express more clearly the holy things which they signify" (SC, 20). Because the texts and rites signify the action of the Trinity in which the Church and her members participate (see translation principle 1, above), they should reflect these divine truths accurately (see translation principle 2, above). Since 1963, the Latin typical editions have been revised according to this schema.

Fidelity to Pope John Paul's guidance here also assures that translations will follow that *lex dicendi* required by Catholic doctrine. Accordingly, it is always the *editio typica* that is translated (LA, 23):

> The Latin liturgical texts of the Roman Rite, while drawing on centuries of ecclesial experience in transmitting the faith of the Church received from the Fathers, are themselves the fruit of the liturgical renewal, just recently brought forth. In order that such a rich patrimony may be preserved and passed on through the centuries, it is to be kept in mind from the beginning that the translation of the liturgical texts of the Roman liturgy is not so much a work of creative innovation as it is of rendering the original texts faithfully and accurately into the vernacular language. (LA, 20)

Sources other than the typical editions may be consulted, yet the original Latin text must be translated, when possible, "integrally and in the most exact manner, without omissions or additions in terms of their content, and without paraphrases or glosses" (ibid., also LA, 60). The challenge, of course, is to translate faithfully while at the same time producing a "flowing vernacular text" (ibid.). Here is where secular culture may chafe against the culture of the Church, for an exact translation is at times difficult to express in the vernacular. The principal concern for translations is fidelity to the original text, and not creativity. It is, moreover, the responsibility of homilies and instructions, and not the task of translations, to provide explanations or catechesis about a text's meaning (LA, 29, 30, 43; RT, 12, 51).

Along these same lines, translations should not restrict the meaning of the original text (LA, 32). Prayers that had ended "*Grant this* through Christ our Lord" and expressed Christ's divinity (as one who can answer prayers), and those that ended with "*We ask this* through Christ our Lord" and conveyed Christ's humanity (as one who speaks for us) now end simply "Through Christ our Lord." With this emphasis on fidelity to the *actual* Latin original, "*Per Christum Dominum nostrum*," the more accurate translation does not "favor" one nature of Christ over the other. Also to be translated accurately and "not sanitized" are "inelegant words or expressions" (LA, 27) that seem awkward or unflattering, such as imprecatory language. The Instruction reminds us that these are the words not of any individual or particular congregation. It is the voice of the Church at prayer (LA, 27) that goes beyond time and place.

Principles Based on the Roman Rite

Liturgical Vernacular Fosters Unity

One of the principal desires of the Second Vatican Council was to "foster whatever can promote union among all who believe in Christ" (SC, 1). A means for unity is heard in the call of her liturgy, particularly the Roman Rite. As has been pointed out previously, the Church in the West uses the Roman Rite almost universally, whereas in the East are found 21 self-governing Churches sharing a variety of liturgical families. Both unity and diversity exist in the Church, even though the former is emphasized in the West and the latter in the East.

This value of unity is expressed within the Roman Rite in the language of the Latin West. As the *Ratio translationis* explains, the Roman Rite "long provided a universal identity in which Latin Catholic[s] in the different parts of the world shared, while vernaculars affirmed the union of the faithful in their own communities" (RT, 15). Even today, following the Second Vatican Council, the Latin language of the Roman Rite serves as a unitive force. Where vernacular languages are used, they are not to completely eliminate the use of Latin but are, on the contrary, "meant to enhance the celebration of the Roman Rite for which Latin was to remain a privileged language" (RT, 16). Through its use in the liturgy or as the basis for vernacular translations, the Latin language symbolizes the unity of the Roman Rite.

In addition to its grounding in theology and ecclesial unity, the unitive principle also emerges from the Roman culture in which the faith in the West developed. After winning a short battle in modern-day Turkey, Julius Caesar famously said, *Veni, vidi, vici:* "I came, I saw, I conquered." Ancient Rome conquered and governed much of its neighboring territories, uniting them, at least under governance, until Rome's fall in the fifth century. In the course of its expansion throughout Europe, North Africa, and the Mediterranean, Rome demonstrated its own ability to inculturate naturally neighboring religions (adopting the cult of Cybele and Attis from Asia Minor, for example), culture (using Greek language, art, and architecture), and governance (spreading the Roman system of law to its colonies). Through "natural inculturation," the Roman Empire united itself with the territories it governed, and united them in a single *pax Romana*.

This give-and-take of Roman culture foreshadows the Roman Rite's ability to inculturate according to the "genius of the peoples" it encountered (RT, 34). While Christianizing the West through her universities (such as the University of Paris), her missionary activity (Saint Augustine of Canterbury in England and Saint Patrick in Ireland), and her arts (Michelangelo and Raphael), the Latin Church simultaneously incorporated elements from these cultures into her rite. From Byzantine and Roman royalty come the practices of carrying lights and incense before the Church's ministers. Stoles, worn over the neck or only one shoulder, find roots in the Roman Senate. When the Roman ritual was carried north into ninth-century Gaul, Holy Roman emperors used it as a means to unite their kingdoms, while at the same time adding dramatic elements to the otherwise austere character. Elements such as the Palm Sunday procession, the veneration of the cross on Good Friday, and the Blessing of the Easter fire enriched the Roman expression. Aristotelian philosophy was reintroduced to the larger European continent in the twelfth century through the cooperation of Arab and Spanish philosophers, and since that time it has aided the Latin Church's explication of sacramental theology (e.g., matter and form, substance and accidents). The Roman Rite "is marked by a signal capacity for assimilating into itself spoken and sung texts, gestures and rites derived from the customs and the genius of diverse nations and particular Churches—both Eastern and Western—into a harmonious unity that transcends the boundaries of any single region" (LA, 5; see also RT, 34). This same unitive quality is to be preserved in the liturgical vernacular of a given language:

> In preparing all translations of the liturgical books, the greatest care is to
> be taken to maintain the identity and unitary expression of the Roman Rite,
> not as a sort of historical monument, but rather as a manifestation of the
> theological realities of ecclesial communion and unity. (LA, 5)

Following closely upon the principle that translations ought to reflect the unity with which the Roman Rite speaks, each liturgical vernacular (whether English, Spanish, or Swahili) should be, when possible, universally accepted throughout the Church. In other words, the English translation of the Roman Rite ought to be uniform, or nearly so, in each country that uses it, be it New Zealand, Pakistan, or the United States (LA, 87). The Order of Mass, especially, and the other parts in which the people participate in speech or song ought to be consistent in every country's English translation (see LA, 88). While each country uses the English language in its own way (and even within a country the manner of speaking it varies: compare the dialects in the American northeast and the American south, for example), the single translation of *The Roman Missal* expresses this unity in three ways: in the faith it professes, the Church that produces it, and the Roman Rite which expresses it.

The Roman Rite also serves the unity of the human person, who is both body and soul. Unlike the classical Greek mind for which the material world seems illusory and deceptive, the Roman mentality (and consequently that of the Roman Rite) is explicitly incarnate: Greeks philosophized abstractly, Romans governed concretely. In a way similar to the ancient Greeks, later reformers saw created matter as fallen and incapable of being a part of Christian worship; for them, sacramental worship was by and large replaced by word-based worship, which is less obviously tied to the material. The "smells and bells" of the liturgy are characteristically Catholic. The unity of body and soul in the human person is expressed in the Roman Rite and should likewise be evident in its liturgical vernacular version:

> The Sacred Liturgy engages not only man's intellect, but the whole person, who is the 'subject' of full and conscious participation in the liturgical celebration. Translators should therefore allow the signs and images of the texts, as well as the ritual actions, to speak for themselves; they should not attempt to render too explicit that which is implicit in the original texts. (LA, 28)

The *Ratio translationis* offers as an example the emotion of the *Exultet* sung at the Easter Vigil. This text ought to sacramentalize the joy of the whole person at our redemption. It is not the nature of the text to be merely intellectual and linguistically concise, like a creed might be, but exuberant and passionate:

> O wonder of your humble care for us!
> O love, O charity beyond all telling,
> to ransom a slave you gave away your Son!
> O truly necessary sin of Adam,
> destroyed completely by the Death of Christ!
> O happy fault,
> that earned so great, so glorious a redeemer! (See RT, 11)

In short, the expression of unity (of the human person, the faith, the Church, and the rite) is characteristic of the Roman Rite, and this same quality must be conveyed in the translation of texts.

Liturgical Vernacular Conveys the Manner of Expression Proper to the Roman Rite

"Ask not what your country can do for you, but what you can do for your country." This line of President John F. Kennedy's inaugural address is one of the most memorable lines in the history of such addresses. But its memorability lies not only in its content, which challenged the President's fellow citizens to take an active part in the progress of the country, but also in his manner of delivering it. Would a different manner of expressing the same challenge (such as, "Instead of wondering what you can get from America, go out and do something for your country") be as meaningful, moving, and memorable? It would not. The value of the content is tied to the way it is expressed.

Liturgiam authenticam directs that not only the contents of the Roman Rite (its theology, ecclesiology, eschatology, etc.) are conveyed to the faithful, but the way in which the rite has come to say them over the centuries is also expressed:

> That notable feature of the Roman Rite; namely, its straightforward, concise and compact manner of expression, is to be maintained insofar as possible in the translation. Furthermore, the same manner of rendering a given expression is to be maintained throughout the translation, insofar as feasible. (LA, 57)

Language is an integral part of any culture. In their desire to become a part of America's "melting pot," immigrants at the end of the nineteenth century sought quickly to learn English and abandon the language of the "old world." This resulted in their mother tongue becoming largely lost to the subsequent generation. The best way to learn a foreign tongue is to live in the culture that speaks it; learning from books or in the classroom does not offer the same effect. Likewise, language is a part of the supernatural culture of the Church, expressed for us in the West in the Roman Rite. To learn the culture of the Church, it is essential to learn how the Latin Church speaks. The manner of her expression is tied to the contents of her faith.

One mark of the Roman Rite is its "straightforward, concise and compact manner of expression" (LA, 57); this comes from ancient Roman culture itself. We noted earlier that the Greeks pondered abstract philosophical thoughts. The people of Gaul dramatized life with wine, cooking, and art. The Romans, in their unique way, organized, planned, and governed. Their system of roads connecting their provinces helped in this task. They thought and acted concisely and concretely; they invented concrete, built arches, buildings, aqueducts, and roads that still exist today. This straight-forward, concise, and compact manner of Roman culture generally found expression in the Roman Rite of the Latin Church. The economy of words and expressions found in the Roman Rite is expressed also in its liturgical vernacular. The *Ratio* provides a draft translation of the Prayer after Communion for December 20 as an example of this style:

> Grant divine protection, O Lord,
> to those you renew with this heavenly gift,
> that to those who delight in your mysteries
> you may give the joy of true peace.
> Through Christ our Lord.

Syntax, the ordering of words and phrases in a sentence, is one element of a language's expression. In this respect, the Latin Church is again influenced by Roman culture; the translations of the Latin Church's liturgy convey the native cultural syntax: "The connection between various expressions, manifested by subordinate and relative clauses, the ordering of words, and various forms of parallelism, is to be maintained as completely as possible in a manner appropriate to the vernacular language" (LA, 57a).

Whereas the English language syntax employs coordinating *sentences* to supplement the idea or information in the main clause, Latin uses subordinate and relative *clauses* in a single sentence. The syntaxes of *The Roman Missal* come not only from Latin, however, but also from the Hebrew of the Old Testament, the Greek of the New Testament, and the influences of Western culture after the classical Roman period (see RT, 102). As a result, a variety of syntaxes have contributed to the Roman Rite as the Church now celebrates it. Not only does a translation need to recognize the unique genius of the various syntaxes, but it must also convey them in the translation. It is worth reiterating that the features of the Latin language (its syntax, style, and grammar) are not simply the language's own peculiarities, but they have become part of the Roman Church's culture and, for this reason, a part of ourselves. The language of the Roman Mass, even in its finest details, is a privileged place of the encounter with Christ. To understand these features of the sacramental language is at the same time to understand and hear the divine dialogue they make real.

By way of example, let's look at the "extended subordination" found in the syntax of the Latin orations. *Liturgiam authenticam* directs that "the theological significance of words expressing causality, purpose or consequence (such as *ut, ideo, enim*, and *quia*) is to be maintained, though different languages may employ varying means for doing so" (LA, 57c). For example, the Prayer over the Offerings for the Eleventh Sunday in Ordinary Time formerly used two sentences to express what the Latin prayer says in a single sentence. The first example comes from the Sacramentary of 1973:

Lord God,
in this bread and wine
you give us food for body and spirit.
May the eucharist renew our strength
and bring us health of mind and body.

The third typical edition of *The Roman Missal*, translating the same Latin text, offers this rendering:

O God, who in the offerings presented here
provide for the twofold needs of human nature,
nourishing us with food
and renewing us with your Sacrament,
grant, we pray,
that the sustenance they provide
may not fail us in body or in spirit.

The first translation reflects the syntax of our current and more conversational English language; it is undoubtedly a more familiar and comfortable formulation. The second example is more characteristic of the syntax of the Roman Rite. The use, there, of subordinating conjunctions in the single sentence reflects not only the Roman manner of speaking, but also signifies through the syntax what happens in reality; namely, that all things depend on God, who is here the sentence's subject. In breaking up the text of the original Latin into two or more sentences, the corresponding theology also loses integrity in the expression (LA, 54; RT, 32, 56).

In addition to respecting the Latin trait of compact expression and syntax, the liturgical vernacular demonstrates a style of language appropriate to public proclamation:

Since liturgical texts by their very nature are intended to be proclaimed orally and to be heard in the liturgical celebration, they are characterized by a certain manner of expression that differs from that found in everyday speech or in texts intended to be read silently. Examples of this include recurring and recognizable patterns of syntax and style, a solemn or exalted tone, alliteration and assonance, concrete and vivid images, repetition, parallelism and contrast, a certain rhythm, and at times, the lyric of poetic compositions. (LA, 59)

Previously we have discussed examples of syntax and speeches with a solemn tone (e.g., Kennedy's first inaugural address), and in the chapters to come we will explore more examples from the Mass itself. At present, it is enough to recall some of the natural qualities of human speech, such as assonance and alliteration mentioned by *Liturgiam authenticam*. Alliteration is the repetition of similar consonant sounds to achieve a rhythmic effect: "Peter Piper picked a peck of pickled peppers." The prosaic device known as assonance repeats vowel sounds: "Old age should burn and rage at close of day; / Rage, rage, against the dying of the light." (Note the striking repetition of the long-A sound in these lines of Dylan Thomas.) Additionally, images should be "concrete and vivid." The *Ratio* points us to a passage from Isaiah which says that *omnis caro* shall see the Lord's glory because the *os Domini* has said so. *Omnis caro* is properly "all *flesh*," not "all people," and the *os Domini* is not simply "the Lord" but "the *mouth* of the Lord."

With attention to the genius of language, we discover that all that goes into the best of human speech and has found its way into the texts of the Roman Rite should also go into the liturgical vernacular of every language.

Liturgical Vernacular Translates Certain Texts Literally

Some words of the Roman liturgy are not translated at all. "Amen," "Alleluia," and *"Kyrie, eleison"* have Hebrew and Greek origins and have found a natural place in the Latin *Missal*. While we could easily translate them as "so be it!" and "praise the Lord!" and "Lord, have mercy," these original, "foreign" words themselves offer a rich nuance because of the scriptural, liturgical, and traditional use. They are so much a part of the Church's liturgical expression, that to translate them into the vernacular would in fact be to bar access to their expansive meaning. This may seem odd, since the point of translation is not to be slavishly literal. But *Liturgiam authenticam* identifies particular words, phrases, and other texts that are so significant in the Latin rite as to demand a more literal rendering:

Certain expressions that belong to the heritage of the whole or of a great part of the ancient Church, as well as others that have become part of the general human patrimony, are to be respected by a translation that is as literal as possible, as for example the words of the people's response *Et cum spiritu tuo,* or the expression *mea culpa, mea culpa, mea maxima culpa* in the Act of Penance of the Order of Mass. (LA, 56)

The Profession of Faith (Creed) is another text requiring a rather literal translation, since the "Symbol of Faith" represents a rule of language developed over the centuries. *Credo* means literally "I believe," not "we believe," and signifies the voice of the one Church confessing a single faith (LA, 31b). The meaning is properly theological; the Creed is not intended to be a social statement. Such special texts are significant because of their intimate connection to the mysteries they articulate (the Church's unity and the body's resurrection) or the imprint they have left on the cultures of the world, such as *mea culpa.*

In examining these principles derived from the Roman Rite, certain questions arise: Why must vernacular translations tie themselves so closely to the original Latin text? Why must English translations incorporate what sounds like a foreign syntax? Why must the quality of modern-American English be checked against the character of a "dead language" such as Latin? Why must the unity of the Roman culture govern the diversity of modern culture? The *Constitution on the Sacred Liturgy* addresses these questions, at least in part, when it directs that provisions be made "for legitimate variations and adaptations to different groups, regions, and peoples . . . , provided that the substantial unity of the Roman Rite is preserved" (SC, 38). The challenge in implementing this principal, whether for ritual language or any other ritual component, is striking the right balance between the "substantial unity of the Roman Rite" and the "legitimate variations and adaptations to different groups." Like the Incarnation of Christ, which, according to John Paul II and *Varietates legitimae,* is the model of authentic inculturation, linguistic inculturation joins the natural and the supernatural in a harmonious unity, each enriching the other. But also like the Incarnate Christ, in whom "God became man so that man might become God," the double movement of inculturation ultimately seeks to make us citizens of heaven, "love-transformed," and divinized. Sacramental signs, including language, make Christ present to us so that we can become like him by participating in his saving work.

For the West, inculturation means that the culture of the Latin Church joins with the human culture of a given time and place (third-century Rome, ninth-century France, or twenty-first-century America) and each is enriched by the other. Linguistically, the voice of the people unites with the voice of the Church in the resounding hymn of praise. The meeting of two languages in the development of the liturgical vernacular *incarnates* the spiritual language of the Church, while at the same time it *divinizes* the human language of the culture. Ultimately, though, it is we who learn to speak with the Church, for her voice is the one resounding in heaven before the throne of the Lamb for all eternity. Our mother tongue on earth is deified and becomes our Mother's tongue, which sings constantly before God, the Logos.

Principles Based on the Character of the English Language

Liturgical Vernacular Is Easily Understandable

As we noted above, one requirement of a liturgical vernacular is its doctrinal precision. The law of language developed by the Church and spoken in the Latin of the Roman Rite authentically expresses the doctrine of the faith. Capturing accurately the substance of supernatural truths in any language, Latin or otherwise, is no small task. It must communicate both simply and truthfully for the faithful such complex theological truths as the hypostatic union of Christ, the formulation of Eucharistic transubstantiation, and

A translation of liturgical texts has an additional challenge that the original and traditional language does not.

the subsistence of the Church of Christ in the Catholic Church. Saint Ephrem suggests that Christ underwent a "double incarnation," one into our flesh and another into our words: the eternal Word that is the source and fulfillment of every meaning condescends to be contained in human words.[17] Liturgical language has, in a sense, an impossible task: it must express the inexpressible. Nevertheless, the *Logos incarnatus* establishes definitively the sacramental principle of the Church in her current age, where the realities of faith are manifested through sacramental signs.

A translation of liturgical texts has an additional challenge that the original and traditional language does not. The liturgical vernacular must express divine truths according to the manner of expression found in the Latin rite, and do so *in a way comprehensible to the modern human ear*:

So that the content of the original texts may be evident and comprehensible even to the faithful who lack any special intellectual formation, the translations should be characterized by a kind of language that is easily understandable, yet which at the same time preserves these texts' dignity, beauty, and doctrinal precision. (LA, 25)

The term liturgical vernacular contains within itself the delicately balanced union of linguistic inculturation: "liturgical" signifies the work of the *divine* Persons, especially the Paschal Mystery of Christ, and "vernacular" identifies the *human* element that participates in the action.

While the Latin Church's ritual language is taken from words of revelation incarnated in Roman culture, it now incorporates living contemporary languages, such as English. The resulting liturgical vernacular "both differs from, yet depends in some way upon everyday or ordinary speech" (RT, 75). *Liturgiam authenticam* therefore discourages a ritual language having an "overly servile adherence to prevailing modes of expression" (LA, 27) or employing "contemporary euphemisms" (RT, 77). And although expressions can be "excessively unusual or awkward" and on that account inhibit understanding, other texts that differ from "ordinary speech" can and at times ought to be included (LA, 27). While most "ordinary speech" doesn't include talk of the Incarnation, that part of the Creed professing our faith in the Incarnation expresses the point in an extra-ordinary manner: "For us men and for our salvation he came down from heaven, and by the Holy Spirit was incarnate of the Virgin Mary, and became man." Easily understandable? With a minimum of catechesis that deliberately connects this fundamental belief (that God condescends, *grounds* himself to take on human flesh) with the universal gesture of genuflecting (grounding ourselves) or bowing at this phrase, not only can it become easily comprehensible, it can also be a powerful and moving sign of the Church's belief. Given the magnitude of this central mystery and the "doctrinal precision" required of its expression, "was incarnate of the Virgin Mary" is perhaps the best and most easily understood expression of this truth.

All in all, an inculturated vernacular strives to do justice to the divine truths as they have come to be expressed in the original language, as well as in the mother tongue to which it is joined. The Mystical Voice of the Church speaks of and to divine Truth, while at the same time it speaks with and to the People of God.

Liturgical Vernacular Is Sacred Language

It is the character of the age of the Church, this "middle" time, that supernatural realities find sacramental expression; presently, the natural symbol *is* the supernatural reality, and the supernatural reality *exists with* its natural symbol. The priest at Mass, for example, not only *symbolizes* Christ, but in a real way is *identified* with him. So while ritual language is spoken and understood by humans, it is also spoken "in accord with the Logos," Jesus himself, the Second Person of the Trinity. Liturgical vernacular is, by its essential connection with the Christ, also sacred language. Other human language—in the classroom, at the market, or around the kitchen table—is *profane* language (which means "before the temple" or "not sacred"; it does not necessarily mean "evil," "sinful," or "wicked," as we have come to recognize it). But in the liturgy we enter a heavenly world, and our language (human though it sounds) speaks in a way that is also heavenly. The Mystical Voice is therefore both "sacred" and "vernacular." The Fifth Instruction hopes that in the process of inculturation a "sacred vernacular" will emerge:

> Liturgical translation that takes due account of the authority and integral content of the original texts will facilitate the development of a sacral vernacular, characterized by a vocabulary, syntax, and grammar that are proper to divine worship, even though it is not to be excluded that it may exercise an influence even on everyday speech, as has occurred in the languages of peoples evangelized long ago. (LA, 47)

The effort to blend sacral language with contemporary usage creates a manner of speaking and praying unique to the Roman Rite in the English language. Here the vernacular remains human (it could not cease to be so) but is elevated and resounds more clearly with the Voice of the Church and the Logos who is her Head. We don't "talk" in the Mystical Body like we talk on the street in our mundane pursuits. At the end of the show, the entertainer says, "Good night, everyone; drive home safely"; at the end of Mass, the priest says, "Go in peace, glorifying the Lord by your life." Our liturgical language sounds different because it *is* different—it is patterned on the divine Word—and it forms us to be different from our worldly existence, to "get beyond ourselves"[18] in what is called our "logification." *Liturgiam authenticam* reiterates the point: "It should cause no surprise that such language differs somewhat from ordinary speech" (LA, 47). The *Ratio* offers the following example of a liturgical or "sacred vernacular," one that speaks of the divine, but in the English language:

Holy Father,
whose Son deigned to wash the feet of his disciples that he might give us
an example, accept, we pray, the gifts of our service,
and grant that in offering ourselves as a spiritual sacrifice
we may be filled with a spirit of humility and zeal.
Through Christ our Lord. (RT, 110, citing the Prayer over the Gifts,
Ordination of Deacons)

Liturgical vernacular has the following characteristics: "1. precision
and completeness; 2. easy intelligibility; 3. beauty and dignity; 4. sacrality;
and 5. a well developed orality" (RT, 114; also LA, 47). A text that combines
these elements is at the same time "a flowing vernacular text suitable to the
rhythm of popular prayer" (LA, 20), and one that fosters the full, conscious,
and active participation of all the faithful in the Logical work of praise. As
a final example, consider the Preface to Eucharistic Prayer IV:

It is truly right to give you thanks,
truly just to give you glory, Father most holy,
for you are the one God living and true,
existing before all ages and abiding for all eternity,
dwelling in unapproachable light;
yet you, who alone are good, the source of life,
have made all that is,
so that you might fill your creatures with blessings
and bring joy to many of them by the glory of your light.

Liturgical Vernacular Fosters Active Participation

The "aim to be considered before all else" in the liturgy's restoration, says the
Constitution on the Sacred Liturgy, is the full, conscious, and active participation (*participatio actuosa*) of the people in the sacramental celebration.
Central to promoting actual participation is knowing *in what* we are participating; namely, the Paschal Mystery of the Logos, in which he joins creation to himself in an obedient "yes" to the Father from the cross. Liturgical
participation, then, joins us with the Logos—logifying our existence—in
his dialogue with the Father in the Voice of the Church. Each of the liturgy's
sacramental signs and symbols facilitates our participation, but *words*
achieve this in a particular way, since they themselves share a unique affinity
with *the Word*.

Because the liturgical vernacular is meant to "engage the whole person" (LA, 28), and not simply the intellect, its texts must possess the qualities found in any speech publicly proclaimed, heard, or sung:

> Since liturgical texts by their very nature are intended to be proclaimed orally and to be heard in the liturgical celebration, they are characterized by a certain manner of expression that differs from that found in everyday speech or in texts intended be read silently. (LA, 59)

The translation's "proclamation nature" adds another consideration to the English text: it must convey the theology of the Church, according to the manner in which it is expressed in the Latin Church, in a way easily understandable to the human ear, *and now in a way facilitating proclamation and hearing.* Translating is one thing; translating *for the demands of liturgical participation* is quite another. Texts for liturgical use are therefore to be "tested orally," regardless of their exactitude on paper (RT, 91).

A further extension of the demands of ritual texts is singability. The normative manner of liturgical proclamation is in song. Singing a text is a more appropriate way to speak to the Logos, for it signifies more authentically the liturgical hymn of the Mystical Body (the "new tongue," in Cardinal Ratzinger's expression), with Christ as the Word and the Holy Spirit the Breath.[19] As a result, the texts of the liturgical vernacular "should be translated in a manner that is suitable for being set to music" (LA, 60), especially those texts for the prayers and dialogues between the minister and the people (LA, 61; see GIRM, 40).

Stability and memorability are especially important for liturgical participation. Much as unity and stability in postures fosters engagement (think how difficult it is to participate when unsure about when to stand or whether to kneel at different points in the celebration of the Mass), so also can our voices join more readily with the sacramental voice of the Church when we know what, exactly, she is going to say and when she is going to say it. Once authentic translations are approved and implemented, therefore, future alterations to the texts should only come when demanded by "real necessity" (LA, 64; RT, 94).

Stable texts become memorable texts. Through the celebration of the Roman Rite, members of the Latin Church are formed—or "cultivated"— to believe, pray, act, and speak like the Incarnate Logos expressed in the Western tradition. The "language of our Mother becomes ours, we learn to speak it along with her, so that, gradually, her words on our lips become our words."[20] Memorable texts live with us and are owned by the memory in such a way that they can go on to shape us further and direct our private prayer; in other words, to *logify* us further and make our prayer more *Logical*. Stability and unity of the texts contributes to memorability, and memorability fosters participation, and actual participation leads to our sanctification and God's glorification, which is the purpose of all things.

Summary of *Liturgiam Authenticam's* Principles of Translation

The Second Vatican Council's *Constitution on the Sacred Liturgy* is the impetus behind *Liturgiam authenticam*; *Liturgiam authenticam* is the Church's most complete articulation of the Council's call for the use of the vernacular language.

   Sacrosanctum concilium calls for "legitimate variations" and adaptations to local cultures, while maintaining the "substantial unity" of the Roman Rite (SC, 38). Twenty-five years after the *Constitution*, Pope John Paul II evaluated the work of liturgical inculturation, including integration of the vernacular, and called for an ongoing and clearer application of the Council's norms. The 1994 publication of *Varietates legitimae*, the Fourth Instruction on the Proper Implementation of *Sacrosanctum concilium*, gave precise direction to the processes of inculturation. The use of a liturgical vernacular is one instance of inculturation, where, after the example of the *Logos incarnatus*, the supernatural culture of the Church unites with the natural culture of man, for the enrichment of the former and the divinization of the latter. In this "double movement" of inculturation, it is ultimately humankind and culture that is to become "love-transformed." What John Paul II says about catechesis, "There would be no catechesis if it were the Gospel that had to change when it came into contact with the cultures" (*Catechesi tradendae*, 53), is equally applicable to the liturgy: there would be no liturgy if it were the ritual expression of the Paschal Mystery that had to change when contacting human cultures.

   Thus, the linguistic inculturation of the Roman Rite into the English language looks to the liturgical culture of the Latin Church, which is the "crystallization" of the liturgical tradition in Roman and Western culture,[21] on the one hand, and to the "particular genius" of the human culture, on the other. *Liturgiam authenticam's* principles, which are further applied to the English language in the *Ratio translationis*, draw upon three sources: theology, its articulation in time in the life and liturgy of the Latin Church, and the exigencies of a human culture at worship. We have considered these principles of translation:

Principles Based on Theology:

1. Liturgical Vernacular Expresses Divine Truths (LA, 19).

2. Liturgical Vernacular is Doctrinally Precise (LA, 25–26).

3. Liturgical Vernacular is Based on the Typical Editions of the Ritual Books (LA, 20, 23).

Principles Based on the Character of the Roman Rite:

4. Liturgical Vernacular Fosters Unity (LA, 5).

5. Liturgical Vernacular Conveys the Manner of Expression Proper to the Roman Rite (LA, 57).

6. Liturgical Vernacular Translates Accurately Special Types of Texts (LA, 31, 56).

Principles Based on the Character of the English Language:

7. Liturgical Vernacular Is Easily Understandable (LA, 25).

8. Liturgical Vernacular Is Sacred Language (LA, 47).

9. Liturgical Vernacular Fosters Active Participation (LA, 59–60).

When the translations are developed according the Voice of the Church, we ourselves are formed according to the same Voice, who is the Logos himself. One component of worshipping in union with the Logos is our speaking, singing, and hearing in harmony with the Logos. Full, active, conscious participation in the speaking Logos divinizes us, trains us to be men and women "fully alive" in the City of God.

Endnotes

1. See *Liturgiam authenticam*, published by the USCCB, Introduction, 4.

2. The West has one Church *sui iuris*, the Latin, while the East finds twenty-one Churches *sui iuris*.

3. Ignatius of Antioch, "Ignatius to the Magnesians," in James A. Kleist, SJ, *The Epistles of St. Clement of Rome and St. Ignatius of Antioch*. Ancient Christian Writers Series. (Mahwah, NJ: Paulist Press, 1946), 70–71.

4. Noteworthy here is the difference in the translations of the titles between the first and second editions of the ordination rites: the English title of the first typical edition (1968) is "Rite for the Ordination of Deacons, Priests, and Bishops" (*De Ordinatione Diaconi, Presbyteri et Episcopi*), while the title of the second typical edition in English (2003) is the

"Rites of Ordination of a Bishop, of Priests, and of Deacons" (*De Ordinatione Episcopi, Presbyterorum et Diaconorum*). The title alone of the second typical edition, with the Bishop listed first and in the singular, best signifies the nature of the Church as taught in the *Constitution on the Sacred Liturgy*.

5. See CNS, "Life Teen Parishes to Make Changes to Mass," August 23, 2004. http://www.catholicnews.com/data/stories/cns/0404616.htm.

6. *Noble* is rooted in the Greek *gno*, meaning "to know" (as in *gnosis*, knowledge) and then, in Latin, *noscere*, "to know."

7. It is unfortunate that the English translation in this instance actually *misleads* the reader, saying that the reform "can be considered already in progress." The Latin text gives the sense of a reform "having been achieved" (VQ, 10).

8. *Inter oecumenici*, September 24, 1964, interprets norms on the sacraments, Divine Office, and churches and altars; *Tres abhinc annos*, May 4, 1967, recalls the authority which oversees the implementation of the *Constitution* and offers more direction on the Mass and Office, as well as notes on vestments, funeral rites, and first uses of the vernacular; and *Liturgicae instaurationes*, September 5, 1970, deals exclusively with the new order of the Mass.

9. Joseph Ratzinger, *The Spirit of the Liturgy,* trans. John Saward (San Francisco: Ignatius Press, 2000), 170.

10. Here we do not mean *only* the Latin language; we mean the language of Christian culture.

11. An important difference between the hypostatic union of the incarnate Christ and inculturation is that the divine nature of Christ is not transformed or "enriched" as, for example, is the liturgical language of the Church.

12. Monophysitism is the heresy that denies the two natures (human and divine) of Christ. It holds that his human nature was taken over by his divine nature. The Catholic position was given its definitive form at the Council of Chalcedon in 451 AD.

13. Nestorianism is the heresy that, while maintaining the two natures of Christ, is weak on the union of the natures. It leads toward two persons (one human, the other divine).

14. See Aidan Kavanagh, "The Role of Ritual in Personal Development," in James D. Shaughnessy, ed., *The Roots of Ritual*, (Grand Rapids, MI: Eerdmans Publishing Company, 1973), 87–101.

15. Mason Locke Weems, *The Life of George Washington* (Amonk, NY: M. E. Sharpe, 1996).

16. See chapter 3 of this book.

17. See Sebastian Brock, *The Luminous Eye: The Spiritual World Vision of Saint Ephrem* (Kalamazoo, MI: Cistercian Publications, revised edition, 1992).

18. Ratzinger, *The Spirit of the Liturgy,* 123.

19. Ratzinger, *The Spirit of the Liturgy,* 140.

20. Ratzinger, *The Feast of Faith: Approaches to a Theology of the Liturgy,* trans. Graham Harrison (San Francisco: Ignatius Press, 1986), 29–30.

21. Ratzinger, *The Spirit of the Liturgy*, 161.

Chapter 5

The Introductory Rites and the Liturgy of the Word

Thus far, we have described Christ the Logos as the meaning and model of all things. He is the Word of the Father through whom creation is made, and he is the Incarnate Word by whom the new creation is brought forth. God's interaction with humanity in Adam reaches a decisive period in Christ, the New Adam. The Church, the New Eve and mother of the new supernatural creation, is drawn from his opened side on the cross. Being Christ's sacrament, the Mystical Body "looks like" him, acts like him, and speaks like him, for he is joined to her as his Head, as the Bridegroom to his Bride. And as Jesus "fulfilled the messianic hope of Israel in his threefold office of priest, prophet and king" (CCC, 436), so now the "Church's deepest nature is expressed in her three-fold responsibility: of proclaiming the word of God . . . , celebrating the sacraments . . . , and exercising the ministry of charity . . ." (DCar, 25).

As we noted in chapter 4, the clearest manifestation of the Church is at the liturgy, especially the Eucharistic liturgy at which presides the diocesan Bishop, surrounded by his priests and ministers, and joined by the faithful (SC, 41). Since the liturgy expresses most brilliantly the nature of the Church, it also actualizes her—and Christ's—threefold offices of prophet, priest, and king. In the Liturgy of the Word, "God speaks to His people and Christ is still proclaiming His gospel" (SC, 33). At the Liturgy of the Eucharist the Church celebrates the "memorial of his death and resurrection: a sacrament of love, a sign of unity, a bond of charity, a paschal banquet in which Christ is eaten, the mind is filled with grace, and a pledge of future glory is given to us" (SC, 47). By the dismissal, which gives the entire celebration the name "Mass" (from Latin *missa*, "sent"), the "missionary nature of the Church" in the world is "succinctly expressed" (SCar, 51).

The liturgy's structure, like the Church herself, symbolizes Christ the Logos: it is ordered to the *Logos*. The words used in each part of the liturgy (whether the Liturgy of the Word, the Liturgy of the Eucharist, or those rites that introduce and conclude them) are also ordered to the *Logos*. That is, liturgical language symbolizes Christ and his sacrificial "yes" to the Father, making them actually present, so that the Mystical Body and her members can speak with him and order themselves to the Logos.

The Second Vatican Council, like the popes and liturgical movement preceding it, worked to make liturgy's reality more present and active in the lives of people: the faithful sanctify themselves and glorify God by their active participation in the Paschal Mystery of Christ made sacramentally present in the Church. Because the faithful actively participate in Christ's work by speaking sacramental language, *Sacrosanctum concilium* allows its adaptation to local cultures while maintaining the unity of language in the Roman Rite (SC, 36, 38). This norm was carried forward by Pope John Paul II to its logical and definitive articulation in the *Constitution's* Fifth Instruction for its Right Implementation, *Liturgiam authenticam*, and the *Ratio translationis* for the English Language.

Bearing all this in mind, we can now examine in detail the English-language texts of the third typical edition of *The Roman Missal* and hear how Christ is present in the words of the Mass. In this chapter, and also in chapters 6 and 7, we will discuss the texts in the following way. We will 1) cite the texts and rubrics as they appear in the third edition of the English-language *Roman Missal*; 2) discuss the theological and supernatural reality (the *res*) of the words and actions, relying in large part on the *General Instruction of the Roman Missal*; 3) point out the scriptural basis of the text, where applicable; 4) show how the Latin Church has inculturated these theological realities in the sacramental language (the *sacramentum*) of her Roman Rite through the ages; and 5) demonstrate how the English-language texts speak the clear voice of Christ the Logos and enable us to encounter him in the words of the Mass.

Reverence to the Altar and Greeting of the Assembled People

When the people are gathered, the Priest approaches the altar with the ministers while the Entrance Chant is sung.

When he has arrived at the altar, after making a profound bow with the ministers, the Priest venerates the altar with a kiss and, if appropriate, incenses the cross and the altar. Then, with the ministers, he goes to the chair.

When the Entrance Chant is concluded, the Priest and the faithful, standing, sign themselves with the Sign of the Cross, while the Priest, facing the people, says:

In the name of the Father, and of the Son, and of the Holy Spirit.

The people reply:

Amen.

Then the Priest, extending his hands, greets the people, saying:

The grace of our Lord Jesus Christ,
and the love of God,
and the communion of the Holy Spirit
be with you all.

Or:

Grace to you and peace from God our Father
and the Lord Jesus Christ.

Or:

The Lord be with you.

The people reply:

And with your spirit.

What the Church Wants Us to Understand

Upon entering the sanctuary at the beginning of Mass, the priest and deacon "reverence the altar" (*salutatio altaris*, GIRM, 49). This may seem like a strange way to describe these early actions about the altar, but it makes clear sense when seen sacramentally. In reality, "the altar is Christ" (Rite for the Dedication of an Altar, 4). Because the altar is in some real way Christ himself, the ordained ministers greet the altar by bowing to it, kissing it, and incensing it (GIRM, 49), each of which signifies love and devotion toward another (GIRM, 275–6). We do not, after all, greet our kitchen table in this way—if at all—because it is *only* a table. The altar, on the contrary, is "initiated" when the Bishop sprinkles it with holy water, anoints it with sacred chrism, and when it receives "the body of Christ" at its dedication (Rite for the Dedication of an Altar, 23). The altar, like the initiated Christian, sacramentalizes Jesus himself, who is the meaning of every liturgical sign and symbol.

After greeting the altar, the priest goes to the chair. All make the Sign of the Cross, a gesture and prayer that wraps them in the salvific power of the Crucifixion and the care of the Trinity. The priest-celebrant greets the people, using one of the three ritual formulas (if the celebrant is a bishop, he uses a single formula, "Peace be with you," imitating the words of the risen Lord). These greetings signify Christ's presence to the gathered community, and with the people's response ("And with your spirit") the "mystery of the Church gathered together is made manifest" (GIRM, 50). We recall here that the Old Testament gathering at Mt. Sinai prefigures the Church. At this first divine assembly, 1) God calls his people together 2) to hear his word; 3) the people give their assent to what they have heard, and they 4) seal their bond or covenant with a sacrifice. Called the "*ecclesia*" in the Septuagint (the Greek version of the Old Testament), this gathering of God's chosen is identified by its first step, the necessary "calling" (*kalein*) "out" (*ek*) of the people: without the call, there can be no *ecclesia*. The same is true for the liturgy of the Church, for the entire *ecclesia* depends upon the Lord's call spoken through the voice of his priests.

Each text of the greeting and response dialogue is scriptural in its source. The divine Persons encountered first at creation are here named at the genesis of the new creation in a formula most explicitly found in Christ's command to baptize: "Go, therefore, and make disciples of all nations, baptizing them *in the name of the Father and of the Son and of the Holy Spirit*" (Matthew 28:19). The first two greeting options are heard in Saint Paul's letters: "The grace of the Lord Jesus Christ and the love of God and the fellowship of the holy Spirit be with all of you" (2 Corinthians 13:13), and "Grace to you and peace from God our Father and the Lord Jesus Christ" (Romans 1:7; see 1 Corinthians 1:3; 2 Corinthians 1:2; Galatians 1:3; Ephesians 1:2; Philippians 1:2; 2 Thessalonians 1:2; Philemon 3). The third greeting ("The Lord be with you") is the greeting of the landowner Boaz to his harvesters (Ruth 2:4). It is a greeting to those who gather their daily bread by working in the field, a greeting to pilgrims like Ruth living off the land as they pass through. It was used by the Hebrews on everyday occasions to express good wishes in the Lord. For Christians, it signifies the fulfillment of the promise: in Christ, the Lord is truly Emmanuel ("God-with-us"; Matthew 1:23). The "peace be with you" said by the Bishop are the words of Christ upon entering the upper room of the apostles after his Resurrection (John 20:19). Conformed most fully to Christ by episcopal ordination, the Bishop is enabled to speak for Christ and with the words of Christ.

Common to each option, the greeting draws some meaning from the nature of human discourse, since it is natural to man's formal communication to begin with a proper greeting (e.g., "Hello, Americans. This is Paul Harvey. Stand by for news!"). But upon this natural demand of human dialogue is a further supernatural requirement of the divine dia-Logos, that the greeting is *in the Lord* who, "where two or three are gathered" in his name, exists in their midst (Matthew 18:20; 28:20). The shape of the greeting, in other words, comes in part from the nature of human discourse, but also from its elevation into the supernatural sphere.

The people's response to each of these greetings is the same: "And with your spirit" (*Et cum spiritu tuo*). Like the greetings that are expressed in Saint Paul's letters, the substance of this traditional response also is found there. Saint Paul concludes his Letter to the Galatians with "The grace of our Lord Jesus Christ be with your spirit, brothers. Amen" (6:18), and his Second Letter to Timothy similarly, "The Lord be with your spirit. Grace be with all of you" (4:22). The fact that these salutations (as well as Second Corinthians' "The grace of the Lord Jesus Christ and the love of God and the fellowship of the holy Spirit be with all of you" mentioned above) appear at the *end* of his letters leads some liturgists to see a parallel between the greeting and response at the Mass' beginning and the same greeting and response in its Concluding Rites.[1]

The response to Boaz's "The Lord be with you" by his land managers was "The Lord bless you," which is inherent in the meaning of the response in the Roman Rite: "And with your spirit." The response signifies the corresponding wish that the Lord's presence and favor be on the one who first spoke. This is the case with Boaz. But more than this, in the Catholic tradition the scripturally based response has come to indicate the "Spirit" of ordination through the imposition of hands: "the name 'spirit' [refers] not to the soul of the priest but to the Spirit he has received through the laying on of hands."[2] The man who greets us is not speaking for himself, but in the person of Christ the Head (*in persona Christi capitis*), to whom he is conformed by the sacramental character of ordination. A layperson, on the contrary, never receives the same response that an ordained man does. For example, the *General Instruction of the Roman Missal* (GIRM) suggests that a person offering the sign of peace at Mass says: "*The peace of the Lord be with you always,*" to which the other responds, "*Amen*" (GIRM, 154). Much as the celebrant's greeting is supernatural in tone, the faithful's response is similarly spiritual, but the response to each symbolizes the spiritual reality of each. The "Good morning" dialogue that takes place around the break room coffee maker can't have the same meaning as the Mystical dialogue that takes place in the Mass. The GIRM points out that by this opening dialogue, "the mystery [or sacrament] of the Church gathered together is made manifest" (#50). In other words, the greeting and response, which is a dialogue between the Mystical Body and her Head, causes the Church to be perceptively present.

The liturgical vernacular of the third edition of *The Roman Missal* captures these theological realities after the manner of speaking developed in the Roman Rite. The response to the priest's greeting in the Latin typical edition (*Et cum spiritu tuo*) is translated as "And with your spirit," and thus gives participants a greater occasion to participate in the authentic liturgy of the Mystical Body, one in which the faithful "logify their existence" according to the Logos himself. "And with your spirit" more clearly sacramentalizes the reality of the priest—that he speaks with the voice of Christ. Other vernacular editions reflect this theological meaning: *E con il tuo spirito* in Italian, *Et avec votre esprit* in French, *Y con tu espíritu* in Spanish, and *Und mit deinem Geiste* in German.[3] The English translation of the third edition of the *Missal*, as a result, not only reflects the theological reality of the initial dialogue as expressed in the Roman Rite, but it also unites itself to other sacred vernaculars, which is an inherent feature of the Roman Rite and also a desire of the Second Vatican Council. On this latter point, let us also note the nuance of using "the communion of the Holy Spirit," rather than "the fellowship of the Holy Spirit" in the priest's first option: "The grace of our Lord Jesus Christ, and the love of God, and the *communion* of the Holy Spirit be with you all." Fellowship belongs more appropriately in the culture of man, "an association of one's fellows," whereas "communion" brings with it a sense of unity not only with others who are equals, but above all, with God. The English "communion" also reflects the Latin of the Roman Rite and the Vulgate "*communicatio Sancti Spiritus*" (2 Corinthians 13:13) in which it has its roots.

Penitential Act (*Confiteor*) and Absolution

Then follows the Penitential Act, to which the Priest invites the faithful, saying:

Brethren *(brothers and sisters)*, let us acknowledge our sins,
and so prepare ourselves to celebrate the sacred mysteries.

A brief pause for silence follows. Then all recite together the formula of general confession:

I confess to almighty God
and to you, my brothers and sisters,
that I have greatly sinned
in my thoughts and in my words,
in what I have done and in what I have failed to do,

And, striking their breast, they say:

through my fault, through my fault,
through my most grievous fault;

Then they continue:

therefore I ask blessed Mary ever-Virgin,
all the Angels and Saints,
and you, my brothers and sisters,
to pray for me to the Lord our God.

The absolution of the Priest follows:

May almighty God have mercy on us,
forgive us our sins
and bring us to everlasting life.

The people reply:

Amen.

What the Church Wants Us to Understand

In addition to establishing the faithful as a communion in the Greeting and forming them into the one Body of Christ, the Introductory Rites "dispose themselves [the faithful] properly to listen to the Word of God and to celebrate the Eucharist worthily" (GIRM, 46). The three forms of the Act of Penitence (the *Confiteor*, "Have mercy on us, O Lord," and the series of invocations with *Kyrie, eleison*) help meet this objective "by means of a formula of general confession" carried out by the newly assembled *ecclesia* (GIRM, 51). After the priest's invitation comes a necessary period of silent reflection and recollection, followed by the collective acknowledgement of sin, and concluded by the wish for pardon: "*May* almighty God (*Misereatur*) . . . ."

The Roman Rite's Penitential Act has its origin in pre-Christian times in the Jewish synagogue.[4] Within the Christian era, mention of the *Confiteor* appears as early as the "Teaching of the Twelve," the *Didache*, in the late first century: the breaking of the bread takes place after "confessing your faults beforehand."[5] Immediately prior to the reforms of the Second Vatican Council, the *Confiteor* had been celebrated by the priest and then the server during the "Prayers at the foot of the altar." It is now carried out publicly and by all as a sign of the communal nature of the Church and of the common priesthood of the baptized deputed to worship God through the Mass.

The faithful admits before God and all others present that he has not only sinned, but as the translation indicates, he confesses that he has "greatly sinned," making the words of King David as his own: "David said to God, 'I have sinned greatly in doing this thing'" (1 Chronicles 21:8). The posture of the tax collector in Jesus' parable likewise impresses upon us the gravity of sin, for he stood not before the altar as we do at Mass, but "off at a distance and would not even raise his eyes to heaven but beat his breast and prayed, 'O God, be merciful to me a sinner'" (Luke 18:13). About posture in particular, history shows that the *Confiteor* was recited either from a low bow or in a prostrate position in a way similar to the opening of today's Good Friday celebration.[6]

Striking the breast has also been a component of the *Confiteor* after the example of the tax collector. Saint Augustine found it necessary to warn his people against the gesture which had become simply automatic upon hearing "*Confiteor*."[7] The penitent's hand is not an accusatory finger as much as it is a stone, meant to crush the evil in one's heart. The striking of the breast as a sign of guilt along with the confession *mea culpa, mea culpa, mea maxima culpa* belongs "to the heritage of the whole or of a great part of the ancient Church" and has "become part of the general human patrimony" (LA, 56). For this reason the triple confession is contained in the English vernacular: "through my fault . . . ." That this *mea culpa* is multiplied three times amplifies its significance, as is found in other places in the order of Mass: "Holy, holy, holy"; "Lamb of God" during the fraction ("Breaking of the Bread"); and when the deacon or server swings the thurible three times when incensing. Even the "Amen" following the Eucharistic Prayer has taken on a triple character in some contemporary musical settings. It is important to note, too, that this common confession is less focused on sin than it is with resounding the plea for God's mercy. The phrase "greatly sinned," makes use of the Latin "*nimis*," which appears only a few times in the *Missal*, most emphasizing the great mercy of God.[8]

The Penitential Act's second option is inspired by scriptural texts. Like each option, the priest (not the deacon) invites those present to call to mind their sins.

The Priest invites the faithful to make the Penitential Act:

Bretheren *(brothers and sisters)*, let us acknowledge our sins,
and so prepare ourselves to celebrate the sacred mysteries.

A brief pause for silence follows.

The Priest then says:

Have mercy on us, O Lord.

The people reply:

For we have sinned against you.

The Priest:

Show us, O Lord, your mercy.

The people:

And grant us your salvation.

The absolution of the Priest follows:

May almighty God have mercy on us,
forgive us our sins,
and bring us to everlasting life.

The people reply:

Amen.

This form of the Penitential Act draws on the psalms and prophets. Baruch, who was the secretary to the prophet Jeremiah, is credited with the first part of the dialogue. Here he expresses the penitential spirit that has fallen upon the Babylonian captives: "Hear, O Lord, for you are a God of mercy; and have mercy on us, who have sinned against you" (Baruch 3:2). Part two of the dialogue echoes Psalm 85:8: "Show us, Lord, your love; / grant us your salvation." In these words of the second Penitential Act, the voice of the scriptures become our own; we express our wish for forgiveness in the same way that the great men and women of the Bible have done.

The words of the priest's "absolution" at the end of each Penitential Act ("May almighty God have mercy on us, forgive us our sins and bring us to everlasting life) are expressed in the form of a *petition* for forgiveness and not as a *declaration* of forgiveness, as in the sacrament of Penance ("I absolve you from your sins . . . "). The history of the Roman Rite shows, however, a close and sometimes confusing relationship between the appeal for forgiveness in the *Confiteor* and its grant in the sacrament of Penance. Early in the second millennium the priest would put on his stole when the *Confiteor* was repeated by the server, and the Sign of the Cross was made during the "words of absolution." The *General Instruction of the Roman Missal*, however, makes clear that this rite "lacks the efficacy of the Sacrament of Penance" (GIRM, 51) and thus does not prescribe a Sign of the Cross either by the priest or the individual.

This form of the Penitential Act draws on the psalms and prophets.

Liturgical words are sacramental, insofar as they make present and active the realities they symbolize. Over the course of centuries, and drawing upon the scriptures of the Old and New Covenants, the Roman Rite has cultivated a language so singularly precise as to convey the realities of the faith. The English translation of the Act of Penitence has captured these same realities—an admission of our wrongdoing in the face of God and the Church, an acknowledgment of our great sorrow for sins of action and omission, and the expression of our desire for mercy and eternal life. These critical moments in our dialogue with God are clearly and authentically made present by the words we say, so that full, conscious, and active participation can be achieved.

The *Kyrie* follows both the first and second options of the Act of Penitence. Unlike the first two options, the *Kyrie* may also be led by the deacon or other minister. The *Kyrie, eleison* (Lord, have mercy) is always included in Mass in one form or another.

Gloria

Then, when it is prescribed, this hymn is either sung or said:
   Glory to God in the highest,
   and on earth peace to people of good will.

We praise you,
we bless you,
we adore you,
we glorify you,
we give you thanks for your great glory,
Lord God, heavenly King,
O God, almighty Father.

Lord Jesus Christ, Only Begotten Son,
Lord God, Lamb of God, Son of the Father,
you take away the sins of the world,
    have mercy on us;
you take away the sins of the world,
    receive our prayer;
you are seated at the right hand of the Father,
    have mercy on us.

For you alone are the Holy One,
you alone are the Lord,
you alone are the Most High,
Jesus Christ,
with the Holy Spirit,
in the glory of God the Father.
Amen.

What the Church Wants Us to Understand

The ultimate purpose of the liturgy is the praise and worship of God, and the *Gloria* does just this. Having celebrated the Penitential Act, the faithful are better disposed to join with the angels and saints in their restored dialogue of praise (see chapter 1 of this book). The *Gloria* is "an ancient and venerable hymn," which has been obligatory in the Roman Rite since the fifth century. In fact, as an indication of the firm position which the *Gloria* enjoys in the liturgical tradition, the GIRM states explicitly that it may not be replaced by any other hymn (GIRM, 53). As a liturgical action that stands alone, no other ritual action is

> Liturgical words are sacramental, insofar as they make present and active the realities they symbolize.

performed during the singing of the *Gloria*; incense is not used, sprinkling is not done (GIRM, 37). Its sole purpose is the praise of the eternal God.

The *Gloria* is closely connected to the *Kyrie*, insofar as both include acclamations of praise to Christ. For example, compare this line in the *Gloria*: "You are seated at the right hand of the Father, have mercy on us" to this line in the Penitential Act: "You are seated at the right hand of the Father to intercede for us: *Kyrie, eleison*." The *Kyrie's* structure has from the very beginning been that of litany (in fact, it was in its original form similar to the General Intercessions we know today), whereas the *Gloria* is a Christian hymn and, at times, had been sung even outside of the Mass.[9] As the *Gloria* resembles the *Kyrie* in its acclamations, the structure of the *Gloria* is similar to that of the Creed: a brief opening dedicated to God the Father, a substantial middle section devoted to the Son, and a short conclusion in which the Holy Spirit is named.[10] In name and structure, the *Gloria* also corresponds to the *Gloria Patri* ("Glory be to the Father . . . "): the former called at times the "Greater Doxology," the latter the "little doxology."[11] On the whole, this hymn of the *Gloria* shifts the Introductory Rites from purification and petition to high praise.[12]

Opening with the words of the angels to the shepherds on the night of the nativity (Luke 2:14), the first part of the *Gloria* praises God in a series of acclamations: "We praise you, we bless you, we adore you, we glorify you, we give you thanks for your great glory." These exclamations had formerly been used for Roman emperors[13] and are now raised to the level of praise for the Trinity, whom the word *God* signifies.[14] The last acclamation ("we give you thanks for your great glory") is peculiar not only in its expression, but also in its content: we *thank God for being great and glorious*, while we simply "appreciate" the great man or woman.

The second part of the *Gloria* directs its praise to Christ the Lamb. Accordingly, the *Gloria* incorporates the scriptural words of John the Baptist: "Behold, the Lamb of God, who takes away the sin of the world" (John 1:29). Also found are words from the "Song of the Lamb" heard in heaven: "Great and wonderful are your works, Lord God almighty. Just and true are your ways, O king of the nations. Who will not fear you, Lord, or glorify your name? *For you alone are holy*" (Revelation 15:3–4). Christ the Lamb is also the *only* Lord (Psalm 83: 19; 1 Corinthians 8:6; Philippians 2:11)—in contradistinction to the many earthly lords and emperors to whom the *Gloria's* first acclamations had been addressed[15]—as well as the Lord "most high" (Psalm 83:19).

In the text of the 2000 Missal, the *Gloria* also incorporates distinctive elements of human speech. The rhetorical *anaphora*, which is the repetition of beginnings of phrases, structures the opening acclamations: "We praise you, we bless you, we adore you, we glorify you, we give you thanks for your great glory." This literary device is also discernable in the acclamations to the Lamb: "For you alone are the Holy One, you alone are the Lord, you alone are the Most High . . . ." The parallel structure of the petitions to Christ is also carried over in the translation (and to a certain extent aligns with the threefold *Agnus Dei*):

> you take away the sins of the world,
>> have mercy on us;
> you take away the sins of the world,
>> receive our prayer;
> you are seated at the right hand of the Father,
>> have mercy on us.

Throughout the text, the elevated linguistic features of the typical edition in Latin are reflected in the liturgical vernacular of English. This correspondence works especially to the advantage of the faithful in the *Gloria,* since it proclaims the mysteries it signifies in a powerful and authentic way.

Because *Liturgiam authenticam's* principles of translation are applied to the *Gloria* (its divine truths, scriptural language, conformity to the original Latin, and figures of speech), the faithful are able to join their own voices with that of the Church in her praise of God, which is liturgical participation in the fullest, most conscious, and most active sense. The *sine qua non* for active participation is the authentic presentation of the Mystery of Christ in the sacramental signs: when the signs (in this case, the words) are insufficient, participation cannot be as full, conscious, and active as possible. The English-language *Gloria*, "in which the Church, gathered together in the Holy Spirit, glorifies and entreats God the Father and the Lamb," authentically verbalizes this supernatural reality so that members of the Church can encounter the divine Persons more intimately.

Collect

When this hymn is concluded, the Priest, with hands joined, says:

Let us pray.

And all pray in silence with the Priest for a while.
Then the Priest, with hands extended, says the Collect prayer,

Almighty ever-living God,
who govern all things,
both in heaven and on earth,
mercifully hear the pleading of your people
and bestow your peace on our times.
Through our Lord Jesus Christ, your Son,
who lives and reigns with you in the unity of the Holy Spirit,
one God, for ever and ever.[16]

at the end of which the people acclaim:

Amen.

What the Church Wants Us to Understand

The Collect or "Opening Prayer" concludes the Introductory Rites and expresses the character of the feast or season (GIRM, 54). Unlike the litany structure of the *Kyrie* or the hymn quality of the *Gloria*, the Collect is a dignified and elevated speaking to God.[17] In the Missal of Saint Pius V, published shortly after the Council of Trent, the

> ...Roman Collects are brief, restrained, and precise...

opening prayer was called the *Oratio*,[18] which "originally means, not 'prayer' (for which the word is *prex*), but solemn public speech. Such speech now attains its supreme dignity through its being addressed to God . . . ."[19] In the Collect, the Mystical Body speaks her praise and petition with the Word, who is her Head, to the Father in heaven, in the Spirit.

The invitation to prayer is brief ("Let us pray") and is followed by a period of silent prayer in order that the faithful can bring to mind their own petitions. In the history of the Roman Rite, the period of silence was on occasion accompanied by the kneeling posture (similar to the General Intercessions on Good Friday). While kneeling no longer remains a part of this recollective silence, the silence itself is deemed essential by the rubrics.[20]

Then, in the person of Christ the Head, the priest gathers, "collects," the intentions together and offers them in the words of the prayer, to which the people assent with their "Amen."

With a character all its own, the style of the Collect is, of all the liturgical texts, the most quintessentially Roman. Where Greek orations are often prolix, lofty, and far-ranging in rhetorical style ("who abide in the saints, whom the seraphim praise with the thrice-holy hymn, whom the cherubim glorify, whom all the heavenly powers worship . . ."[21]), Roman Collects are brief, restrained, and precise: "Almighty everlasting God," or simply "O God."[22] The prayer following the address is also equally compact and concise, and lacks that emotive and flamboyant quality that characterizes Gallican compositions and other non-Roman compositions, such as the *Exultet*.

In fact, the Collect is so deeply rooted in Roman culture that its structure predates Christian times. While Jewish prayers influence the prayers of the Roman Rite (as from the Sabbath and Passover *seders*, or meals), the Roman prayer's pattern is found also in pagan religion as follows:

1) The address to God

2) A relative clause of description

3) A petition, along with

4) A fuller description of the petition or an expression of its motivation, followed by

5) A devout closure, expressing hope of divine action (RT, 32).

Given the family tree to which the Collect belongs, it is no surprise that, for instance, the Collect from the Second Sunday of Ordinary Time (mentioned above) follows this pattern precisely:

1) The address:	Almighty ever-living God,
2) Relative clause of description:	who govern all things, both in heaven and on earth,
3) A petition:	mercifully hear the pleading of your people
4) Development of petition:	and bestow your peace on our times.
5) A devout closure:	Through our Lord . . .

Roman Collects are almost exclusively directed to God the Father (rarely to God the Son) through our Lord, in the Holy Spirit, and invoke Christ the Mediator near the end:[23] "Through our Lord . . ." Among the three orations of the Mass, the ancient tradition of the Church concludes only the Collect with a Trinitarian ending; the prayer over the offerings and the prayer after communion are concluded simply "Through Christ" our Lord. No longer does the translation begin, as in earlier translations, "Grant this" or "We ask this." Christ the priest is both God (who *grants* prayers) and man (*through* whom prayers are addressed). The conclusion "Through Christ our Lord" doesn't restrict the fullness of his mediatorial power by underemphasizing one or the other of his natures.

While it stands as a prime example of supernatural and graced speech to God, the Collect also contains many features found in the best of natural, human speech. Here the Collect exhibits the original inculturation of the Logos of faith with what is in many ways the original culture of Western Civilization—the culture of Rome: the Word finds fitting articulation in the oratory of Roman culture, and the human greatness of Roman culture is divinized in the Mystical Voice of the Latin Church. The *Ratio translationis*, for example, identifies a number of classical figures of speech incorporated into the Collect from the Second Sunday in Ordinary Time (given above):

Asyndeton, the listing of words or clauses without conjunctions: "Almighty everliving God" (versus "Almighty *and* everliving God").

Balance, the pairing elements: "both *in heaven* and *on earth*."

Parataxis, the juxtaposition of unequal phrases: 1) "mercifully hear the pleading of your people" and 2) "on our times bestow your peace" (the first clause, "mercifully hear the pleading of your people" is the more significant of the two).

Chiasmus, the use of antithetical phrases that reflect one another in an inverse manner (from the Greek letter Chi, χ): "our times . . . your peace" (the "peace of God" corresponds here to the "times of man")

Antithesis, the comparing of dissimilar ideas: "upon *our times* bestow *your peace*"

Colometry, the division of the line to reflect the syntax and meaning of the text (RT, 108).

The Collect from Midnight Mass also contains many of these same elements:

O God,
who have made this most sacred night
radiant with the splendor of the true light,
grant, we pray, that we, who have known the mysteries of his light
   on earth
may also delight in his gladness in heaven.

Who lives and reigns with you in the unity of the Holy Spirit,
one God, for ever and ever.

The placing together of *night* and *radiant* is an example of antithesis, and their juxtaposition makes the meaning of "this most sacred night" stand out, unlike any ordinary night. These first two lines also offer a *chiasmus*, taking the hearer from "sacred night" into its converse "true Light"; despite their opposition, "night" and "Light" are tied together by their rhyme. In the petition part of the prayer, the "light on earth" is balanced with the "delight in his gladness in heaven." Each of these figures of speech gives the Collect a heightened and beautiful form, which is not only fitting but necessary when speaking to God who from his height is the source of all beauty.

There are a number of principles of translation at work in the Collects, including the articulation of divine truths, fidelity to the *editio typica* and the Roman Rite's manner of expression, a sacral quality, and comprehensibility. Each of these principles produce a translation that is both "adapted to the genius of the people" and faithful to "the substantial unity of the Roman rite" and, consequently, allows members of the Mystical Body of Christ to engage actively in the Logical worship of the Latin Church to which they belong.

Gospel Preparation Prayers

Meanwhile, if incense is used, the Priest puts some into the thurible. After this, the Deacon who is to proclaim the Gospel, bowing profoundly before the Priest, asks for the blessing, saying in a low voice:

Your blessing, Father.

The Priest says in a low voice:

May the Lord be in your heart and on your lips
that you may proclaim his Gospel worthily and well,
in the name of the Father, and of the Son, ✠ and of the Holy Spirit.

The Deacon signs himself with the Sign of the Cross and replies:

Amen.

If, however, a Deacon is not present, the Priest, bowing before the altar, says quietly:

Cleanse my heart and my lips, almighty God,
that I may worthily proclaim your holy Gospel.

What the Church Wants Us to Understand

The proclamation of the Gospel belongs properly to the ministerial function of the deacon. Several ritual corollaries follow from this. First, in concelebrating when a deacon is not present, this diaconal function is taken by one of the concelebrants. Second, the greeting, whether given by a deacon or priest, is done with hands joined. The ritual gesture of extending hands belongs properly to the presidential role; when the one who presides takes on the ministerial role, he follows the gestures proper to the ministerial role. Finally, although Gospel and homily are related, their connection is not so much in the person reading them as in the mystery being presented. The model liturgy, in fact, has the proclamation of the Gospel and the preaching of the homily accomplished by *different* ministers.

The relationship between the internal and the external (between the heart and the word) is necessary in the liturgical proclamation of the Word of God. By the sacrament of Baptism, men and women become living cells of the Mystical Body and, as a consequence, are enabled to join their voices with that Mystical Voice of the Church as she carries on the restored dialogue of love through the Logos within the Trinity. The entire liturgy, as described in chapter 1, is *Logical:* it re-presents in the Church's sacramental signs the sacrificial "yes" of the Logos to his Father from the cross. What makes Christ's Paschal Sacrifice efficacious, unlike any sacrifice before his, is the internal desire of his heart completely represented in the external giving of himself. Christ's sacrifice is not the destruction of his body but the union of his will with the Father. The dialogue which is the Liturgy of the Word demands that our wills and our words, like Christ's, are seeking union with God.

In the Liturgy of the Word, "God speaks to his people and Christ is still proclaiming his gospel," to which his people respond in word and song (SC, 33). The dialogue between God and man demands that the words spoken are true representations of the heart, and not merely "lip service": like the redeeming sacrifice of Christ, there is no division between the internal and the external. For this reason, the Liturgy of the Word avoids "any kind of haste such as hinders recollection" (GIRM, 56), and, instead, periods of silence are included so that "the Word of God may be grasped by the heart and a response through prayer may be prepared" (GIRM, 56). Not unlike the ongoing dialogue between God and the Chosen People through the centuries, the liturgical conversation is deliberate, meditative, and unhurried. Before a response arises, the word itself must be internalized. As Saint Paul reminds us, "For one believes with the heart and so is justified, and one confesses with the mouth and so is saved" (Romans 10:9).

In addition to the necessary silence within the liturgical dialogue, other prayers, postures, and gestures foster the union of heart and words. Immediately before proclaiming the Gospel, the priest or deacon, and all of the faithful with him, makes the Sign of the Cross on the forehead, lips, and breast. These blessings on the mind, the mouth, and heart express and foster their proper dispositions (intelligent, clear, and sincere, respectively) and the unity of mind, mouth, and heart together.[24] The prophet Isaiah experiences the same before his own proclamation of God's Word:

> Then I said, "Woe is me, I am doomed! For I am a man of unclean lips, living among a people of unclean lips; yet my eyes have seen the King, the Lord of hosts!" Then one of the seraphim flew to me, holding an ember which he had taken with tongs from the altar. He touched my mouth with it. "See," he said, "now that this has touched your lips, your wickedness is removed, your sin purged." (Isaiah 6:5–7)

(It is worth noting here that the sinful to whom Isaiah spoke could not see with their eyes, hear with their ears, nor could they understand with their heart: they needed harmony to receive the Word of God rightly.) While we are not called upon literally to purify our mouths "with burning embers," the purifying effect is the same, that our mouths speak clearly of our heart's desire for God. These ritual expressions also echo the Scrutinies in the Rite of Christian Initiation for Adults and the Ephpheta prayer in the Rite of Baptism for Children.

Prior to the smaller blessing made on the forehead, mouth, and breast, the ordained minister seeks a first blessing. If the reader is a deacon, he asks the priest to bless him: "Your blessing, Father." The priest or bishop then says in a low voice: "May the Lord be in your heart and on your lips that you may proclaim his Gospel worthily and well, in the name of the Father, and of the Son, ✠ and of the Holy Spirit." Once again, the union of interior and exterior, of the heart and word, is necessary to proclaim "worthily and well." The minister's worthy proclamation also bears upon the faithful's own active participation in the Word, for believing depends upon hearing, and hearing requires preaching (Romans 10:14): if the proclamation is unclear, the hearing likewise suffers. If the minister is a priest, he blesses himself in the spirit of Isaiah, asking, as does the deacon, for unity of heart and mouth: "Cleanse my heart and my lips, almighty God, that I may worthily proclaim your holy Gospel."

It is interesting to note here that there are two classic Latin terms for what we translate as "word." They are *scriptum* and *verbum*. The *scriptum* is the word printed on the page. The *verbum* is the spoken word. *Scriptum* preserves the tradition; religious traditions need scribes in order to reliably hand on the faith. The *verbum*, on the other hand, is dynamic. It is through the *verbum* that God "created the universe."[25] This is the sense given by the letter to the Hebrews: "Indeed, the word[26] of God is living and effective" (Hebrews 4:12). Without it, our faith would be lifeless. This is also why there is no rubric directing the lector to point to the Lectionary and say "this is the word . . . ." The *Verbum Domini* is not the written text; it is the scripture's proclamation. This insight comes from Brazilian author Alberto Manuel:

> The classic phrase *scripta manet verba volat*—which has come to mean, in
> our time, "what is written remains, what is spoken vanishes into air"—used to
> express the exact opposite; it was coined in praise of the word said out loud,
> which has wings and can fly, as compared to the silent word of the page, which
> is motionless, dead. Faced with a written text, the reader had a duty to lend
> voice to the silent letters, the *scripta*, and to allow them to become, in the delicate
> biblical distinction, *verba*, spoken words—spirit.[27]

Like grains of incense that become dynamic only when tossed on burning embers, words need the fire of the Spirit; only then do they become prayer.

The *General Instruction of the Roman Missal* encourages a few moments of silence after the dynamic communication of the readings "so that all may mediate on what they have heard" (GIRM, 128). This is the occasion to marvel at the wonders of God in a kind of speechless awe.

Worship is "in accord with the Logos," who is Jesus himself. Each element of the Church's worship is also carried out "in accord with the Logos." In the Liturgy of the Word, the Church enters a unique dialogue with the Father, through her Head, in the Holy Spirit: she therefore speaks in accord with the Logos, hears in accord with the Logos, and responds in accord with the Logos. All of these Logical acts demand of us intelligent minds, clean lips, and pure hearts.

The Profession of Faith (Creed)

At the end of the homily, the Symbol or Profession of Faith or Creed, when prescribed, is sung or said:

I believe in one God,
the Father almighty,
maker of heaven and earth,
of all things visible and invisible.

I believe in one Lord Jesus Christ,
the Only Begotten Son of God,
born of the Father before all ages.
God from God, Light from Light,
true God from true God,
begotten, not made, consubstantial with the Father;
through him all things were made.
For us men and for our salvation
he came down from heaven,

At the words that follow up to and including and became man, *all bow.*

and by the Holy Spirit was incarnate of the Virgin Mary,
and became man.

For our sake he was crucified under Pontius Pilate,
he suffered death and was buried,
and rose again on the third day
in accordance with the Scriptures.
He ascended into heaven
and is seated at the right hand of the Father.
He will come again in glory to judge the living and the dead
and his kingdom will have no end.

I believe in the Holy Spirit, the Lord, the giver of life,
who proceeds from the Father and the Son,
who with the Father and the Son is adored and glorified,
who has spoken through the prophets.

I believe in one, holy, catholic and apostolic Church.
I confess one Baptism for the forgiveness of sins
and I look forward to the resurrection of the dead
and the life of the world to come. Amen.

What the Church Wants Us to Understand

Following the readings and the homily, proclaimed and heard in sincerity of heart, comes the Creed. "The purpose of the Creed or the Profession of Faith is that the whole gathered people may respond to the Word of God proclaimed in the readings taken from Sacred Scripture and explained in the Homily and that they may also honor and confess the great mysteries of the faith by pronouncing the rule of faith in a formula approved for liturgical use, and before the celebration of these mysteries in the Eucharist begins" (GIRM, 67). The word *creed* comes from the Latin *credo*, itself a contraction of *cor*, meaning "heart" (as in "cardiac" and "cordial"), and *do*, "I give" (as in "donor" and "donation"). Having received the Logos from the Father in the readings and explained in the homily, the Mystical Body "gives her heart" back to God, so genuine is her response to him. Together, the Gospel and the Creed represent the high points in the dialogue between God and man at this part of the Mass, for both capture the heart of the liturgy: God and man effecting a union of wills.

The Creed is called the Symbol of Faith because its words authentically express the faith it symbolizes. The GIRM (67) speaks of "the rule of faith in a formula approved" by the Church. (Recall that the *lex credendi* [law of believing] is necessarily connected to the Church's *lex orandi* [law of prayering] and *lex dicendi* [law of speaking].) In the Symbol of Faith, we are to take the Church at her Word: the Church says what she believes and means what she says. It is, in fact, such a "substantial" summary of the faith, that some in the tradition have likened the Profession of Faith to the Eucharistic Prayer itself: both contain the substance of the faith; the one in words, the other in sacrament.[28] The Creed had even been designated *Eucharistia* by some in the Patristic Church.[29]

Sung or said by the entire assembly, the Creed is used on Sundays, solemnities, and other solemn celebrations. It can be intoned by priest, cantor, or choir, and then "sung either by everybody together or by the people alternating with the choir" (GIRM, 68).

In its origins, the Creed was a baptismal formula, which accounts in part for its first-person singular beginning: "I believe."[30] Today, the "I believe" is the confession of the Church, the belief of the one Mystical Body, as well as the profession of individual faith. As alive as the Church herself, the Creed developed and became more precise through the centuries as the divine truths of faith were articulated. At the Council of Nicaea in 325, Christ was declared "one in being" with the Father: *homo-ousious* in Greek, *con-substantialem* in Latin (see the "iota controversy" mentioned in chapter 3). Later, when the divinity of the Holy Spirit was questioned, the Council of Constantinople (in 381) occasioned further clarifications of the Creed. Prior to Constantinople, Christ "came down from heaven, was incarnate of the Virgin Mary, and became man." Now the Church professes Christ "came down from heaven, *and by the Holy Spirit* was incarnate of the Virgin Mary, and became man." Later in the text, the Creed had professed belief in "the Holy Spirit, the holy catholic Church" (similar to the wording found in the Apostles' Creed). In light of Constantinople's decrees, the Creed professed more of its belief about the Holy Spirit: "the Holy Spirit, *the Lord [2 Corinthians 3:7], the giver of life [2 Corinthians 3:6], who proceeds from the Father [John 15:26], who with the Father and the Son is adored and glorified, who has spoken through the prophets [2 Peter 1:21]*." In light of these two Councils, the Creed is named the "Niceno-Constantinopolitan." The *filioque* expresses the origin of the Holy Spirit not only from the Father, but from the Father "and the Son" (*filioque*), and is seen in parts of the West as early as 589.[31] To this day, the doctrine and profession concerning the Holy Spirit's origins divides the Catholic and Orthodox Churches, the latter believing the Holy Spirit proceeds from the Father alone (see CCC, 247).

As a baptismal profession, the Creed only gradually became a part of the Mass between the sixth and tenth centuries. When the Germanic Emperor Henry II came to Rome for his coronation in 1014, he was disturbed to find that the Creed was not used at the coronation Mass, and he imposed upon the Pope to henceforth include it. Why so long for the Creed to be used in Rome? "The Roman clerics explained to him [the emperor] that the Roman Church had never been disturbed by error and therefore had no reason to profess the Credo so often."[32] The fact that the Niceno-Constantinopolitan Creed did incorporate significant theological teachings through the centuries gives it a doctrinally high tone. And since both Nicaea and Constantinople safeguarded the divinity of Christ and the Holy Spirit, respectively, their Creed has been a banner of orthodoxy safeguarding the *supernatural*. The Apostles' Creed, which is also an option at all Masses when the Profession of Faith is called for, maintained its traditional character, not incorporating (although of course, not denying) later formulations. It consequently is more *earthy, less philosophical* in its emphasis.[33]

Its origin as a baptismal profession explains in part why the Creed says, "I believe," and not "we believe," as we noted earlier. Later theology saw the singular profession as coming from the one Church: "the confession of faith is handed down in the Creed, as it were, as coming from the person of the whole Church, united by means of the Faith" (LA, 65, quoting Saint Thomas Aquinas). Saint Paul's Letter to the Ephesians bears this out, speaking of the "one body and one Spirit . . . , one Lord, one faith, one baptism" (4:4–5). Perhaps in an effort to make the point of ecclesial unity clearer still, some Eastern Churches had the Creed "recited by one person as representing the community."[34]

The center of the Creed is the profession of the Incarnation. The Church instructs all the faithful to bow or, on the solemnity of the Annunciation and the solemnity of Christmas, to kneel. Imitating the condescension of the Second Person of the Blessed Trinity, they touch their bodies to the ground: "He emptied himself, taking the form of a slave, coming in human likeness" (Philippians 2:7). The faithful demonstrate their great devotion to this mystery, fulfilling the requirement of Saint Paul "so that at the name of Jesus every knee should bend" (Philippians 2:10). Some of the Latin Church's greatest musical treasures exult these central words of the Symbol ("and by the Holy Spirit was incarnate of the Virgin Mary, and became man"), further sacramentalizing the great mystery of the *Logos incarnatus*.[35]

There are a number of *Liturgiam authenticam's* translation principles in action here. First, the English vernacular goes to great pains in this most important of texts to reflect divine realities (the divinity of Christ and the Holy Spirit, for example), which in truth is the entire subject and emphasis of the Creed. The translation also employs doctrinally precise language handed down through the centuries and found in the typical edition of *The Roman Missal:* things "visible and invisible," rather than things "seen and unseen" (for that which is unseen may, by changing one's perspective, become seen; an angel, however, remains invisible). The phrase "was incarnate" also speaks more clearly to Jesus' *actual Incarnation*, rather than his birth and becoming man, simply. Particular words identified by *Liturgiam authenticam* are also rendered "according to the precise wording that the tradition of the Latin Church has bestowed upon it" (LA, 65), such as "I believe" and "consubstantial with" the Father (LA, 53).

In the sacramental liturgy, words signify Christ: liturgical words "sound like" *the* Word. But not all words can bear such a high calling, for not all words are "in accord with the Logos." "We believe in one God" may be good, but "*I* believe in one God" is more attuned with the truth. "One in being with the Father" gets us close to the mystery, but "consubstantial with" brings us nearer. "Was born of the Virgin Mary" is true, but "was incarnate of the Virgin Mary" is more nuanced, more authentic to our faith and liturgical expression. In short, each of the phrases in the great Symbol of the Faith must be "in accord with the Logos," who is the reality of all sacramental words. Early Church authors, as noted above, compared the Profession of Faith to the Eucharist Prayer, since both "contained" the substance of the faith, who is Christ himself. In both cases, Christ is realized in the sacramental sign, for without it, his presence ceases. It is incumbent on the Church, consequently, to see that her words, especially those professing her belief, harmonize with the Word, are attuned to the Word, and resound with the Word. In learning the Church's language, her faithful are learning Christ himself.

Conclusion

In the words of the Mass, the Church and her members join with *the* Word in his unreserved "yes" to the Father and "share in the dialogue which God is."[36] This Mystical Voice of the Mystical Body speaks "in accord with the Logos," who has become incarnate for us. As the seeds of faith in the *Logos incarnatus* spread, various liturgical families sprouted (what Cardinal Ratzinger calls "points of crystallization"[37]),and these rites grew and developed over time, so that each expressed in ways characteristic to its particular place (e.g., Alexandria, Antioch, Rome) the one faith in the one Lord. For the Latin Church of the West, her voice has been formed not only from divine revelation, but also from the Roman and Western cultures in which the faith took root. Today's Roman Rite of the Latin Church (like the rites of the Eastern Churches) is the fruit of a long and organic development, one begun by God and nurtured in his providence.

For us, to encounter the Logos and to speak with him is to learn the language of the Latin Church. Christ is the fundamental Word, full of meaning and purpose; the words that sacramentalize him, and which come to us in the Roman Rite, likewise are charged with meaning and purpose. The more these words are "in accord with the Logos," the more we can speak with the Logos, and become ourselves "logified" in our existence.

The English language of the third typical edition of *The Roman Missal* seeks God's glory and, at the same time, our sanctification, divinization, and logification. Founded upon the principles derived from *Sacrosanctum concilium*, guided by the Papal Magisterium since the Council, and shaped by the documents *Varietates legitimae* and *Liturgiam authenticam*, the words we use at the Mass express authentically the Logos and foster his image in those who speak with him. At the Introductory Rites and the Liturgy of the Word, the restored dialogue of love with the Father in the Spirit begins and, like the disciples on the road to Emmaus, our hearts burn within us. The divine dialogue between God and man finds its sacramental perfection in the Eucharistic sacrifice of Christ. It is to that great mystery that we now turn.

Endnotes

1. See Johannes H. Emminghaus, *The Eucharist: Essence, Form, Celebration*, trans. Linda M. Maloney, revised and edited by Theodor Mass-Ewerd (Collegeville: Liturgical Press, 1997), 115.

2. "Narsai of Nisibis," in Robert Cabié, *The Eucharist*, ed. Aimé Georges Martimort, trans. Matthew J. O'Connell (Collegeville: Liturgical Press, 1986), 51. See also Chrysostom, Homily on Galatians: "By this last word he hath sealed all that preceded it. He says not merely, 'with you,' as elsewhere, but, 'with your spirit,' thus withdrawing them from carnal things . . . ."

3. See *Bishops' Committee on the Liturgy Newsletter*, August 2005, 31–32.

4. Emminghaus, *The Eucharist*, 116.

5. *Didache*, 14.1; Harold W. Attridge, ed., translation by Linda M. Maloney, *The Didache* (Minneapolis, MN: Fortress Press, 1998).

6. See Emminghaus, *The Eucharist*, 116; Joseph A. Jungmann, *The Mass of the Roman Rite: Its Origins and Development*, trans. Francis A. Brunner, 2 vols. (New York: Benzinger, 1951), 303.

7. Jungmann, *The Mass of the Roman Rite*, 303.

8. The term appears eight other times: in the Reproaches Hymn on Good Friday, thrice in Communion Antiphons and four times in Entrance Antiphons.

9. See Jungmann, *The Mass of the Roman Rite*, 346; Emminghaus, *The Eucharist*, 124.

10. Emminghaus, *The Eucharist*, 124–26.

11. See Jungmann, *The Mass of the Roman Rite*, 347.

12. The history of the *Gloria's* liturgical use in the Latin Church illustrates the variance between Roman culture and Frankish culture: the austere and economical Roman liturgy of the sixth century used the *Gloria* sparingly, only in Masses celebrated by the Pope, while the dramatic and expressive Gallican liturgy liberally included the *Gloria* in Masses, even those celebrated by presbyters (see Joseph A. Jungmann, *The Mass: An Historical, Theological, and Pastoral Survey*, trans. Julian Fernandes, ed. Mary Ellen Evans [Collegeville: Liturgical Press, 1976], 169).

13. See Emminghaus, *The Eucharist*, 125.

14. See Jungmann, *The Mass: An Historical, Theological, and Pastoral Survey*, 170.

15. See Jungmann, *The Mass: An Historical, Theological, and Pastoral Survey*, 171.

16. Order of Mass; Collect from the Second Sunday in Ordinary Time.

17. See Jungmann, *The Mass: An Historical, Theological, and Pastoral Survey*, 172; Emminghaus, *The Eucharist*, 129.

18. See Cabié, *The Eucharist*, 196.

19. Joseph Ratzinger, *The Spirit of the Liturgy*, trans. John Saward (San Francisco: Ignatius Press, 2000), 172.

20. See Jungmann, *The Mass: An Historical, Theological, and Pastoral Survey*, 172.

21. Prayer of the Thrice Holy Hymn, Liturgy of Saint Basil.

22. See Jungmann, *The Mass: An Historical, Theological, and Pastoral Survey*, 172.

23. See Jungmann, *The Mass: An Historical, Theological, and Pastoral Survey*, 172.

24. See Jungmann, *The Mass of the Roman Rite*, 455.

25. Preface, Eucharistic Prayer II: "*Verbum tuum per quod cuncta fecisti.*"

26. The Latin gives "*Dei sermo,*" which also has the sense of the spoken word: it is the word vocalized.

27. Alberto Manguel, *A History of Reading* (New York: Penguin, 1997), 45.

28. See Jungmann, *The Mass: An Historical, Theological, and Pastoral Survey*, 181.

29. See Jungmann, *The Mass of the Roman Rite*, 473.

30. See Jungmann, *The Mass of the Roman Rite*, 463; Emminghaus, *The Eucharist*, 150.

31. See Jungmann, *The Mass: An Historical, Theological, and Pastoral Survey*, 181.

32. Jungmann, *The Mass of the Roman Rite*, 469–70.

33. See Jungmann, *The Mass: An Historical, Theological, and Pastoral Survey*, 182; *The Mass of the Roman Rite*, 465.

34. Jungmann, *The Mass: An Historical, Theological, and Pastoral Survey*, 183.

35. See Jungmann, *The Mass of the Roman Rite*, 465–6.

36. Ratzinger, *The Feast of Faith: Approaches to a Theology of the Liturgy*, trans. Graham Harrison (San Francisco: Ignatius Press, 1986), 25.

37. Ratzinger, *The Spirit of the Liturgy*, 160–61.

Chapter 6

Liturgy of the Eucharist

Liturgy exists for divine glory and human sanctification; the words of the Mass "speak" for these reasons. Members of the Church become sanctified or, in the well-known expression of Saint Ireneaus, men and women become "fully alive" by actively speaking and listening to words of the Mass, from the Entrance Chant, Sign of the Cross and Greeting, to the final dismissal. Since sanctification depends on our participation, the Second Vatican Council considered participation paramount in the liturgy's reform, designating it the "aim to be considered before all else," and further, calling pastors to "zealously strive to achieve it, by means of the necessary instruction, in all their pastoral work" (SC, 14). The "true Christian spirit" (ibid.) is realized by uniting ourselves with the action of Christ made present in the sacramental signs. First among these signs are words.

In our appreciation of words, therefore, we realize before all else that our active participation is a cooperation *in the work of Christ*. "The real 'action' in the liturgy, in which we are all supposed to participate, is the action of God himself. This is what is new and distinctive about the Christian liturgy: God himself acts and does what is essential."[1] Christ's saving action, as we said in chapter 1, is his sacrificial "yes" to the Father, spoken on our behalf from the wood of the cross, and his "yes" continues to resound with the Church in the liturgy, especially in the Eucharistic Prayer.

The Eucharistic Prayer is the heart of the liturgy, for in it the action of God is really, truly, and substantially made present to us in the Church. Here, the "Sacrifice of the Word" appears on the altar, the "voice of Someone Else"—Christ—continues to speak, and we are enabled to "be transformed into the Logos (*logisiert*), conformed to the Logos, and so be made the true Body of Christ."[2] Conformity with the Logos (the "logicizing" of existence)[3] is possible in the Eucharistic Prayer not only because the Logos and his sacrifice are made present, but also because of our baptismal obligation to

158

cooperate with him. Christ's sacrifice here becomes ours; his obedient "yes" to the Father we make our own; and his holiness reflects itself in each of us. "Ultimately, the difference between the *actio Christi* and our own action is done away with. There is only *one* action, which is at the same time his and ours."[4] When the faithful fully, consciously, and actively participate in the liturgy—especially the Eucharistic Prayer—their sanctification is at hand, for the "Sacrifice of the Logos"[5] is itself before them.

To effect this sanctification, the Roman Rite's Eucharistic Prayers, whether in Latin or in English, express the "Logical" Sacrifice, and as a result foster our participation in it. In this age of the Church, Christ acts through the sacraments. The sacramental words are therefore the means by which we come into contact with the Logos and participate in his sacrifice. "Christ transformed his death into a verbal form."[6] Eucharistic Prayers *verbalize his sacrifice,* so their texts must speak "in accordance with the Logos" who himself speaks for us. Words that do not clearly sacramentalize Christ's saving work can thwart active participation, hinder holiness, and deprive God of the glory owed him. Like the original Latin, the Eucharistic Prayers of the English-language *Roman Missal* use a sacramental language that rightly conveys the reality of Christ, for they are part of the authentic liturgy (*liturgiam authenticam*) cultivated by the Latin Church. The English translation takes particular care to provide this authentic language for each of the following elements of the Liturgy of the Eucharist and the Concluding Rites:

Presentation and Preparation of the Gifts
Prayer over the Offerings
The Eucharistic Prayer:
    Preface Dialogue
    Thanksgiving: The Preface Text
    Preface Acclamation
    Epiclesis
    Institution Narrative and Consecration (and the Mystery of Faith)
    Anamnesis and Oblation
    Intercessions
    Concluding Doxology
Communion Rite:
    Lord's Prayer and Embolism
    Sign of Peace

> Lamb of God (or Fraction of the Bread)
> Communion
> Concluding Rites

In the sections of the Eucharistic Prayer (considered here) and Concluding Rites that follow (discussed in chapter 7), we continue the approach followed in chapter 5, on the Introductory Rites and the Liturgy of the Word:

1. Citing the words and their accompanying instructions as found in *The Roman Missal,* third edition, in English;

2. Showing the supernatural reality (or *res*) of the *Missal's* words and actions;

3. Pointing out the scriptural sources of the sacramental words;

4. Seeing how the Roman Rite has incorporated these theological realities in the language (the *sacramenta*) of the Mass through time; and

5. Demonstrating how the English-language texts express the Mystical Voice of Christ with his Church and allow us to encounter him today in the words of the Mass.

Presentation and Preparation of the Gifts

When all this has been done, the Offertory Chant begins. Meanwhile, the ministers place the corporal, the purificator, the chalice, the pall, and the Missal on the altar.

It is desirable that the faithful express their participation by making an offering, bringing forward bread and wine for the celebration of the Eucharist and perhaps other gifts to relieve the needs of the Church and of the poor.

The Priest, standing at the altar, takes the paten with the bread and holds it slightly raised above the altar with both hands, saying in a low voice:

> Blessed are you, Lord God of all creation,
> for through your goodness we have received
> the bread we offer you:
> fruit of the earth and work of human hands,
> it will become for us the bread of life.

Then he places the paten with the bread on the corporal.

If, however, the Offertory Chant is not sung, the Priest may speak these words aloud; at the end, the people may acclaim:

> Blessed be God for ever.

*The Deacon, or the Priest, pours wine and a little water into the chalice,
saying quietly:*

> By the mystery of this water and wine
> may we come to share in the divinity of Christ
> who humbled himself to share in our humanity.

*The Priest then takes the chalice and holds it slightly raised above the altar
with both hands, saying in a low voice:*

> Blessed are you, Lord God of all creation,
> for through your goodness we have received
> the wine we offer you:
> fruit of the vine and work of human hands
> it will become our spiritual drink.

Then he places the chalice on the corporal.

*If, however, the Offertory Chant is not sung, the Priest may speak these words
aloud; at the end, the people may acclaim:*

> Blessed be God for ever.

After this, the Priest, bowing profoundly, says quietly:

> With humble spirit and contrite heart
> may we be accepted by you, O Lord,
> and may our sacrifice in your sight this day
> be pleasing to you, Lord God.

*If appropriate, he also incenses the offerings, the cross, and the altar.
A Deacon or other minister then incenses the Priest and the people.*

*Then the Priest, standing at the side of the altar, washes his hands,
saying quietly:*

> Wash me, O Lord, from my iniquity
> and cleanse me from my sin.

What the Church Wants Us to Understand

At the beginning of the Liturgy of the Eucharist, the altar, bread, wine (as well
as the priest and people) are prepared for Christ's sacrifice. As the Offertory
Chant is sung, the offerings are presented by the faithful. At this moment,
the words of the Ordination Rite should resound in the priest's ears: the
bishop hands him the paten and chalice saying, "Receive the oblation of the
holy people to be offered to God." In the past, these gifts of bread and wine

were given from the faithful's own possessions (which at certain times and places meant their names were mentioned during the Eucharistic Prayer; see the "Intercessions" section below), but now they are provided from the parish's resources. Nevertheless, the laity's presentation of the gifts is "praiseworthy" and "still keeps its spiritual efficacy and significance" (GIRM, 73) since the offerings symbolize the hearts of those who give them. If we recall the sacrificial offerings of the Old Covenant, and then that of Jesus, we hear the prophetic entreaty to make the gift a true representation (versus a "replacement") of the giver: "For it is love that I desire, not sacrifice" (Hosea 6:6). In other words, our true offering is an authentic sign of the heart's desire. The laity's presentation of the gifts signifies its desire to give themselves to God and, along with the bread and wine, to become divinized by the power of Christ's sacrifice.

When the gifts reach the sanctuary, it is the priest's own hands that place them on the altar; he himself presents to God "the bread we offer you," "the wine we offer you." Acting in the person of Christ the Head, the priest is the mediator between God and the people, speaking and acting in the person of the Logos. Consequently, humble gifts of bread and wine reach the altar through his mediation, and God's "'eucharisted' bread" (CCC, 1345, 1355) returns to the faithful also through the priest's anointed hands.[7] Before placing the bread upon the altar, the priest first elevates the paten slightly and says the blessing prayer which is rooted in the Sabbath and Passover meals of the Jews of Christ's time. At the beginning of a meal, the father would take bread, break it, and say a short *berakah*, or blessing: "Blessed are you, Lord our God, King of the universe, who bring forth bread from the earth."[8] By indicating what the gift will become, "the bread of Life" (John 6:48), the Roman Rite adapts these words of the *berakah* as its own: "Blessed are you, Lord God of all creation, for through your goodness we have received the bread we offer you: fruit of the earth and work of human hands, it will become for us the bread of life." In response to this short blessing over the bread, if the Offertory Chant or song is not being sung during the prayer of the priest, the people respond, "Blessed be God forever," words inspired by Saint Paul's Letter to the Romans, where God the creator over all "is blessed forever" (1:25; 9:5).

Next during the Preparation of the Gifts, the deacon (or in his absence, the priest) prepares the chalice, pouring into it wine and "a little water." The original purpose of mixing water with wine was, perhaps, the practice of cutting an otherwise dense wine in order to make it more drinkable; yet in the blessing prayers at the Jewish sacred meals, certain cups of wine were mixed with water, while others were not.[9] In any case, the mixing of water with the wine in the different Christian traditions came to symbolize 1) the restoration of human nature (symbolized by the water) by its union with the divine nature (symbolized by the wine) in the Incarnate Christ, which is evident in the words said during the mixing or commingling: "By the mystery of this water and wine may we come to share in the divinity of Christ who humbled himself to share in our humanity"—this prayer itself is taken from the Mass for the Nativity of the Lord. 2) The mixing also signifies the blood and water that flowed from Christ's side on the cross. The text of the Medieval Carthusian Missal says during the mixing, "From the side of our Lord Jesus Christ blood and water flowed for the forgiveness of sins," or 3) Finally, the action symbolizes the divine blessing, since according to some early rubrics the water was poured "in the form of a cross."[10]

The words of the Last Supper inform the prayer that accompanies the chalice at the altar. When offering the chalice, the priest mentions the "fruit of the vine," a phrase used by Jesus at the Last Supper: "I tell you, from now on I shall not drink this *fruit of the vine* until the day when I drink it with you new in the kingdom of my Father" (Matthew 26:29). Then, recalling Saint Paul's First Letter to

> The Church's speaking, then, is rooted in the scriptures. She speaks as Christ and the apostles spoke . . .

the Corinthians, the prayer petitions that the wine become our "spiritual drink": "all drank the same *spiritual drink*, for they drank from a spiritual rock that followed them, and the rock was the Christ" (10:4). The Church's speaking, then, is rooted in the scriptures. She speaks as Christ and the apostles spoke ("the fruit of the vine" and the "spiritual drink") and by participating in her prayer, we too learn the sacred language of the scriptures.

The prayers for the bread and for the wine parallel each other. In both prayers, the words symbolize 1) the goodness of creation and our natural lives ("creation" and "fruit of the earth" and "vine"); 2) our labors in the natural order of creation ("the work of human hands"); and 3) our desire for union with God, our divinization ("the bread of life" and "our spiritual drink").[11] These prayers are ordinarily said "in a low voice." They may be said "aloud" if the Offertory Chant is not sung. The two possibilities speak to the meaning of the gift's preparation: on the one hand, the prayers accompanying the placement of the bread and wine upon the altar are not themselves the "offering" of the sacrifice, so their audible inclusion is not required; on the other hand, the audible recitation can truly foster the people's participation, calling them to prepare their hearts for the sacrifice to come. The option also honors the various practices found in the history of the Roman Rite. The original preparation of the gifts was a merely practical action, and the bread and wine were placed on the altar by the priest without ceremony. Only later, whether in an attempt to emphasize the "goodness of creation" against extreme spiritualism or under the influence of a more dramatically inclined French liturgy, did the offertory and preparation become more elaborate.[12] Whatever the cause of the Preparatory Rites, they help us understand what we should contemplate; namely, the great goodness of God in creation—and the ultimate gift of the new creation in Christ himself, when the gifts are prepared on the altar. The *Novus Ordo* Missal maintains elements of the tradition in its prayers beyond the minimum, yet keeps the preparation of the gifts a simple action as well.[13]

Once the gifts have been set apart for worship, the priest bows profoundly, offering a prayer of humility and surrender: "With humble spirit and contrite heart may we be accepted by you, O Lord, and may our sacrifice in your sight this day be pleasing to you, Lord God." The priest prays that the hearts of those who participate may offer a genuine sacrifice, and, imitating the sacrifice of Christ, they may be one with the gift offered. This prayer brings the Church to the book of Daniel. Azariah, after having been thrown into the white-hot furnace, is the author of these words to God. Lamenting Israel's Babylonian captivity and the loss of the Temple and its material sacrifices, Azariah asks instead that *their own hearts* might serve a fitting sacrifice to the Lord: "But with contrite heart and humble spirit let us be received; as though it were holocausts of rams and bullocks, or thousands of fat lambs, so let our sacrifice be in your presence today as we follow you unreservedly . . ." (Daniel 3:39–40). The Church prays these words in the Divine Office,[14] recalls the fidelity of the three young men every Sunday,[15] and makes their prayer of selfless sacrifice her own at every Mass. We, too, in our exile on earth, imitate captive Israel who is "brought low" because of sin. The priest himself makes his own lowliness incarnate by "bowing profoundly" as he says the prayer.

This prayer is called an *apologiae,* not in the sense of "explanation" or "defense," but as a prayer of contrition and acknowledgment of fault. In it, the priest seeks forgiveness from sin before the holy action of the sacramental sacrifice; similar prayers appear before the priest's reception of communion. To understand the purpose of these prayers, it is necessary to understand how the sacrament of confession developed in the history of the Church. In the early centuries of the Church, sacramental Penance was offered only for the gravest sins; it was not until the seventh century that frequent confession became the norm (see CCC, 1447). Until regular confession was observed, multiple prayers for forgiveness were a customary part of the Mass, for these were deemed necessary for purification.[16] From early forms of the sacrament of Penance, the Mass integrated its own confessional prayers, and they continued through the ages to their present form in the Roman Rite.

Closely associated with the priest's prayer of humility is the washing of his hands, "a rite in which the desire for interior purification finds expression" (GIRM, 76). While his hands are washed, the priest prays: "Wash me, O Lord, from my iniquity and cleanse me from my sin." He echoes the psalm of David, "Wash away all my guilt; from my sin cleanse me" (51:4). Like other actions, such as the offering and preparation of the gifts, the washing of hands at first may have been a mere pragmatic measure, necessary after having handled the smoky thurible or the gifts of the faithful, which sometimes included oil and candles.[17] It should neither be disregarded as archaism nor turned into an obsession of "hand sanitizing." The words of the prayer indicate the meaning of the gesture: this washing symbolizes most profoundly the purity of heart that is the essential component of any genuine sacrifice.

Taken together, the Preparation of the Gifts and its texts express and foster the desire of the Church and her members to unite themselves with Christ in his perfect offering to the Father. When placing the bread and wine on the altar, the priest draws his words from the Old Testament tradition, blessing God for creation and looking ahead to a supernatural re-creation. As he bows low and prays for acceptance, he echoes the three young men in the furnace whose hearts were raised entirely to the Lord. And when asking for purity while washing his hands—hands that will be used as Christ's own in mere moments—the priest prays Psalm 51, speaking for all the assembled who desire forgiveness of sin and purity of intention. Each prayer text is rendered in such a way that interior and otherwise unheard sentiments are expressed authentically. All of the liturgy, but especially the Eucharistic Prayer anticipated by the preparation of the gifts, enables the Mystical Body and her members to actively participate in the work of the Logos. Liturgical language, which is a key component of the liturgy, connects us to Christ and his work: to hear the Mystical Voice of the Church at prayer is to hear the

Logos, and to speak with the Church's voice is to speak *to* the Logos as our God, and *with* the Logos as our Head.

Prayer over the Offerings

Standing at the middle of the altar, facing the people, extending and then joining his hands, he says:

> Pray, brethren (brothers and sisters),
> that my sacrifice and yours
> may be acceptable to God,
> the almighty Father.

The people rise and reply:

> May the Lord accept the sacrifice at your hands
> for the praise and glory of his name,
> for our good
> and the good of all his holy Church.

Then the Priest, with hands extended, says the Prayer over the Offerings, at the end of which the people acclaim:

> Amen.

What the Church Wants Us to Understand

The Prayer over the Offerings concludes the rites of preparation and transitions into the Eucharistic Prayer (GIRM, 77). This conclusion is in part signaled by the fact that the priest addresses the people. The invitation to pray (*Orate, fratres,* "Pray brethren") introduces the larger Eucharistic Prayer similar to the *Oremus* ("Let us pray") before other presidential prayers[18] but in a manner that is more familiar, more intimate: "brothers and sisters." In particular, the "Pray brethren" asks intercession for the priest himself, who in a real and sacramental way is about to speak the "voice of Someone Else"[19] in a way that the rest of the assembly does not. For this reason, he asks the prayers of others before "stepping through the door of the Preface"[20] into the Holy of Holies, the Eucharistic Prayer. In fact, the *Orate, fratres* was originally spoken only to the priest's assisting ministers, so personal was its character.[21] The invitation was also the last prayer spoken aloud before the Prayer over the Gifts (*Oratio super oblata*), which was the first of the eucharistic orations said silently, from which its other name—*Secreta*—arose.

Since the prayer is intended for the priest and his action *in persona Christi*, his invitation distinguishes his unique place in the offering—"my sacrifice"—from the position of the assembly—"and yours." In essence, the invitation to pray reflects the difference between the ministerial priesthood of the ordained and the common priesthood of the baptized. As a result, the prayer sacramentalizes the "many parts" of the single Mystical Body of Christ. There are neither two priesthoods nor two sacrifices, but only different relations to the single sacrifice of the one High Priest. While that which belongs *to you* and *to me* can rightly be called "ours," the translation of *meum ac vestrum sacrificium* as "my sacrifice and yours" is doctrinally precise and appreciates the different orders and roles in the Church. Furthermore, to acknowledge the essential differences between the priest and people in the sacramental action fosters the active participation of all. "The liturgy," says Pope John Paul II, "like the Church, is intended to be hierarchical and polyphonic, respecting the different roles assigned by Christ and allowing all the different voices to blend in one great hymn of praise."[22] The more authentically the liturgy's reality resonates in the sacramental words, the greater possibility for the faithful to know it and to speak with it.

The people stand before verbalizing their response to the priest's invitation to pray. Standing is the posture of readiness. Like the Israelites in Egypt ready to depart for the forty-years' wandering, we put ourselves on our feet after the invitation to demonstrate that we are ready to enter into the sacrifice. A ritual parallel exists here to the rite of ordination where the candidates are called by name, stand and only then reply "Present!" Our first response is a bodily one. We put into our bodies what we believe. When the *General Instruction of the Roman Missal* was released in March 2000, two years prior to the actual texts of *The Roman Missal* in March 2002, the rubric that indicates the people's rising after the invitation: "The people rise and make the response *May the Lord accept the sacrifice*, etc." (GIRM, 146) was misunderstood. In practice, many parishes began standing *before* the priest's invitation, indicating that the meaning of the posture as a response to the invitation was not clear. The rising of the assembly *after* the invitation "Pray, brethren" matches body language with words. Both express the ardent desire that the sacrifice "be accepted." As our choice of words symbolizes the reality before us, so too our gestures reflect the reality's dignity. In no instance during the liturgy do we pray to God collectively from a seated position; rather, when entreating the Lord, our respectful and attentive posture conveys as much as our words. Moreover, our prayer at this point in the Mass is especially meaningful, as we ask God that our sacrifice obtain the end for which we and all things exist: "for the praise and glory of his name, for our good and the good of all his holy Church." Our posture and words express our heart's prayer—for God's glory—which is rendered by our holiness in his holy Church.

When all are standing, the priest says the Prayer over the Offerings. This prayer is said aloud and serves as a transition into the Eucharistic Prayer, summing up the preparatory rites and inaugurating the central action that follows. The *Missal's* "*super oblata*" prayers are drawn from "the treasures of antiquity,"[23] and although similar to the Collect they rarely have a clause of description or praise. They include only an invocation, petition, and short conclusion. (The Trinitarian conclusion is used only at the Collect.) The Prayer over the Offerings for Friday within the octave of Easter illustrates the typical form:

> Perfect within us, O Lord, we pray,
> the solemn exchange brought about by these paschal offerings,
> that we may be drawn from earthly desires
> to a longing for the things of heaven.
> Through Christ our Lord.

Although not every Prayer over the Offerings mentions the "solemn exchange," many, in fact, do invoke it (e.g., "Receive our oblation, O Lord, by which is brought about a glorious exchange, that by offering what you have given we may merit to receive your very self. Through Christ our Lord."[24] "O God, who by the wonderful exchange effected in this sacrifice have made us partakers of the one supreme Godhead . . ."[25]). Explicitly or not, each prayer does in some way ask God for our ongoing transformation into divinity. In this way, the prayer reflects the same spirit with which the water was mixed with wine in the Preparation of the Gifts, which in condescending to our condition, Christ allows us to rise to his own. The prayer concludes with the "Amen" of the people, by which the faithful acknowledge the sentiments of the prayer, expressing in the response their own wish to become divinized, "love-transformed" citizens of the Heavenly Jerusalem.

Through the Preparation of the Gifts and the Prayer over the Offerings, the Catholic faithful are drawn into the heart of the Church's action, which is the sacramental offering of the "Logical" Sacrifice, and are prepared to engage it fully, consciously, and actively. As always, the clear voice of the Church is one of the sacramental means of our participation. The words of the Roman Rite, grown in the soil of Tradition and prayer over centuries, express uniquely and—insofar as is possible—precisely the reality of *the* Word. By Christ's command, his one sacrifice is actualized by the ordained priest surrounded by his people; accordingly, the priest invites those gathered to pray that God accept "my sacrifice and yours." The people, in turn, enter the sacrifice when, standing, they beg God to accept it. Words signify realities, and in the case of *The Roman Missal*, they signify clearly, "for the praise and glory of his name, for our good and the good of all his holy Church."

Eucharistic Prayer

Jesus' redemptive sacrifice is his obedient and wholehearted response of love to the Father. From the agony of the Garden of Gethsemane through his death on the cross, Christ remains faithful to the Father and his plan: he thirsts entirely for God, longs to pass over to the Father's paradise, and commends his spirit entirely to him. This same sacrificial "yes" of Jesus the Logos still sounds today in the Eucharistic Prayer of the Church. "The Eucharistic prayer is an entering-in to the prayer of Jesus Christ himself; hence it is the Church's entering-in to the Logos, the Father's Word, into the Logos' self-surrender to the Father, which, in the Cross, has also become the surrender of mankind to him."[26] In the once-and-for-all Sacrifice of the Word, the Logos "sums up our existence" and addresses himself to the Father, proclaiming our unconditional desire for him. Now in the miraculous context of the Eucharist at Mass, that same Word places his sacrificial "yes" before us so that we can join our existence, our "yes," to his.

The Sacrifice of the Word is sacramentally represented in the Church's words of sacrifice: "The eucharistic canon is a sacrifice in the form of the word."[27] Of all the words spoken in the Mass of the Roman Rite, the Eucharistic Prayer is especially significant, for as the action is Word-based (Logical), our commensurate participation is Word-based. We join with the Word by listening, interiorizing, and acclaiming the Mystical Voice of the Church, here expressed in the Roman Rite. As the *General Instruction of the Roman Missal* (GIRM) explains, "the meaning of this Prayer is that the whole congregation of the faithful joins with Christ in confessing the great deeds of God and in the offering of Sacrifice. The Eucharistic Prayer requires that everybody listens to it with reverence and in silence" (GIRM, 78). This is why the chanting or recitation of the Eucharistic Prayer must not be ornamented by musical accompaniment. It is the naked voice, without adornment, that offers the pleasing sacrifice to the Father. Hearing the crucified Christ offer himself to the Father, we seek to identify ourselves with his sacrifice, and become holy by his work.

The *General Instruction of the Roman Missal* identifies and describes the eight principle elements making up the Eucharistic Prayer; these now direct our own discussion:

a) The *thanksgiving* (expressed especially in the Preface), in which the Priest, in the name of the whole of the holy people, glorifies God the Father and gives thanks to him for the whole work of salvation or for some particular aspect of it, according to the varying day, festivity, or time of year.

b) The *acclamation*, by which the whole congregation, joining with the heavenly powers, sings the *Sanctus (Holy, Holy, Holy)*. This acclamation, which constitutes part of the Eucharistic Prayer itself, is pronounced by all the people with the Priest.

c) The *epiclesis,* in which, by means of particular invocations, the Church implores the power of the Holy Spirit that the gifts offered by human hands be consecrated, that is, become Christ's Body and Blood, and that the unblemished sacrificial Victim to be consumed in Communion may be for the salvation of those who will partake of it.

d) The *Institution Narrative and Consecration*, by which, by means of the words and actions of Christ, that Sacrifice is effected which Christ himself instituted during the Last Supper, when he offered his Body and Blood under the species of bread and wine, gave them to the Apostles to eat and drink, and leaving with the latter the command to perpetuate this same mystery.

e) The *anamnesis,* by which the Church, fulfilling the command that she received from Christ the Lord through the Apostles, celebrates the memorial of Christ, recalling especially his blessed Passion, glorious Resurrection and Ascension into heaven.

f) The *oblation,* by which, in this very memorial, the Church, in particular that gathered here and now, offers the unblemished sacrificial Victim in the Holy Spirit to the Father. The Church's intention, indeed, is that the faithful not only offer this unblemished sacrificial Victim but also learn to offer their very selves,* and so day by day to be brought, through the mediation of Christ, into unity with God and with each other, so that God may at last be all in all.[†]

---

*. Cf. Second Vatican Ecumenical Council, Constitution on the Sacred Liturgy, *Sacrosanctum Concilium*, no. 48; Sacred Congregation of Rites, Instruction, *Eucharisticum mysterium*, 25 may 1967, no. 12: *Acta Apostlice Sedis* 59 (1967), pp. 548–549.

†. Cf. Second Vatican Ecumenical Council, Constitution on the Sacred Liturgy, *Sacrosanctum Concilium*, no. 48; Decree on the Ministry and Life of Priests, *Presbyterorum*

g) The *intercessions,* by which expression is given to the fact that the Eucharist is celebrated in communion with the whole Church, of both heaven and of earth, and that the oblation is made for her and for all her members, living and dead, who are called to participate in the redemption and salvation purchased by the Body and Blood of Christ.

h) The *concluding doxology,* by which the glorification of God is expressed and which is affirmed and concluded by the people's acclamation *Amen.* (GIRM, 79)

There are four main Eucharistic Prayers in the *Novus Ordo Roman Missal.* The first Eucharistic Prayer, called the Roman Canon, acquired its essential form in the fourth century under Pope Damasus I (d. 384), the Pope who commissioned Saint Jerome to produce an official version of the Latin Bible, the Vulgate. The Roman liturgy (not unlike the Vulgate) was more or less in the Greek language until Pope Damasus. Henceforth it would use Latin (that is to say, the vernacular of the age) in its prayers. Among the unique features of the first Eucharistic Prayer is the insertion of intercessions for various people and groups, as well as lists of saints solicited to intercede on our behalf.[28] Another mark of this first prayer is *chiasmus*, a rhetorical structure where the first half of the prayer is reflected inversely in the second half (*chiasmus* appears also in the Collect discussed in chapter 5). From the central account of the words of institution, both before and after it, are found the offering and epiclesis, intercessions and lists of saints, transitional words, and lastly (and firstly) words of praise (in the preface and *Sanctus* at the beginning and in the concluding doxology at the end).[29] The style of the Roman Canon, like all things Roman, is compact, efficient, and ordered. The *General Instruction of the Roman Missal* recommends its use on Sundays and solemnities in which special forms of texts within the prayer should be used (e.g., the ". . . *Communicantes, (In communion with those whose memory we venerate),*" or "*Hanc igitur (Therefore, Lord, we pray)*" (GIRM, 365).

The *Apostolic Tradition* attributed by some to Saint Hippolytus of Rome (d. 236) is the source of Eucharistic Prayer II. Written at the beginning of the third century,[30] the *Apostolic Tradition*, as its name suggests, records practices that had been in existence for some time. There was a great deal of theological confusion in Rome (and elsewhere) at the time, and the author desired to set down clearly the true teaching handed down from the apostles.[31] Following the *Apostolic Tradition*'s lead, the second Eucharistic Prayer

---

ordinis, no. 5; Sacred Congregation of Rites, Instruction *Eucharisticum mysterium*, 25 May 1967, no. 12: *Acta Apostlice Sedis* 59 (1967), pp. 548–549.

recounts in its preface a short history of salvation, and the prayer as a whole is brief. The *Sanctus* and the intercessions are two significant additions to the Prayer in the *Apostolic Tradition*. Eucharistic Prayer II is appropriately used on weekdays or "in special circumstances" (GIRM, 365).

Of the three Eucharistic Prayers introduced after the Council, the third prayer most resembles the Roman Canon insofar as it uses a variable preface (unlike Eucharistic Prayer IV and, to some degree, the prayer patterned on the *Apostolic Tradition*). Eucharistic Prayer III is similar to Eucharistic Prayer II in its seamless account of Christ's sacrifice and the Church's place in it,[32] which it achieves by avoiding the many insertions of intercessions and saints as found in the Roman Canon. According to the *General Instruction of the Roman Missal*, the preferred use of the Eucharistic Prayer III is Sundays and festive days (GIRM, 365).

Eucharistic Prayer IV is inspired by the Eucharistic Prayers of the Antiochene and Byzantine tradition, called *anaphora* in the East.[33] Characteristic of this Eastern tradition is the use of an invariable preface, which itself initiates part of the entire economy of salvation recounted by the prayer: the Preface begins the account, after which the *Sanctus* plays an essential part. The Eucharistic Prayer proper continues the recounting immediately after the *Sanctus*. The Roman tradition, represented by Eucharistic Prayers I–III, focuses more precisely on particular aspects of salvation history, expressed in their various prefaces and proper texts for feasts. The fourth Eucharistic Prayer includes the *Sanctus*, but does so in the context of the entire prayer's recalling of God's divine plan. Because the fourth Eucharistic Prayer also precludes naming the deceased, it is not recommended in Masses for the dead. But since it is an invariable text, it is suitable on Sundays in Ordinary Time and at Masses without a proper preface (GIRM, 365).

As we examine these prayers more carefully, the beginning of each of the following sections provides texts from one of the four Eucharistic Prayers cited in full; elements proper to the remaining prayers will be noted as necessary. On the whole, however, what is said about a given section of one prayer (e.g., intercessions, epiclesis) is applicable to each prayer, since all four share the same overall structure and the same principle divisions.

Thanksgiving and Acclamation
(Preface Dialogue and *Sanctus*)

Although it is provided with its own Preface, this Eucharistic Prayer may also be used with other Prefaces, especially those that present an overall view of the mystery of salvation, such as the Common Prefaces.

V.:   The Lord be with you.

R.:   And with your spirit.

V.:   Lift up your hearts.

R.:   We lift them up to the Lord.

V.:   Let us give thanks to the Lord our God.

R.:   It is right and just.

PREFACE I OF THE SUNDAYS IN ORDINARY TIME

It is truly right and just, our duty and our salvation,
always and everywhere to give you thanks,
Lord, holy Father, almighty and eternal God,
through Christ our Lord.

For through his Paschal Mystery
he accomplished the marvelous deed,
by which he has freed us from the yoke of sin and death,
summoning us to the glory of being now called
a chosen race, a royal priesthood,
a holy nation, a people for your own possession,
to proclaim everywhere your mighty works,
for you have called us out of darkness
into your own wonderful light.

And so, with Angels and Archangels,
with Thrones and Dominions,
and with all the hosts and Powers of heaven,
as we sing the hymn of your glory
without end we acclaim:

Holy, Holy, Holy Lord God of hosts.
Heaven and earth are full of your glory.
Hosanna in the highest.
Blessed is he who comes in the name of the Lord.
Hosanna in the highest.

What the Church Wants Us to Understand

Each Eucharistic Prayer begins with the Preface, which has three parts: 1) it starts in a dialogue, 2) is followed by the thanksgiving, and 3) concludes with the *Sanctus-Benedictus* acclamation. In general, the Roman tradition supplies many prefaces to focus on a particular aspect of the mystery of Christ (e.g., his conception, epiphany, or transfiguration), and so the first and third Eucharistic Prayers, which embody the Roman mind most fully, allow the option of particular preface texts. Eucharistic Prayer II, although itself Roman, predates the Canon and contains its own preface, even though other prefaces may be substituted for it. Eucharistic Prayer IV, from the Eastern inspiration, has an invariable preface. Let us take a closer look at the Preface's three parts: the Preface Dialogue, the Thanksgiving, and the *Sanctus-Benedictus* acclamation.

Preface Dialogue

Similar to the Greeting and Dialogue that began the Mass (see chapter 5), the beginning of the Preface Dialogue is meant to animate and unite the priest and people, thus symbolizing the ecclesial unity of the Church herself.[34] The words of the Preface Dialogue also encourage those present to engage in the Paschal Sacrifice at hand. The priest's invitation, "The Lord be with you," and the people's response, "And with your spirit," first appeared in the Introductory Rites and were repeated prior to the proclamation of the Gospel. Those short dialogues signified Christ's presence among the priest and people who are gathered in his name. In the same way, here the dialogue places Christ in the midst of the gathering, while the acknowledgment of the priest's "spirit" signifies his ordination and conformity to Christ the Priest. Dialogues between priest and people demonstrate the acting Church, where the one Body engages in a Christ-centered dialogue, responding to his voice and actively participating in his praise.

The invitation "Lift up your hearts" is inspired by God's word in the scriptures: "Let us reach out our hearts toward God in heaven!" (Lamentations 3:41).[35] As noted earlier, what the Church in the West calls the "Eucharistic Prayer," the East calls the *anaphora*, meaning "lifting up" or "offering," as in the Greek *anō tas kardias*, "let us lift up (*anō*) our hearts (*kardias*)."[36] The people's response to the *sursum corda* ("Lift up your hearts") is: "We lift them up to the Lord." Saint Cyprian explains the dialogue thus: "Therefore the priest precedes the eucharistic prayer with a few words of introduction and prepares the hearts of the sisters and brothers by saying: 'Lift up your hearts,' and the congregation, which answers this with: 'We have them with the Lord' may be reminded that they are to think of nothing except the Lord."[37] Our sacramental words at this point simultaneously express and foster the movement of the heart. "Our heart is restless," says Saint Augustine in the first lines of the *Confessions*, "until it rests in you." The Church is leading our hearts at this moment to the core of life, the "pierced heart of the Crucified" open for us during the Eucharistic sacrifice.

A third verse and response complete the Preface Dialogue: V. "Let us give thanks to the Lord our God." R. "It is right and just." The Greek term *eucharistia* means "thanksgiving," so the priest's entreaty speaks to the essence of the Eucharist itself. Another name for the Eucharistic Prayer is the Canon, meaning "norm." Its fuller name is *Canon actionis gratiarum*, the norm or "order of the thanksgiving," a name inspired by this present invitation to give thanks to the Lord.[38] The phrase "Let us give thanks" is found among the early Christians[39] and may have its origins in Jewish prayer,[40] whereas the response "It is right and just" derives from the agreement of civic assemblies of ancient Greece.[41]

We might pause here to consider why Catholics today speak like ancient Romans and Greeks and Jews; we are not, after all, their contemporaries, nor do we share their cultural and linguistic environment. If language is culturally bound, why do we use elements of ancient culture rather than our own? First, we must remember that when we talk about liturgical language, we are inextricably tied to the religious culture that produced it. The language of the liturgy is not so much Latin or Greek, Copt or English. We use the Christian language.[42] It is the Roman Rite itself that connects

> . . . we must remember that when we talk about liturgical language, we are inextricably tied to the religious culture that produced it.

members of the Latin Church with the ancients. This rite has taken elements of Greek, Roman, and Jewish culture to itself and developed an ecclesial, Christian culture that is now our own. The Church's culture has grown in part from other human cultures; her "family tree" is rooted in Roman, Greek, and Jewish soil. The "relatives" of the Church are now our relatives, and the affinities between us are expressed in the ways we think, act, and speak. Our adoption of the Greek civic phrase "It is right and just" to express our communal assent is one example. As every family has an album or collection of images that celebrates its history, the "family album" of the Latin Faithful is the Roman Rite, which contains our history, our identity, and communicates our values. Hence, the Preface Dialogue not only unites the assembly with the priest, or both of them with God, but the whole family of the Church with itself through all the ages.

Thanksgiving: The Preface Text

In the text of the Preface, the Mystical Body continues to thank God, particularly the Father, for the saving works of his salvific plan. Earlier we noted that the prayers accompanying the preparation of the gifts resemble the shorter *berakah* prayers of the Jewish meals at Christ's time. A longer *berakah* prayer, called the *birkat ha mazon*, situates the thanksgiving of the Preface at the beginning of the Eucharistic Prayer. Said by the father at the end of the meal over a cup of water and wine mixed, the *birkat ha mazon* is first a *blessing* (*eulogia* in Greek) for the gifts of creation; second, a *thanksgiving* (*eucharistia* in Greek) for the gift of revelation, the covenant, and God's saving works; and third, a *petition* (*proseuche* in Greek) for the fulfillment of God's plan.[43] For example:

Blessed are you, Lord our God, King of the universe,
who feed us and the whole world with goodness, grace,
    kindness and mercy.
Blessed are you, Lord, who sustain all things.

We thank you, Lord our God, for giving us as our heritage
a desirable, good and broad land,
the covenant and the Torah, life and food.
For all this we thank you and bless your name for ever and beyond.
Blessed are you, Lord, for the land and our food.

Have mercy, Lord our God, on Israel your people,
on Jerusalem your city, on your sanctuary and your dwelling,
on Zion, the place where your glory dwells,
and on the great and holy house upon which your name is
    invoked . . . Blessed are you, Lord, who rebuild Jerusalem.[44]

This same pattern found in the *birkat ha mazon*—of 1) blessing God for creation, 2) thanking him for his saving works, and 3) petitioning him, for consummation of his plan—guides the eucharistic liturgy. At the Preparation of the Gifts, God was *blessed* for "all creation," the "fruit of the earth," and the "fruit of the vine." Later in the Eucharistic Prayer we will *petition* God to fill us with the Holy Spirit and make us "one body, one spirit in Christ" and so "obtain an inheritance with your elect" (Eucharistic Prayer III). In this prelude, the Preface *thanks* God for his saving work. The Preface I of the Sundays of Ordinary Time, for example, thanks the Father for Christ's Paschal Mystery:

> It is truly right and just, our duty and our salvation,
> always and everywhere to give you thanks,
> Lord, holy Father, almighty and eternal God,
> through Christ our Lord.
>
> For through his Paschal Mystery
> he accomplished the marvelous deed,
> by which he has freed us from the yoke of sin and death,
> summoning us to the glory of being now called
> a chosen race, a royal priesthood,
> a holy nation, a people for your own possession,
> to proclaim everywhere your mighty works,
> for you have called us out of darkness
> into your own wonderful light.

The texts of *The Roman Missal* allow us to thank (*eucharistein*) God during the Preface in a way consonant with the Jewish tradition that the Church has made her own. Faithful to the Latin typical edition, the English translation also reflects the Roman Rite's characteristic expression of the liturgy (its use of relative words and clauses in a single sentence), which help form us in the abiding culture of the Church. By learning to speak clearly with the scripture, history, and the style of the rite, we are at the same time participating fully with Christ's own individual voice of thanks to the Father.

Preface Acclamation (Holy, Holy, Holy)

Our thanks to God in the Preface continues with the saints and the angels or, as the Preface example at the beginning of this section says concretely, "with Angels and Archangels, / with Thrones and Dominions." In fact, this oldest of congregational hymns[45] employs the words of the heavenly Church as recounted in the prophet Isaiah and the book of Revelation: "'Holy, holy, holy is the Lord of hosts!' they cried one to the other. 'All the earth is filled with his glory!'" (Isaiah 6:3); "Holy, holy, holy is the Lord God almighty"

(Revelation 4:8). While not all records show the *Sanctus* as a part of the Eucharistic Prayer (that of the *Apostolic Tradition*, for example), the *Sanctus* is thought to have existed in the Mass of the earliest Christian communities, and perhaps even in those communities that identified with the apostles themselves.[46] The English text sings of the "Holy Lord God of *hosts*" (*Sabaoth*) rather than the God of "power and might" as it might be translated. This reflects the concrete style of Roman language. "Hosts" signifies an army or multitude of angels and saints, giving the hearer a vivid image of the heavenly choir; "power and might," on the other hand, are more abstract terms, denoting general qualities of substantial realities. The text also renders exactly the passage from Isaiah. In short, the translation speaks clearly the mother tongue, so that we, her children, can make it our own. In the life of faith, our voices are to imitate Christ's, and so the Church's liturgy forms our voice to be like his.

While the *Sanctus* had originated within the first Christian communities, the *Benedictus* ("Blessed is he . . .") was introduced in the West around the sixth century.[47] The words used in the acclamation are found in Saint Matthew's Gospel account. The crowds welcome Jesus upon his triumphal entry into Jerusalem, where he will complete his Paschal Sacrifice: "The crowds preceding him and those following kept crying out and saying: 'Hosanna to the Son of David; blessed is he who comes in the name of the Lord; hosanna in the highest'" (Matthew 21:9). The words of the *Benedictus* also have an echo in other parts of the New Testament. Compare the *Benedictus,* for example, to Saint John's account of heavenly worship in the book of Revelation: ". . . every creature in heaven and on earth and under the earth and in the sea, everything in the universe, [cries] out: 'To the one who sits on the throne and to the Lamb be blessing and honor, glory and might, forever and ever'" (Revelation 5:13). Inspired by God's Word, the words of the liturgy in this case repeat the words of the Heavenly City in order that we may live comfortably in it, walking its golden streets (Revelation 21:21), eating its manna (Revelation 2:17), and singing its unending Song of the Lamb (Revelation 15:3). The English-language *Roman Missal* fosters heavenly speech, our participation in it, and our logification to the heavenly Lamb. Languages are best learned when one is immersed in a culture. When acquiring heavenly language through the liturgy, we are therefore acclimating ourselves to heaven's culture and its own life. Its words divinize us and make us capable of living within its walls and joining its eternal praise.

Epiclesis

EUCHARISTIC PRAYER I

The Priest, with hands extended, says:

> To you, therefore, most merciful Father,
> we make humble prayer and petition
> through Jesus Christ, your Son, our Lord:

He joins his hands and says:

> That you accept

He makes the Sign of the Cross once over the bread and chalice together, saying:

> and bless ✠ these gifts, these offerings,
> these holy and unblemished sacrifices,

With hands extended, he continues:

> which we offer you firstly
> for your holy catholic Church . . . .

[*In primis, Momento Domine, Communcantes,* and *Hanc igitur* follow]
> *Holding his hands extended over the offerings, he says:*

> Be pleased, O God, we pray,
> to bless, acknowledge,
> and approve this offering in every respect;
> make it spiritual and acceptable,
> so that it may become for us
> the Body and Blood of your most beloved Son,
> our Lord Jesus Christ.

He joins his hands.

What the Church Wants Us to Understand

Epiclesis means "to call upon," from the Greek *kalein* ("to call"), and the prefix *epi,* "upon,"[48] and here indicates the calling down of the Holy Spirit upon the gifts, and later in the Eucharistic Prayer, the Spirit will be invoked on the people so that they too become one in the Mystical Body. Accompanying the words of epiclesis is the extension of the priest's hands over the gifts, itself a sacramental gesture embodying the descent of the Holy Spirit. This expression is found in each liturgy of the Church's sacraments: in confession, for instance, the confessor raises his hands above the head of the penitent; during the administration of confirmation, the bishop extends his hands over the *confirmandi.*

As the *General Instruction of the Roman Missal* indicates, there are in fact two epicleses in the Roman Rite Mass: the first, called the *consecratory* epiclesis, occurs prior to the words of institution and "implores the power of the Holy Spirit that the gifts offered by human hands be consecrated, that is, become Christ's Body and Blood" (GIRM, 79). The second, known as the *communion* epiclesis, follows the institution narrative. The priest extends his hands and asks that "the unblemished sacrificial Victim to be consumed in Communion may be for the salvation of those who will partake of it" (GIRM, 79).

It is perhaps no surprise, given the Roman tendency for terrestrial conquering, organizing, and managing, that the Western and Roman liturgical tradition focuses on the compact and concrete realities of the world and in particular emphasizes the Person of the Incarnate Christ and his saving work in history. The Eastern tradition, drawn to more transcendent realities, accentuates the work of the Holy Spirit. Again, compared to the law and order prized by the Romans, the Greeks were philosophizers and thinkers, perpetually fascinated with abstraction, contemplation, and nuanced distinctions. When held in balance, the tendencies of each area respect the integrity of the faith;[49] only when given to extremes do the trends obscure the faith. As discussed in chapter 4, the Western and Antiochene theology sympathized with the humanity of Christ, while the Eastern and Alexandrian position championed the divinity of Christ. These same tendencies in Eastern and Western theology find their expressions in their respective Eucharistic Prayers. The Roman Canon (which is the most characteristically "Roman" of any of the four Prayers) does not explicitly mention the Holy Spirit except at the concluding doxology: "Through him, and with him, and in him, O God, almighty Father, in the unity of the Holy Spirit, all glory and honor is yours, for ever and ever." The Eastern Anaphoras (and that of the Roman *Apostolic Tradition* prior to the fully developed Roman Canon), on the contrary, each include an explicit mention of the Holy Spirit, particularly at the point of the consecratory and communion epicleses. This relative silence should not be understood to mean that prayers of epiclesis are missing from the first Eucharistic Prayer; rather, the work of the Holy Spirit is implicitly invoked during the "calling down," for it is by the Holy Spirit's action that the priest begs the Father to "accept and bless these gifts" and to "bless, acknowledge, and approve this offering."

> To you, therefore, most merciful Father,
> we make humble prayer and petition
> through Jesus Christ, your Son, our Lord:
> that you accept
> and bless ✠ these gifts, these offerings,
> these holy and unblemished sacrifices,
> which we offer you firstly
> for your holy catholic Church. (Roman Canon)

From this point follows a series of intercessions for the living (*In primis*), prayers for the deceased (*Memento Domine famulorum*), invocations to the saints (*Communicantes*), and prayers to the Father for acceptance of the offering (*Hanc igitur*) (more on these individual parts will follow). Then, immediately prior to the words of institution in the Roman Canon, the priest extends his hands over the offerings and completes the consecratory epiclesis (the *Quam oblationem*):

> Be pleased, O God, we pray,
> to bless, acknowledge,
> and approve this offering in every respect;
> make it spiritual and acceptable,
> so that it may become for us
> the Body and Blood of your most beloved Son,
> our Lord Jesus Christ.

Noteworthy in this latter section is the phrase "make it *spiritual* and acceptable." The Latin text uses *rationabilem*, or "rational," hearkening to the *logike latreia* of Saint Paul in his Letter to the Romans: "I urge you therefore, brothers, by the mercies of God, to offer your bodies as a living sacrifice, holy and pleasing to God, your spiritual worship [*logikē latreia*]" (Romans 12:1). "Logical liturgy" has been our consistent theme: living in accord with the Logos (i.e., logification), speaking in accord with the Logos, and worshipping in accord with the Logos. Now, at the consecratory epiclesis, the Church asks the Father to make her sacrifice in accord with the Logos, a "Sacrifice of the Word," one that is logical, rational, and spiritual.

The remaining Eucharistic Prayers in the Roman Rite are more heavily influenced by Eastern spiritualism. Each prayer mentions the Holy Spirit explicitly in its epiclesis. For instance, in Eucharistic Prayer II, the priest implores God:

> Make holy, therefore, these gifts, we pray,
> by sending down your Spirit upon them like the dewfall,
> so that they may become for us
> the Body ✠ and Blood of our Lord Jesus Christ.

An expression that is foreign to our daily speech appears in this epiclesis. We ask the Spirit to be sent "like the dewfall" (*rore*, in the Latin). Its inclusion, apart from being faithful to the typical edition, is scripturally and theologically significant.[50] It brings to mind a number of biblical allusions, including the dew that fell upon the camp of the Chosen People on their way to the Promised Land which, when evaporated, revealed the heavenly manna (Exodus 16:13–17). This dewfall yields food from heaven for Israel on its pilgrimage to a land they could call their own. In Catholic liturgy, at the threshold of the reception of our true bread from heaven,[51] this dewfall of the Holy Spirit precedes the food (*Viaticum*) for the journey to our true home, heaven. The dew also symbolizes refreshment and hope of new life. God likens himself to "the dew for Israel," which produces much fruit in a godly life (Hosea 14:6).

Eucharistic Prayer III invokes the Holy Spirit in these words:

> Therefore, O Lord, we humbly implore you:
> by the same Spirit graciously make holy
> these gifts we have brought to you for consecration,
> that they may become the Body and ✠ Blood
> of your Son our Lord Jesus Christ,
> at whose command we celebrate these mysteries.

The calling down of the Holy Spirit in the Eucharistic Prayer IV takes the following form:

> Therefore, O Lord, we pray:
> may this same Holy Spirit
> graciously sanctify these offerings,
>
> that they may become
> the Body ✠ and Blood of our Lord Jesus Christ
> for the celebration of this great mystery,
> which he himself left us
> as an eternal covenant.

A second epicletic prayer, a "Communion epiclesis," follows the words of institution. Where the consecratory epiclesis invokes the Holy Spirit to transform our offering on the altar into "the Body and Blood of your most beloved Son, our Lord Jesus Christ" (Eucharistic Prayer I), the Communion epiclesis asks the same Spirit to refashion those who receive the sacrament into the same Body of Christ:

> In humble prayer we ask you, almighty God:
> command that these gifts be borne
> by the hands of your holy Angel
> to your altar on high
> in the sight of your divine majesty,
> that all of us, who through this participation at the altar
> receive the most holy Body and Blood of your Son,
> may be filled with every grace and heavenly blessing.

Saint Paul, in his First Letter to the Corinthians, emphasizes that eating the sacrifice is a "participation at the altar" (1 Corinthians 10:18), and, moreover, that "Because the loaf of bread is one, we, though many, are one body, for we all partake of the one loaf," which is precisely the intent of the Communion ("union with") epiclesis. The epiclesis asks that "all of us who through this participation at the altar" may be filled with the grace that unites recipients into one heavenly Body.

The Communion epicleses of the remaining Eucharistic Prayers also call upon the Holy Spirit to unite participants within the unity of Christ and his Church:

IN EUCHARISTIC PRAYER II

> Humbly we pray
> that, partaking of the Body and Blood of Christ,
> we may be gathered into one by the Holy Spirit.

IN EUCHARISTIC PRAYER III

> Look, we pray, upon the oblation of your Church
> and, recognizing the sacrificial Victim by whose death
> you willed to reconcile us to yourself,
> grant that we, who are nourished
> by the Body and Blood of your Son
> and filled with his Holy Spirit,
> may become one body, one spirit in Christ.

IN EUCHARISTIC PRAYER IV:

> Look, O Lord, upon the Sacrifice
> which you yourself have provided for your Church,
> and grant in your loving kindness
> to all who partake of this one Bread and one Chalice
> that, gathered into one body by the Holy Spirit,
> they may truly become a living sacrifice in Christ
> to the praise of your glory.

This final epiclesis asks the Spirit to transform participants into a "living sacrifice," recalling once again the *logikē latreia* (spiritual worship) of Saint Paul. With Paul's encouragement, we are to enter into the liturgy to become logified in mind *and* body. Since man is made of both body and spirit, the Church which forms us in the Christian life speaks of both in her prayers. The epiclesis of Eucharistic Prayer IV therefore asks the Spirit to make Christ's sacrifice present not only on the altar, but a "living sacrifice" in the world.

How does one call down the Holy Spirit? Happily the Church knows how to do so, for she herself is animated by this same Spirit. She has developed a clear and powerful language over time suitable for this purpose. It is a language based on scriptural texts, apostolic and patristic teachings, and the deposit of faith. The English translations of the epicletic prayers render faithfully this manner of speaking found in the Latin edition of the *Missal* and allow the faithful to join their own hearts to the prayer of the Church. We speak of "dew" because God speaks of it; we ask clearly for transubstantiation and transformation since these works are attributed to the Spirit; and we pray in elevated tones because they reflect the elevated position of the Holy Spirit whom we desire. And we "say" all of these things according to the Logos, the Word who gives meaning to all liturgical words.

Institution Narrative and Consecration

EUCHARISTIC PRAYER I

In the formulas that follow, the words of the Lord should be pronounced clearly and distinctly, as the nature of these words requires.

On the day before he was to suffer,

He takes the bread
and, holding it slightly raised above the altar, continues:

he took bread in his holy and venerable hands,

He raises his eyes.

> and with eyes raised to heaven
> to you, O God, his almighty Father,
> giving you thanks, he said the blessing,
> broke the bread
> and gave it to his disciples, saying:

He bows slightly.

> TAKE THIS, ALL OF YOU, AND EAT OF IT,
> FOR THIS IS MY BODY,
> WHICH WILL BE GIVEN UP FOR YOU.

He shows the consecrated host to the people, places it again on the paten, and genuflects in adoration.
After this, the Priest continues:

> In a similar way, when supper was ended,

He takes the chalice
and, holding it slightly raised above the altar, continues:

> he took this precious chalice
> in his holy and venerable hands,
> and once more giving you thanks, he said the blessing
> and gave the chalice to his disciples, saying:

He bows slightly.

> TAKE THIS, ALL OF YOU, AND DRINK FROM IT,
> FOR THIS IS THE CHALICE OF MY BLOOD,
> THE BLOOD OF THE NEW AND ETERNAL COVENANT,
> WHICH WILL BE POURED OUT FOR YOU AND FOR MANY
> FOR THE FORGIVENESS OF SINS.
> DO THIS IN MEMORY OF ME.

He shows the chalice to the people, places it on the corporal, and genuflects in adoration.

What the Church Wants Us to Understand

As indicated in chapters 2 and 3, the meaning of sacramental signs is found in the economy of salvation: in creation, human culture, the Old Covenant, Christ, heaven, and generally in their use by the Church through time. But it is Jesus himself who gives sacramental signs their definitive meaning. The Eucharist's institution narrative is the supreme example of this.

In examining the institution narrative, we must recall the scriptural sources that repeat Christ's own words. These words are used by the Church as she joins herself to the Paschal Sacrifice, her Bridegroom, Christ himself. Christ's words at the Last Supper are now the Church's words at the Supper of the Lamb. The institution narratives of the Last Supper are recorded in the Synoptic Gospels (Matthew, Mark, and Luke), and also in the First Letter of Saint Paul to the Corinthians. One thing to note is that the scriptural accounts (written in the second half of the first century) are themselves not strictly historical accounts, but liturgical ones as well. That is, by the time Jesus' words at the Last Supper are recorded by Saint Paul and the evangelists, the institution narrative had established itself within the early Christians' weekly Eucharists. Also, of the four accounts, those of Saint Matthew and Saint Mark resemble each other, while the narratives of Saint Luke and Saint Paul share an affinity. In the Roman Eucharistic Prayers both trends are present, as we will see below.

Christ's central words of institution are the same for each Eucharistic Prayer, although the introductory and transitional words vary slightly. In the Roman Canon, the narrative follows upon the consecratory epiclesis and begins with the words "On the day before he was to suffer" (*Qui pridie*). The rubric at this point reminds us that "the words of the Lord should be pronounced clearly and distinctly, as the nature of these words requires" (Order of Mass, 89). Continuing, the prayer says, "he took bread in his *holy and venerable* hands," after the Latin text *accepit panem in sanctas ac venerabiles manus suas*. While the *Missal*'s initial translation rightly conveyed the meaning of "holy and venerable" as "sacred," the vernacular *interpreted* rather than *translated* the Latin text that had for centuries been the practice of the Church. To use the words "holy and venerable" does more than satisfy the demands of Latin teachers: it connects our voice to the voices of Catholics before, fashioning our voices into one timeless prayer.

Following the priest's rubric, "He raises his eyes," the celebrant continues:

and with eyes raised to heaven
to you, O God, his almighty Father,
giving you thanks, he said the blessing,
broke the bread
and gave it to his disciples, saying: . . . .

Et elevates oculis in caelum: **"And with eyes raised to heaven."** The
liturgical vernacular at this point reflects the Roman manner of thinking
and speaking in a way that simply "looking up" cannot. Romans,
remember, are detail people: practical, explicit, and concrete. Roman
Catholics, who are offspring of the Latin Church and its Roman Rite, in
many ways share the same Roman culture. We saw earlier, in the Preface
Acclamation (Holy, Holy, Holy [*Sanctus*]), that *"Domine, Deus Sabaoth"*
is masterfully translated as "Lord, God of *hosts*." "Hosts," in this
instance, evokes images of the heavenly band or the "army of heaven"
(Revelation 19:14). Here also "eyes raised to heaven" describes clearly
the action of Christ, something which the more vague action of
"looking up" is not able to do. Raising our eyes to heaven, whether those
of the priest at this moment or those of the laity with him, is, as Pope
Benedict has said, "to fix our gaze upwards, detaching it from the things
of this world, to direct ourselves in prayer towards God and thus to raise
ourselves."[52] "To raise ourselves" or, as he says elsewhere, to "get beyond
ourselves"[53] is the goal of the Christian life and liturgy. A "liturgical
asceticism" through authentic participation forms our spirits, souls, and
bodies for heaven, makes us "capable of resurrection."[54] To lift our eyes
is also to lift our hearts,[55] much as we were encouraged to do during the
Preface Dialogue: Lift up your hearts! (*Sursum corda!*) Lifting our eyes
and hearts after the example of Jesus in the Church's Eucharistic Prayer,
we become like him (the Logos), Logical. In short, when the faithful
attend to "eyes raised to heaven" and "holy and venerable hands," we
more easily focus our vision and our voices on the sacrifice of Jesus, who
never lost sight of his Father and for him offered a once-fallen creation
into his own hands. In the person of the priest, the "praying Church
gazes upon the hands and eyes of the Lord," says Pope Benedict. "It is as
if she wants to observe him, to perceive the form of his praying and acting
in that remarkable hour, she wants to encounter the figure of Jesus even,
as it were, through the senses."[56] As the Pope suggests, the words of our

liturgical vernacular lead us to hear the voice of the Logos at this moment of his sacrificial "yes" to the Father.

Christ's "yes" to the Father (his "sacrifice in verbal form") becomes reality in the words of consecration over the bread: [57]

TAKE THIS, ALL OF YOU, AND EAT OF IT,
FOR THIS IS MY BODY,
WHICH WILL BE GIVEN UP FOR YOU.

In these words, Christ gives new meaning to the Passover bread: no longer is it the "bread of affliction" eaten by the ancestors in the desert and described in the Passover story, or *haggadah*, but it is now Christ's glorified body, once sacrificed on the cross.[58] The priest, acting in the person of Christ, speaks in a real and sacramental way for the Logos: there are not two voices, but one. For the members of the Church, too, the matchless moment has arrived to unite themselves to Christ's sacrificial union with God. "We must still pray for [his sacrifice] to become *our* sacrifice, that we ourselves . . . may be transformed into the Logos, conformed to the Logos, and so be made the true Body of Christ. That is the issue, and that is what we have to pray for."[59]

After showing the consecrated host to the people, the priest places it on the paten, genuflects, and then continues with the chalice:

In a similar way, when supper was ended,
he took this precious chalice
in his holy and venerable hands,
and once more giving you thanks, he said the blessing
and gave the chalice to his disciples, saying:

Once again focusing in typical Roman manner on the concrete, the liturgical vernacular emphasizes "his holy and venerable hands," but the translation also directs our attention to what these hands contain; namely, a "precious chalice" (or simply "chalice" in Eucharistic Prayers II–IV). From the level of human culture, the "precious chalice" delivers more meaning than the more generic "cup." While earthly wedding feasts may use cups, they more probably include specific types of drinking vessels like glasses, goblets, and champagne flutes. Important events express themselves in beautiful surroundings. A liturgical event is no different. At the Wedding Feast of the Lamb, the "precious chalice" has more sacramental weight than a mere cup. Does it matter that Christ may not have used a "precious chalice" at the Last Supper? That he used *a chalice* is imperative for the Church and her re-presentation of his sacrifice; and while it may be that the chalice was not outwardly *precious*, it was made precious by its contents. For while the Mass and its Eucharistic Prayer hearken back to actions of Christ in the upper room some two thousand years ago, that historical action currently exists in *heavenly* splendor, which is why it can be made present to us at all. The cup of the first Paschal meal in time is now furnished with divine splendors and is "the chalice of great joy, of the true feast, for which we all long,"[60] and it is this divine chalice that our sacramental chalice emulates. The "precious chalice" (*praeclarum calicem* in the *editio typica*) also alludes to the "overflowing cup" at the feast set by God:[61]

> The Lord is my shepherd; there is nothing I lack.
> In green pastures you let me graze; to safe waters you lead me;
>   you restore my strength.
> You guide me along the right path for the sake of your name.
> Even when I walk through a dark valley, I fear no harm for you are
>   at my side; your rod and staff give me courage.
> You set a table before me as my enemies watch;
> You anoint my head with oil; my cup (*calix*) overflows. (Psalm 23)

In sum, the "precious chalice" taken into the Lord's "holy and venerable hands" conveys to the assembly the authentic reality playing out in the liturgy before them. Christ's hands, which will be nailed to the cross for the salvation of the world, are hands unlike any other, and their blood ("of the new and eternal covenant") contained in the chalice is precious indeed. Before one can fully, consciously, and actively participate in the sacrificial act of Christ presenting himself now to the Church, that sacrifice must be sacramentalized. The true achievement of the English-language *Roman Missal* is that its translation, in fact, captures this sense of sacrifice in an equally significant liturgical vernacular.

The third edition's success in communicating sacrifice is no better demonstrated than at the heart of the liturgy, in the words of consecration over the chalice for each of the Eucharistic Prayers:

> TAKE THIS, ALL OF YOU, AND DRINK FROM IT,
> FOR THIS IS THE CHALICE OF MY BLOOD,
> THE BLOOD OF THE NEW AND ETERNAL COVENANT,
> WHICH WILL BE POURED OUT FOR YOU AND FOR MANY
> FOR THE FORGIVENESS OF SINS.
> DO THIS IN MEMORY OF ME.

As Jesus gave new meaning to the bread (it is has become his body), so now does he signify the new reality of the chalice, for it becomes the sign of a "new and everlasting covenant" in his own blood, and not that of sheep, goats, and bulls.[62] Entering into a covenant unites two parties in an intimate and personal way different from a legal contract. That the covenant between God and man is in blood signifies closeness of the new bond, one that Pope Benedict likens to a "spiritual consanguinity," a sharing of blood: "Through the incarnation of Jesus, through the outpouring of his blood, we have been drawn into an utterly real consanguinity with Jesus and thus with God himself. The blood of Jesus is his love, in which divine life and human life have become one."[63] This bond is borne out in the institution accounts of Saint Matthew and Saint Mark who both speak of the "blood of the covenant" and recall the Mosaic covenant in blood: "This is the blood of the covenant which the Lord has made with you in accordance with all these words of his" (Exodus 24:8). On the other hand, the narratives of Saint Luke and Saint Paul speak of the *new* covenant in my blood," alluding to the prophet Jeremiah: "The days are coming, says the Lord, when I will make a new covenant with the house of Israel and the house of Judah" (31:31). The Church's liturgical words of consecration, then, reflect the somewhat differing accounts of the evangelists and Saint Paul in an enriching manner.

Another difference among the texts is the identity of the intended recipient of the sacrifice. Saint Luke says that the sacrifice will be poured out "for you," while Saint Matthew and Saint Mark record "for many." Saint Paul, by contrast, recalling Jesus' words at the Last Supper, does not record for whom the chalice is offered (1 Corinthians 11:25). He does, however, speak in the Letter to the Romans of "the many" who fell in Adam and are graced in Christ: "But the gift is not like the transgression. For if by that one person's transgression the many died, how much more did the grace of God and the gracious gift of the one person Jesus Christ overflow for the many" (5:15). Saint John, while not offering a version of institution at the Last Supper, records in the Bread of Life discourse that "the bread of God is that which comes down from heaven and gives life *to the world*" (John 6:33), which indicates the constant teaching of the Church and which is meant by each of the Gospel accounts: that Christ died for all (see John 11:52; 2 Corinthians 5:14–15; Titus 2:11; 1 John 2:2). As the texts describing "the blood of the new and everlasting covenant" call to mind the figures of Moses and Jeremiah, the sacrifice "for many" echoes the words of the Prophet Isaiah:

Because of his affliction
 he shall see the light in fullness of days;
Through his suffering, my servant shall justify *many*,
 and their guilt he shall bear.
Therefore I will give him his portion among the great,
 and he shall divide the spoils with the mighty,
Because he surrendered himself to death
 and was counted among the wicked;
And he shall take away the sins *of many*,
 and win pardon for their offenses. (Isaiah 53:11–12, emphasis added)

Saint Matthew's Gospel account is written from a Jewish perspective and for a Jewish readership, so what may seem to us an obscure reference to Isaiah would for the Jews be entirely clear. In the larger context of Isaiah, it is clear for whom the Suffering Servant will offer his life: *for all*.[64] Saint Matthew's account is similar to Saint Mark's, written not for a Jewish audience but for a Roman one, and this may explain why the Roman Canon has used "for many" (in Latin, *pro multis*) from time immemorial. What had been translated "for all" may *explain* the original *pro multis*, but it is not an authentic *translation* of *pro multis*. It is the job of catechesis—not of translation—to explain the meaning of liturgical texts to the people (LA, 29). Liturgical texts form the faithful to hear and to speak the language of the Church, but they are not on this account instructive and merely conduits of information.

Another benefit of the vernacular's "for many" is its emphasis on the requisite participation of the faithful in the saving act of Christ, here made present in the Eucharist. In an October 17, 2006, letter from Cardinal Arinze, then Prefect for the Congregation for Divine Worship and the Discipline of the Sacraments, explains:

> The expression "for many," while remaining open to the inclusion of each human person, is reflective also of the fact that this salvation is not brought about in some mechanistic way, without one's own willing or participation; rather, the believer is invited to accept in faith the gift that is being offered and to receive the supernatural life that is given to those who participate in this mystery, living it out in their lives as well so as to be numbered among the "many" to whom the text refers.

The "full and active participation by all the people is the aim to be considered before all else" in the restoration of the liturgy (SC, 14), and the authentic rendering of *pro multis* as "for many" reminds the faithful of their needed cooperation with Christ and encourages each to unite with the sacrifice of Christ, to achieve that "consanguinity" desired by God, and become one in the family of God.

The Mystery of Faith

He says:

> The mystery of faith.

And the people continue, acclaiming:

> We proclaim your Death, O Lord,
> and profess your Resurrection
> until you come again.

Or:

> When we eat this Bread and drink this Cup,
> we proclaim your Death, O Lord,
> until you come again.

Or:

> Save us, Savior of the world,
> for by your Cross and Resurrection
> you have set us free.

What the Church Wants Us to Understand

At this point in the Mass, following Christ's command to "do this in memory of me," the priest calls on those gathered to join their own voices with the Sacrifice of the Word now substantially present upon the altar. The *Mysterium fidei* ("The mystery of faith") has a long history. It is found first within the words of consecration of the chalice already in the seventh century in Eucharistic Prayers of Roman origin.[65] Despite its history, however, the meaning of the phrase is unclear. Scholars associate "the mystery of faith" with Saint Paul's exhortation concerning deacons, who must hold fast "to the mystery of the faith with a clear conscience" (1 Timothy 3:9). Whatever the origin of the phrase's meaning, it has been embellished to serve now as an invitation for those present to acclaim the substance of the faith in the sacrament of the altar, which is "the entire spiritual wealth of the Church, namely Christ himself our Pasch and our living bread."[66]

The priest's invitation, "The mystery of faith," evokes the people's acclamation; it is dialogical in character. This is why the priest does not join in the acclamation: *"And the people continue, acclaiming . . . ."* The vernacular maintains the original formulation (simply, "The mystery of faith") to affirm the nature of the sacrament—it *is* the Mystery of Faith, Christ himself. The current rendering in the form of a declarative statement ("The mystery of faith") not only invites the faithful to acclaim the sacramental truth (in any one of the formulas that follow), but it also acclaims the mystery of Christ's sacrifice already present on the altar. "*Let us proclaim* the mystery of faith," on the other hand, would change the affirmation into a command.

In response to the priest's invitation, the faithful respond with one of three formulas, each of which recalls Christ's saving work and its redemptive effects on his people. The first acclamation ("We proclaim your death, O Lord, and profess your Resurrection until you come again") finds its source in Saint Paul's First Letter to the Corinthians: "For as often as you eat this bread and drink the cup, you proclaim the death of the Lord until he comes" (11:26). The second response is like the first, appealing to Jesus' historical Paschal Mystery and his prophetic final coming: "When we eat this Bread and drink this Cup, we proclaim your death, O Lord, until you come again." A final acclamation incorporates the words of John's Gospel account where the Samaritans profess their belief in Christ: "We have heard for ourselves, and we know that this is truly the savior of the world" (John 4:42). Inspired by the Samaritans' own faithful profession, we acclaim: "Save us, Savior of the world, for by your Cross and Resurrection you have set us free." In each version of the Memorial Acclamation, the faithful participate fully and actively in the Logical Sacrifice in words inspired by theological and sacramental teaching (i.e., the Eucharist contains the Church's mystery of faith) articulated by the history of the Latin Church and contained in the prayers of the *Missal*. With Christ and his Church, the faithful announce this central truth of the faith, conform their hearts to it, are lifted up and divinized by it. Underscoring the importance of the liturgical language of the Mass, the liturgical vernacular of the Mass serves as a sort of "liturgical lexicon" with which our voice becomes one with Christ's and with him sings perfect praise to the Father.

Anamnesis and Oblation

EUCHARISTIC PRAYER I

Then the Priest, with hands extended, says:

Therefore, O Lord,
as we celebrate the memorial of the blessed Passion,

the Resurrection from the dead,
and the glorious Ascension into heaven
of Christ, your Son, our Lord,
we, your servants and your holy people,
offer to your glorious majesty
from the gifts that you have given us,
this pure victim,
this holy victim,
this spotless victim,
the holy Bread of eternal life
and the Chalice of everlasting salvation.

What the Church Wants Us to Understand

Christ commanded his disciples to "Do this in *memory* of me." Therefore, the words of consecration end with the command to *remember*; the acclamation that concludes "The mystery of faith" is called the "*Memorial* Acclamation." The Eucharist Prayer continues, immediately noting that we "celebrate the *memorial*" of Christ's saving work yet again. In the Greek New Testament, Christ tells us to "Do this as an *anamnesis* of me."[67] In fact, this part of the Eucharistic Prayers still bears this Greek name, "*anamnesis*." An anamnetic memory is not one that "recollects"; it is not synonymous with our own ordinary understanding of the term "memory."[68] Rather, anamnesis is the process of bringing an object of memory to mind in the same instant that it makes the memory itself "come to life," thereby inducing action in the individual. Moses, for example, begs an angry God to "*Remember* your servants Abraham, Isaac and Israel, and how you swore to them by your own self" (Exodus 32:13).[69] It's not as if God had forgotten the patriarchs or the promises made to them. They have not somehow "slipped his divine mind." Moses prays for God to act on his earlier promises to the patriarchs, making his covenant with them come alive at that moment, despite the infidelity of the people. The Passover meal of the Jews is likewise anamnetic: for to share in the meal is also to actually share in the liberation from Egypt. For Catholics present at the climax of the Mass, the "remembering" or "memorial" of the Eucharist, especially at the prayers immediately following the consecration, is a living participation in Christ's "blessed Passion, glorious Resurrection and Ascension into heaven" (GIRM, 79).

Before citing the texts themselves, let us look at another element closely associated with the anamnesis—the oblation. Through a sharing in the Paschal Mystery of Christ, we ourselves are transformed and "logified," capable of passing over with Christ to the heavenly world of the Father. As the *General Instruction of the Roman Missal* explains:

> [I]n this very memorial, the Church, in particular that gathered here and now, offers the unblemished sacrificial Victim in the Holy Spirit to the Father. The Church's intention, indeed, is that the faithful not only offer this unblemished sacrificial Victim but also learn to offer their very selves, and so day by day to be brought, through the mediation of Christ, into unity with God and with each other, so that God may at last be all in all. (GIRM, 79)

Our own transformation according to the Logos is also the intention of the communion epiclesis spoken of earlier. Not until the sacrifice is actually made present before us can we invoke the Holy Spirit to unite us and offer us along with it. In it "the difference between the *actio Christi* and our own action is done away with. There is only *one* action, which is at the same time his and ours—ours because we have become 'one body and one spirit' with him."[70] We can participate in the eternal Logical Sacrifice only because that same sacrifice is actually present on the altar. As a consequence, the prayers of anamnesis include the oblation of "the spotless Victim" and then, by the power of the Holy Spirit, the oblation of ourselves. Accordingly, the anamnesis of the Roman Canon (*Unde et memores*) prays:

> Therefore, O Lord,
> as we celebrate the *memorial* of the blessed Passion,
> the Resurrection from the dead,
> and the glorious Ascension into heaven
> of Christ, your Son, our Lord,
> we, your servants and your holy people,
> *offer* to your glorious majesty
> from the gifts that you have given us,
> this pure victim,
> this holy victim,
> this spotless victim,
> the holy Bread of eternal life
> and the Chalice of everlasting salvation. (emphasis added)

The offering is then further developed in the two subsequent prayers in the Roman Canon (*Supra quae* and *Supplices te rogamus*), the latter of which combines with the communion epiclesis:

Be pleased to look upon these offerings
with a serene and kindly countenance,
and to accept them,
as once you were pleased to accept
the gifts of your servant Abel the just,
the sacrifice of Abraham, our father in faith,
and the offering of your high priest Melchizedek,
a holy sacrifice, a spotless victim.

In humble prayer we ask you, almighty God:
command that these gifts be borne
by the hands of your holy Angel
to your altar on high
in the sight of your divine majesty,
so that all of us who through this participation at the altar
receive the most holy Body and Blood of your Son,
may be filled with every grace and heavenly blessing.

The prayers of anamnesis and offering in Eucharistic Prayers II–IV also "celebrate the memorial," that is, offer the sacrifice of the Lamb, and conclude with the prayer of self-offering of the participants gathered in unity by the Holy Spirit:

EUCHARISTIC PRAYER II

Therefore, as we celebrate

the *memorial* of his Death and Resurrection,
we *offer* you, Lord,
the Bread of life and the Chalice of salvation,
giving thanks that you have held us worthy
to be in your presence and minister to you. (Emphasis added.)

EUCHARISTIC PRAYER III

Therefore, O Lord, as we celebrate the *memorial*
of the saving Passion of your Son,
his wondrous Resurrection and Ascension into heaven,
and as we look forward to his second coming,
we *offer* you in thanksgiving
this holy and living sacrifice. (Emphasis added.)

Eucharistic Prayer IV

> Therefore, O Lord,
> as we now celebrate the *memorial* of our redemption,
> we remember Christ's Death
> and his descent to the realm of the dead,
> we proclaim his Resurrection
> and his Ascension to your right hand,
> and, as we await his coming in glory,
> we *offer* you his Body and Blood,
> the sacrifice acceptable to you
> which brings salvation to the whole world. (Emphasis added.)

The anamnesis and offering make us contemporaries with Christ. They let us offer Jesus to the Father for the forgiveness of our sins, and give us the opportunity to become one with him in his perfect sacrifice.

An authentic sacrifice unites us to God, because the human heart itself is in the gift handed over ("Lift up your hearts"). Precisely for this reason is Christ's sacrifice perfect: every part of Christ is contained in the gift of himself upon the cross—he holds nothing back. In the sacrifice of the Mass, we strive to identify ourselves with that perfect Sacrifice of the Word, so that nothing of the secular world (our worldly allurements, unhealthy attachments, and sinful actions) threatens our union with God, our divinization. The anamnesis and offering (the formula for being transformed, body and soul, into love) is prayed clearly in each celebration of the Mass. Once again, the Mystical Voice of the Church at prayer is also the Voice of the Bridegroom. Through participation, that voice becomes our own.

Intercessions

Eucharistic Prayer I
Commemoration of the Dead

With hands extended, the Priest says:

> Remember also, Lord, your servants N. and N.,
> who have gone before us with the sign of faith
> and rest in the sleep of peace.

He joins his hands and prays briefly for those who have died and for whom he intends to pray.

Then, with hands extended, he continues:

> Grant them, O Lord, we pray,
> and all who sleep in Christ,
> a place of refreshment, light and peace.

He joins his hands.

> (Through Christ our Lord. Amen.)

He strikes his breast with his right hand, saying:

> To us, also, your servants, who though sinners

And, with hands extended, he continues:

> hope in your abundant mercies,
> graciously grant some share
> and fellowship with your holy Apostles and Martyrs:
> with John the Baptist, Stephen,
> Matthias, Barnabas,
> (Ignatius, Alexander,
> Marcellinus, Peter,
> Felicity, Perpetua,
> Agatha, Lucy,
> Agnes, Cecilia, Anastasia)
> and all your Saints:
> admit us, we beseech you,
> into their company,
> not weighing our merits, but granting us your pardon,

He joins his hands.

> Through Christ our Lord.

What the Church Wants Us to Understand

Next in the Eucharistic Prayer we ask that others intercede on our behalf, and we do so in communion with the whole Church. As an expression of ecclesiology, the Eucharistic Prayer includes prayers for the Church, the Pope and Bishop, all of the faithful present and absent, the entire world, and the deceased. Moreover, the prayer invokes the angels and saints in its petitions. United by the Holy Spirit around the one sacrifice of the Lamb, the petitions express and foster the communion of the whole Church.

Although the intercessions have always found a place in the Mass, they do not appear to have been a part of the Eucharistic Prayer in its original form. Saint Justin Martyr (d. 165) mentions intercessions after the homily, similar to the General Intercessions prayed today,[71] but their inclusion at that point was not long lived. In the Roman liturgy, the intercessions migrated closer to the heart of the sacrificial action, that is, within the Eucharistic Prayer itself.[72] Other historical evidence finds the names of those who had offered the bread and wine for the sacrifice being read in the course of the Eucharistic Prayer, at least in Rome and North Africa.[73] These particularly Roman practices (unlike the liturgical forms found at this time in France, Spain, and the East)[74] may explain why the list of saints is most fully developed in the Roman Canon. It may also explain why the saints in the Canon are either Roman themselves or venerated by the early Roman Church. Whatever their origin, as the *General Instruction of the Roman Missal* explains, the intercessions express "the fact that the Eucharist is celebrated in communion with the whole Church, of both heaven and of earth, and that the oblation is made for her and for all her members, living and dead, who are called to participate in the redemption and the salvation purchased by the Body and Blood of Christ" (GIRM, 79).

As we have seen in other parts of the Mass, the structure of this prayer also evinces a certain profound meaning and purpose. In fact, the first Eucharistic Prayer, as has been mentioned previously, is structured as a *chiasm*, with the consecration of the bread and wine at its center and parallel structures surrounding it on both sides. As a result, the Roman Canon has two corresponding sets of intercessions, one before the institution and one after; the remaining Eucharistic Prayers contain only one set of intercessions, and these follow the words of institution.

In the first set of intercessions in the Roman Canon, it is the visible members of the Church who are prayed for:

With hands extended, he continues:

> which we offer you firstly
> for your holy catholic Church.
> Be pleased to grant her peace,
> to guard, unite and govern her
> throughout the whole world,
> together with your servant *N.* our Pope
> and *N.* our Bishop,

and all those who, holding to the truth,
hand on the catholic and apostolic faith.

Commemoration of the Living.

Remember, Lord, your servants *N.* and *N.*

The Priest joins his hands and prays briefly for those for whom he intends to pray.
Then, with hands extended, he continues:

and all gathered here,
whose faith and devotion are known to you.
For them, we offer you this sacrifice of praise
or they offer it for themselves
and all who are dear to them:
for the redemption of their souls,
in hope of health and well-being,
and paying their homage to you,
the eternal God, living and true.

While this prayer is a familiar one for Catholics, the section recommending the living presents an enigmatic phrase: "For them, we offer you this sacrifice of praise / or they offer it for themselves / and all who are dear to them . . . ." Historically, this intention was to reference those who had brought the actual gifts for Mass, as noted above. The original wording appears to have mentioned "*they* offer it for themselves" and did not include "*we* offer you this sacrifice." When the Roman Canon was adopted in eighth-century France, the phrase "*we* offer you" was added to that intercession for the gift bearers, thus including a wider community in the Eucharistic intentions.[75] Also integrated in this period was the mention of the local Bishop in addition to the name of the Pope.[76]

What are we to make of this odd-sounding phrase? Since the purpose of translation is not to revise history but to render accurately the prayer, we must use the opportunity to remind ourselves of the great richness of our liturgical tradition and the wideness of God's mercy in the mystery of salvation. As members of the baptized, when praying these intercessions of the Canon we should bring to mind, each time, all of the Church's living members. As a result of the prayer's migration from Rome to France, we pray with greater fervor these intercessions that have expanded to include even more members—not only the Pope but also the local Bishop, and not only those who have brought the gifts but also all those who are present.

Next, the prayer invokes the saints, beginning with Mary, Joseph, then listing the 12 apostles and 12 other martyrs. This invocation, called in Latin the *Communicantes* ("In communion"), has special texts used on particular solemnities (e.g., Epiphany) and the octave days of Easter and Christmas.

In the Roman Canon's chiasmic structure, following the institution narrative is another set of intercessions; these remember the dead:

Remember also, Lord, your servants *N.* and *N.*,
who have gone before us with the sign of faith
and rest in the sleep of peace.
Grant them, O Lord, we pray,
and all who sleep in Christ,
a place of refreshment, light and peace.
(Through Christ our Lord. Amen.)

Like the intercessions for the living, those for the dead invoke more saints, seven male martyrs and seven female. When taken with the previous list, the saints represent a cross section of Church life, representing men and women; virgins, married, widowed, ordained and lay; young and old. The range of heavenly saints parallels the assortment of the Church's earthly members, sacramentalizing the Heavenly City we are called to inhabit.

The other Eucharistic Prayers place all of their intercessions for the living and dead and their invocations to the saints after the consecration, anamnesis, offering, and epiclesis.

Eucharistic Prayer II

Remember, Lord, your Church,
spread throughout the world,
and bring her to the fullness of charity,
together with *N.* our Pope and *N.* our Bishop
and all the clergy.
Remember also our brothers and sisters
who have fallen asleep in the hope of the resurrection,
and all who have died in your mercy:
welcome them into the light of your face.
Have mercy on us all, we pray,
that with the Blessed Virgin Mary, Mother of God,

with the blessed Apostles,
and all the Saints who have pleased you throughout the ages,
we may merit to be coheirs to eternal life,
and may praise and glorify you
through your Son, Jesus Christ.

Eucharistic Prayer III

May this Sacrifice of our reconciliation,
we pray, O Lord,
advance the peace and salvation of all the world.
Be pleased to confirm in faith and charity
your pilgrim Church on earth,
with your servant N. our Pope and N. our Bishop,
the Order of Bishops, all the clergy,
and the entire people you have gained for your own.

Listen graciously to the prayers of this family,
whom you have summoned before you:
in your compassion, O merciful Father,
gather to yourself all your children
scattered throughout the world.
✠ To our departed brothers and sisters
and to all who were pleasing to you
at their passing from this life,
give kind admittance to your kingdom.
There we hope to enjoy for ever the fullness of your glory
through Christ our Lord,
through whom you bestow on the world all that is good. ✠

Eucharistic Prayers II and III have special texts for use in Masses with the dead, in which the name or names of the deceased are given specific mention.

Eucharistic Prayer IV

Therefore, Lord, remember now
all for whom we make this sacrifice:
especially your servant, N. our Pope,
N. our Bishop, and the whole Order of Bishops,
all the clergy,
those who take part in this offering,

those gathered here before you,
your entire people,
and all who seek you with a sincere heart.

Remember also
those who have died in the peace of your Christ
and all the dead,
whose faith you alone have known.

To all of us, your children,
grant, O merciful Father,
that we may enter into a heavenly inheritance
with the Blessed Virgin Mary, Mother of God,
and with your Apostles and Saints in your kingdom.
There, with the whole of creation,
freed from the corruption of sin and death,
may we glorify you through Christ our Lord,
through whom you bestow on the world all that is good.

Like the previous sections of the Eucharistic Prayer, the intercessions express the theology of the Church, that is, her ecclesiology, which in this case is her identity as the Mystical Body of Christ. All of the baptized, living and dead, and even "all who seek [God] with a sincere heart" (Eucharistic Prayer IV), are gathered together with Mary, Joseph, and the saints in a voice of perfect praise. To commune with the Logos is at the same time to join with others in his Body, the Church. Our communion within the Mystical Body is wrought by the Sacrifice of the Word, which is actualized in the Mass and its words. The vernacular that expresses the Church's communion is theologically accurate, faithful to the Roman tradition, and accessible to the very members it unites. To hear these words is to hear Christ's words, which gather all into "the fullness of charity" (Eucharistic Prayer II, see 1 John 4:18).

Concluding Doxology

He takes the chalice and the paten with the host and, elevating both, he says:

Through him, and with him, and in him,
O God, almighty Father,
in the unity of the Holy Spirit,

all glory and honor is yours,
for ever and ever.

The people acclaim:

Amen.

What the Church Wants Us to Understand

In this final action of the Eucharistic Prayer, the Church's entire theology of worship is summed up, for in it the Mystical Body, united by the work of the Holy Spirit, joins the Logos in his eternal "yes" to God the Father. The name for this action (doxology) has a significance which adds to the profound nature of the prayer itself. At its roots the word means "praise" or "worship," from the Greek *doxa* (we see the root also in the word *orthodoxy*, "right worship"), and "to speak," from *logos*. Quite literally, then, the Logical worship is summed up and reiterated in this short prayer which serves as an "exclamation" mark upon the entire Eucharistic Prayer.

While the priest announces the doxology, he lifts the chalice and paten—not to show them to the people, but to present the sacrifice to the Father.[77] This gesture says with the body what the words themselves proclaim: that through, with, and in Christ our voices—and ourselves—are lifted up to the Father.

The "honor and glory" spoken in the doxology is then confirmed with the "Amen" of the people. Saint Justin Martyr, writing in the second century, attests to the assembly's affirmation at this point: "When the prayers and eucharist are finished, all the people present give their assent with an 'Amen!' 'Amen' in Hebrew means 'So be it!'"[78] In giving their assent, the people are sacramentally (which is to say, really and truly) entering into the dialogue of Trinitarian Love. "God himself is speech,"[79] and Christ himself is the Word spoken. By the Incarnation and Sacrifice of the Logos, that same divine Word speaks in human overtones, joining our own voices to his perfect voice. To adapt Saint Athanasius's phrase, "God speaks like us so that we might speak like him." The whole liturgy—indeed, the entire Christian life— "speaks" according to the Logos, through, with, and in him. At the concluding doxology, this reality is verbalized, and by it our actual participation in the Sacrifice of the Word resounds, not only in the nave and sanctuary of our churches, but also in the temple of our hearts.

Endnotes

1. Joseph Ratzinger, *The Spirit of the Liturgy,* trans. John Saward (San Francisco: Ignatius Press, 2000), 173.

2. Ratzinger, *The Spirit of the Liturgy,* 171–73.

3. Ratzinger, *The Spirit of the Liturgy,* 58.

4. Ratzinger, *The Spirit of the Liturgy,* 174; see also Joseph Ratzinger, *The Feast of Faith: Approaches to a Theology of the Liturgy,* trans. Graham Harrison (San Francisco: Ignatius Press, 1986), 37.

5. Ratzinger, *The Spirit of the Liturgy,* 173.

6. Joseph Ratzinger, *God Is Near Us: The Eucharist, the Heart of Life,* ed. Stephan Otto Horn and Vinzenz Pfnür, trans. Henry Taylor (San Francisco: Ignatius Press, 2003), 49.

7. For this reason, the priest (and, as his ordained assistant, the deacon) is the "ordinary" minister of Holy Communion: his duty to distribute the sacred species expresses his power to mediate between God and man.

8. See Robert Cabié, *The Eucharist,* ed. Aimé Georges Martimort, trans. Matthew J. O'Connell (Collegeville: Liturgical Press, 1986), 21.

9. See Aidan Kavanagh, "Jewish Roots of Christian Worship," in *New Dictionary of Sacramental Worship* (Collegeville, MN: The Liturgical Press, 1990), 617.

10. Cabié, *The Eucharist,* 158–9, 162; See also Joseph A. Jungmann, *The Mass: An Historical, Theological, and Pastoral Survey,* trans. Julian Fernandes, ed. Mary Ellen Evans (Collegeville: Liturgical Press, 1996), 191; Johannes H. Emminghaus, *The Eucharist,* 166–67.

11. Joseph A. Jungmann, *The Mass: An Historical, Theological, and Pastoral Survey,* trans. Julian Fernandes, ed. Mary Ellen Evans (Collegeville: Liturgical Press, 1976), 190–1.

12. Jungmann, *The Mass: An Historical, Theological, and Pastoral Survey,* 186, 188.

13. Jungmann, *The Mass: An Historical, Theological, and Pastoral Survey,* 190.

14. Liturgy of the Hours, At Morning Prayer, Tuesday Week IV.

15. Liturgy of the Hours, At Morning Prayer on each Sunday of the four-week cycle.

16. See Cabié, *The Eucharist,* 131.

17. See Jungmann, *The Mass: An Historical, Theological, and Pastoral Survey,* 188.

18. Jungmann, *The Mass: An Historical, Theological, and Pastoral Survey,* 191.

19. Ratzinger, *The Spirit of the Liturgy,* 173.

20. The expression is Joseph Jungmann's; *The Mass: An Historical, Theological, and Pastoral Survey,* 189.

21. See Jungmann, *The Mass: An Historical, Theological, and Pastoral Survey,* 190; Cabié, *The Eucharist,* 162, 206; Emminghaus, *The Eucharist: Essence, Form, Celebration,* trans.

Linda M. Maloney, revised and edited by Theodor Mass-Ewerd (Collegeville: Liturgical Press, 1997), 169.

22. *Ad limina* discourse to the Bishops of the Northwestern United States, 9 October 1998.

23. Cabié, *The Eucharist*, 206.

24. Twentieth Sunday in Ordinary Time.

25. Wednesday of the Sixth Week of Easter.

26. Ratzinger, *The Feast of Faith*, 37.

27. Rev. Msgr. Richard Malone, "Eucharist: Sacrifice According to the Logos," in *Antiphon* 13:I (2009): 80.

28. See Emminghaus, *The Eucharist*, 172.

29. See Emminghaus, *The Eucharist*, 172, 229–30.

30. See Jungmann, *The Mass: An Historical, Theological, and Pastoral Survey*, 200, and Cabié, *The Eucharist*, 26.

31. In fact, suspecting the successive popes of his day (Zephyrinus, Callistus, and Pontius) of unorthodoxy, Hippolytus broke for a time from the Church, putting himself forward as the true Pope. Banished to Sardinia along with Pope Pontius, Hippolytus eventually reconciled with the Church and became a martyr, along with Pope Pontius, for the faith. The shared feast day of Saint Hippolytus and Saint Pontius is August 13.

32. See Emminghaus, *The Eucharist* 189–90; Jungmann, *The Mass: An Historical, Theological, and Pastoral Survey*, 201.

33. See Emminghaus, *The Eucharist* 189; Jungmann, *The Mass: An Historical, Theological, and Pastoral Survey*, 200–1.

34. See Emminghaus, *The Eucharist*, 180.

35. Ibid.

36. See Emminghaus, *The Eucharist* , 171.

37. *De oratione dominica*, 31 (PL 4:557), in Emminghaus, *The Eucharist* 180.

38. See Emminghaus, *The Eucharist,* 171.

39. See Jungmann, *The Mass: An Historical, Theological, and Pastoral Survey*, 201.

40. See Emminghaus, *The Eucharist,* 180.

41. Ibid.

42. See Bernard Botte, "*La liturgie de Vatican II. Une mise au point du R. P. Botte*" in *La libre Belgique*, 25 août 1976, 1, 5.

43. See Aidan Kavanagh, "Jewish Roots of Christian Worship," 617.

44. Cabié, *The Eucharist*, 21–22.

45. See Jungmann, *The Mass: An Historical, Theological, and Pastoral Survey*, 203.

46. See ibid., 202.

47. See ibid., 203.

48. The term resembles the name for the Church, *ecclesia*, also from the root *kalein*, "calling," but with the prefix *ek*, meaning "out": the ecclesia is a "calling out," prefigured first at Mt. Sinai and later fulfilled in the Body of Christ called together by God.

49. It is not, it should be emphasized, as if the West disregards the Holy Spirit and the East is unconcerned about Christ, for both ecclesial traditions fully profess the Persons and attributes of both.

50. See the remarks of Cardinal Rigali on this point at the June 2009 USCCB Conference; *Adoremus Bulletin*, Vol. XV No. 5, August 2009, p. 9.

51. "My Father gives you the true bread from heaven" (John 6:32).

52. Homily during the Mass of the Lord's Supper of Pope Benedict XVI, April 9, 2009. www.vatican.va.

53. Ratzinger, *The Spirit of the Liturgy*, 123.

54. Ratzinger, *The Spirit of the Liturgy*, 176.

55. Homily during the Mass of the Lord's Supper of Pope Benedict XVI, April 9, 2009. www.vatican.va.

56. Homily during the Mass of the Lord's Supper of Pope Benedict XVI, April 9, 2009. www.vatican.va.

57. Ratzinger, *God Is Near Us*, 49.

58. See Roch Kereszty, ocist, *The Wedding Feast of the Lamb* (Chicago: Hillenbrand Books),25.

59. Ratzinger, *The Spirit of the Liturgy*, 173.

60. Homily during the Mass of the Lord's Supper of Pope Benedict XVI, April 9, 2009. va.www.vatican.va.

61. Ibid.

62. See Roch Kereszty, *The Wedding Feast of the Lamb*, 26.

63. Ibid.

64. See Kereszty, *The Wedding Feast of the Lamb*, 32–33, 38.

65. See Jungmann, *The Mass of the Roman Rite*, 199–200.

66. *Sacramentum caritatis*, 16, citing the Second Vatican Council's "Decree on the Ministry and Life of Priests," *Presbyterorum ordinis*, 5.

67. The root of the word is *mnesis*, meaning "memory" (as when we speak of a mnemonic device that helps us recall a person's name). The prefix *a-* negates the memory (as in amnesia, or forgetfulness). Another prefix, *ana-*, signifies "back again": so *ana-mnesis* might literally be rendered "to remember again."

68. See Cabié, *The Eucharist*, 28.

69. In the Greek version of the Hebrew Scriptures, the Septuagint, the present form of anamnesis is translated in the English as "remember."

70. Ratzinger, *The Spirit of the Liturgy*, 174.

71. See Emminghaus, *The Eucharist*, 152.

72. See Jungmann, *The Mass: An Historical, Theological, and Pastoral Survey*, 197.

73. See Cabié, *The Eucharist*, 81.

74. See ibid.

75. See Cabié, *The Eucharist*, 134.

76. Ibid.

77. Compare this doxological action to the more practical, showing "the consecrated host to the people," and to the gesture where he "takes the host and, holding it slightly raised above the paten or above the chalice, while facing the people, says, "*Ecce Agnus Dei*" ("Behold the Lamb of God") (see GIRM, 151, 157).

78. See Cabié, *The Eucharist*, 15.

79. Ratzinger, *The Feast of Faith*, 25.

Chapter 7

Communion Rite and Concluding Rites

Communion Rite

The fullest form of active participation imagined by the Church is the faithful's worthy reception of the Body and Blood of Christ in Holy Communion.[1] Worship is *Logical* (i.e., rational and spiritual) because Christ is the Logos; but it is also *incarnational* since Christ is the Word *become flesh*, the *Logos incarnatus*. If worship were merely logical, the Eastern and Platonic impulse to withdraw from the fallen and misleading material world would be true. But as Christ is both spirit (divine Logos) and body (via the Incarnation), our corresponding liturgy is both spiritual and bodily, Logical and incarnational, transcendent and sacrificial. Pope Benedict sees the logical-sacrificial reality expressed neatly by Saint Paul as "spiritual worship," *logikē latreia*, in which our spirits, souls, and bodies undergo transformation unto his likeness (see SCar, 70).[2] The preparatory rites for Communion prepare us to receive the Incarnate Word most efficaciously, allowing us, in the words of Saint Augustine, to be transformed into him (SCar, 70). In these rites, as in every other, words are significant. By reflecting *the* Word, the liturgy's words lead us to him and with him to the Father.

Lord's Prayer and Embolism

After the chalice and paten have been set down, the Priest, with hands joined, says:

At the Savior's command
and formed by divine teaching,
we dare to say:

He extends his hands and, together with the people, continues:

> Our Father, who art in heaven,
> hallowed be thy name;
> thy kingdom come,
> thy will be done
> on earth as it is in heaven.
> Give us this day our daily bread,
> and forgive us our trespasses,
> as we forgive those who trespass against us;
> and lead us not into temptation,
> but deliver us from evil.

With hands extended, the Priest alone continues, saying:

> Deliver us, Lord, we pray, from every evil,
> graciously grant peace in our days,
> that, by the help of your mercy,
> we may be always free from sin
> and safe from all distress,
> as we await the blessed hope
> and the coming of our Savior, Jesus Christ.

He joins his hands.
The people conclude the prayer, acclaiming:

> For the kingdom,
> the power and the glory are yours
> now and for ever.

What the Church Wants Us to Understand

The first part of the preparatory rites for Communion is the Lord's Prayer, which is found in the Roman Rite as early as the late fourth century.[3] At this early time, however, the Prayer was said after the breaking of the bread (the fraction); it wasn't until Pope Gregory the Great's intervention that the Our Father was moved to its current position. The Pope moved the Our Father closer to the Eucharistic Prayer, he says, because it seemed to him "quite inappropriate, on the one hand, to say over the offering a prayer composed by one or other writer and, on the other, not to say over the redeemer's body and blood the prayer which he himself composed . . . ."[4] Christ's own words are also employed next in the Sign of Peace: "Lord Jesus Christ, / who said to your Apostles: / Peace I leave you . . . .'" Using his words (or scriptural words referring directly to him, as at the Lamb of God) during the Communion Rite is only "logical," for as we prepare to receive the Sacrifice of the Word, we prepare ourselves with the words of the Word.

The Lord's Prayer is preceded by the priest's introduction, in which he speaks of the "daring" (*audemus*) we show by calling God "Our Father." But we are daring because we are undergoing a transformation into the Logos. As we participate in the Son's sacramental re-presentation in the Eucharistic Prayer and prepare to unite with him in the most powerful way in the reception of Communion, our conformity with Christ is actualized: we begin to "look like" him and "talk like" him. Our "daring," consequently, results from our identity with the Son and his sacrifice.

It is Saint Matthew's version of the Lord's Prayer (which differs somewhat from Saint Luke's) that is used during the Communion Rite. According to the instructions of the *Ratio translationis for the English Language*, the prayer also resembles that version most widely used in popular devotions and private prayer (RT, 107). Seven petitions are found in the Lord's Prayer, but the tradition emphasizes three of them at this point of the Mass: the giving of daily bread, the forgiveness of sins, and the deliverance from evil. In his teaching to the newly baptized, for example, Saint Ambrose calls the daily bread "supersubstantial." "It is not the bread which passes into the body, but that *bread of eternal life,* which supports the substance of our soul."[5] Saint Augustine (as well as Saint Ambrose and others) elaborates upon the petition for forgiveness: "As a result of these words we approach the altar with clean faces; with clean faces we share in the body and blood of Christ."[6] The final petition of the Lord's Prayer, deliverance from evil, is developed more fully in what is called the embolism, which means "insertion" (between the end of the Lord's Prayer and the concluding doxology: "Deliver us, Lord, we pray, from every evil . . . "). Linguistically, the translation of the embolism reflects that Roman manner of speaking, where selective conjunctions and subordinate clauses do grammatically what the prayer seeks liturgically. For example, the text first makes use of *asyndeton* (as found in the discussion of the Collect, chapter 5), where words or phrases are joined without a coordinating conjunction, "and." Rather than saying (as most English speakers would), "Deliver us, Lord, we pray, from every evil, *and* graciously grant peace in our days . . . ," the Mass' embolism omits the "and," thus making a stronger connection between the deliverance of evil and the granting of peace: "Deliver us, Lord, we pray, from every evil, graciously grant peace in our days." The true peace of God, in other words, *is* the exclusion of evil, sin, and disobedience to the divine plan. Rather than breaking up the phrases of the embolism into shorter, separate sentences, its use of subordination in a single sentence (employing the relative pronoun "that") shows how its remaining petitions are the result of deliverance from evil and the granting of peace: "Deliver us, Lord, we pray, from every evil, graciously grant peace in our days, *that*, by the help of your mercy . . . ." Freedom from sin and safety from distress are tied—both theologically and syntactically—to freedom from evil. Finally, the embolism keeps the liturgy's forward momentum by looking ahead to the full consummation of the divine economy, which is our eternal union with Christ: "as we await the blessed hope and the coming of our Savior, Jesus Christ." Here, as elsewhere, the text incorporates scripture, this time from Saint Paul's letter to Titus, where the apostle encourages Titus to exhort others to live upright lives "as we await the blessed hope, the appearance of the glory of the great God and of our savior Jesus Christ" (Titus 2:13). The people respond with "For the kingdom, the power and the glory are yours now and for ever," an expression found very early in the liturgy, and even in the margins of some of the earliest manuscripts of Saint Matthew's Gospel account where the teaching of the Lord's Prayer is found (Matthew 6:13).[7]

On the whole, the words of this part of the Communion Rite (the introduction, the Lord's Prayer, the embolism, and the people's response) unite us ever closer to the very Word we are about to receive in Holy Communion. The theology that the words reflect, their origins in Christ and the scriptures, their use throughout the history of the Latin Church and other Churches, and even their grammatical expression, convey to the "mystagogical ear" the meaning of the Word before us. Our preparation is a preparation to communicate with the Incarnate Logos and to enter into the eternal dialogue of the Trinity and which the Trinity is.[8] The Mystical Voice of the Church attunes our own voices, our own ears, and our own hearts to the Logical Sacrifice of the Word of God.

Sign of Peace

Then the Priest, with hands extended, says aloud:

Lord Jesus Christ,
who said to your Apostles,
Peace I leave you, my peace I give you;
look not on our sins,
but on the faith of your Church,
and graciously grant her peace and unity
in accordance with your will.

He joins his hands.

Who live and reign for ever and ever.

The people reply:

Amen.

The Priest, turned towards the people, extending and then joining his hands, adds:

The peace of the Lord be with you always.

The people reply:

And with your spirit.

Then, if appropriate, the Deacon, or the Priest, adds:

Let us offer each other the sign of peace.

And all offer one another a sign, in keeping with local customs, that expresses peace, communion, and charity. The Priest gives the sign of peace to a Deacon or minister.

What the Church Wants Us to Understand

As we prepare to communicate with Christ in the Blessed Sacrament, our words also communicate more directly with him. Nearly every prayer text of the Roman liturgy is addressed to God the Father; only rarely is a Collect directed to the Son (e.g., on the solemnity of *Corpus Christi*: "O God, who in this wonderful Sacrament / have left us a memorial of your Passion . . ."). But in the preparatory rites of the Communion Rite, our words begin to address Christ himself (as well as taking his own words, as in the Lord's Prayer). The Church's words (and with them, ourselves) take on a different character, a Logical character, since they are spoken to the Word substantially before us.

The embolism mentioned in the preceding section asked deliverance from evil and the consequent granting of peace (a petition which anticipates the third trope of the Lamb of God), and the present Sign of Peace sustains this same divine theme. As the *General Instruction of the Roman Missal* describes this preparatory rite, "the Church entreats peace and unity for herself and for the whole human family, and the faithful express to each other their ecclesial communion and mutual charity before communicating in the Sacrament" (GIRM, 82). While the *General Instruction* locates the exchange of peace immediately prior to sacramental communion, this was not its original place. Both Saint Justin Martyr (d. 165) and Saint Hippolytus (d. 236) describe the exchange of peace following the intercessions and before the offertory procession, and here the Sign of Peace reflects Christ's exhortation in the Gospel account of Matthew: "if you bring your gift to the altar, and there recall that your brother has anything against you, leave your gift there at the altar, go first and be reconciled with your brother, and then come and offer your gift" (Matthew 5:23–24). Tertullian (who died around 220) likens the exchange of peace to a "seal on the prayer," and whether following the Prayers of the Faithful (General Intercessions) or the Eucharistic Prayer, the "seal" of peace is a meaningful gesture.[9]

The first words of the exchange of peace are the priest's introduction. These words were once a private prayer for the priest's own preparation,[10] but are now addressed to Christ on behalf of all and recall his words recorded in Saint John's Gospel account: "Peace I leave with you; my peace I give to you" (John 14:27). The same passage continues, "Not as the world gives do I give it to you. Do not let your hearts be troubled or afraid," and here resembles the embolism, insofar as God's peace is not simply the absence of conflict but is the total abolition of evil. Christ's peace, in other words, cannot exist along with evil, even when no apparent conflict exists. Furthermore, Christ's words of peace are said at the Last Supper, where he encourages his disciples to have courage and to know that they are not abandoned: he will send the Advocate and will himself take them to the Father's house. The Sign of Peace, then, is an eschatological one, leading us ever closer to heavenly union where we become "love-transformed mankind."

After the priest's offering of peace to the people ("The peace of the Lord be with you always") those gathered respond as before ("And with your spirit"), signifying his sacramental conformity to the person of Christ the

Head and Priest. Then, "if appropriate," the deacon or priest may invite those present to exchange a Sign of Peace with one another. The gesture used to exchange peace among the Church's members at the Mass has varied from time to time and place to place. The fourth-century *Apostolic Constitutions* describes how in segregated congregations (men from women) the clergy would "embrace the bishop, the laymen the laymen, and the women the women."[11] Later, the exchange was limited to communicants, and then only to the clergy, where the celebrant would receive the *pax* (peace) from the altar, and through the deacon pass it along to the other clergy who were present. In the thirteenth-century the "passing of the peace" was symbolized by a "kissing board" or "pax board" which would receive the kiss of peace from one cleric before being passed to the next. Today the Sign of Peace is exchanged in a manner "established by the Conferences of Bishops in accordance with the culture and customs of the peoples," but only to those who are near, and always "in a sober manner" (GIRM, 82). The *General Instruction* suggests, "While the Sign of Peace is being given, it is permissible to say, *The peace of the Lord be with you always*, to which the reply is *Amen*" (GIRM, 154). As has been observed previously, the reply to the invitation is simply "Amen," unlike that given to the same invitation of the priest ("And with your spirit"). The people's response speaks to the priest's spiritual reality, namely, the spirit received at the priest's ordination; the layperson does not possess the character of the ordained priest.

The Mystical Voice, which is the Voice of Christ with his Church, is a voice of concord and harmony; a voice of truth, goodness, and beauty; in a word, a voice of peace. "The Church gives voice to the hope for peace and reconciliation rising up from every man and woman of good will," says Pope Benedict XVI, "directing it towards the one who 'is our peace' (Ephesians 2:14) and who can bring peace to individuals and peoples when all human efforts fail" (SCar, 49). The Sign of Peace is a gesture of exchange, and the words which introduce it, offer it, and respond to it are meaningful, sacramentalizing the "peace, communion, and charity" (GIRM, 154) of Christ himself. To say other words is to mean other things, and to speak in accord with the Logos is to mean the Logos, Christ himself.

Lamb of God (or Fraction of the Bread)

Then he takes the host, breaks it over the paten, and places a small piece in the chalice, saying quietly:

> May this mingling of the Body and Blood
> of our Lord Jesus Christ
> bring eternal life to us who receive it.

Meanwhile the following is sung or said:

> Lamb of God, you take away the sins of the world,
>   have mercy on us.
> Lamb of God, you take away the sins of the world,
>   have mercy on us.
> Lamb of God, you take away the sins of the world,
>   grant us peace.

The invocation may even be repeated several times if the fraction is prolonged. Only the final time, however, is grant us peace *said.*

What the Church Wants Us to Understand

There are certain words or actions in the Mass that have such great meaning (either in themselves or from Christ's own command) that the entire celebration takes its name after them. *Mass* comes from the very last words of the celebration, *Ite, missa est*, signifying the command to "Go out!" (more on the dismissal will follow). *Eucharist*, as we have seen, means "thanksgiving" and signifies during the Preface and Eucharistic Prayer the Church's thankful praise for the saving work of Christ. "Breaking of the bread" was the term used already by the earliest Christians. They devoted themselves to the teaching of the apostles and to the communal life, to the breaking of the bread and to the prayers (Acts 2:46; 46) and spoke of the action of Jesus at the Last Supper (see CCC, 1328–1332). In our Mass today, the words and actions of the breaking of the bread (also called the fraction of the bread) signify unity: the unity of Christ, the unity of the Church, and the unity of her members in Christ and in the Church.

Following the exchange of peace, and accompanied by the singing or recitation of the "Lamb of God," the priest breaks the host and places a small piece in the chalice. While liturgical history suggests that the breaking of the consecrated bread and its mixing with the consecrated wine may be merely practical, the actions came to speak great meaning. First, the "commingling,"

which is the uniting of the host with the consecrated wine, has come to signify "the unity of the Body and Blood of the Lord in the work of salvation,
namely, of the Body of Jesus Christ, living and glorious" (GIRM, 83). As the
double-consecration of the bread and the wine represented the separation of
the body from the blood of the crucified Christ, so now the commingling
signifies the union of the resurrected and heavenly Lamb. Second, the breaking of the bread symbolizes the unity of the many members in the one
Church of Christ. Saint Paul, in his First Letter to the Corinthians, teaches
that "because the loaf of bread is one, we, though many, are one body, for we
all partake of the one loaf" (1 Corinthians 10:17). In a famous passage from
the early second-century *Didache* ("Teaching of the Twelve"), a Eucharistic
Prayer, asks: "Just as the bread broken was first scattered on the hills, then
was gathered and became one, so let your Church be gathered from the ends
of the earth into your kingdom . . . ."[12] The Body of Christ, the Church, is
united by the Body of Christ, the sacrament. In the early Roman Church,
her unity was signified further by sending a small piece of the host, called the
fermentum, from the Pope to his priests in the city of Rome at their individual Sunday celebrations: the *fermentum* from the Pope's Mass was added
to the priest's chalice, so that, in the words of Pope Innocent I (d. 417), he
"may not feel separated from communion with us."[13] Third, members who
receive the broken Bread are united within the Church and through her
with Christ. "The cup of blessing that we bless," asks Saint Paul, "is it not a
participation in the blood of Christ? The bread that we break, is it not a participation in the body of Christ?" (1 Corinthians 10:16). As the priest breaks
the host and places a small piece of it in the chalice, he prays that the commingling will "bring eternal life to us who receive it," where we may gather
with the blessed around the slain Lamb of God (see Revelation 5:6, 13:8).

Unity (of the glorified Christ, of the Church with Christ, and of us in
the Church with Christ) is the meaning of "Communion," and the current
rites prepare us to become united with Christ in his representational sacrifice. The Lamb who was slain, which is the Lamb we are to receive, is now
reigning in heaven, so our oneness with him draws us to heaven with him.
The *Agnus Dei* ("Lamb of God") was sung in the Roman Rite Mass by the
end of the seventh century, and by the twelfth century it was the custom to
repeat the invocation three times.[14] The words accompanying the fraction
are not only those of John the Baptist as he heralds the coming of his cousin
("Behold, the Lamb of God, who takes away the sin of the world" [John
1:29]), but also of Revelation as anticipating the glorious and eternal Lamb

before whom all in heaven worship and sing: "Worthy is the Lamb that was slain to receive power and riches, wisdom and strength, honor and glory and blessing" (Revelation 5:12; also 13:8). We ask Jesus, "the *true* paschal lamb who freely gave himself in sacrifice for us" (SCar, 9), to have mercy on us and grant us peace, as he has done to the heavenly host with whom we now sing.

Communion

Then the Priest, with hands joined, says quietly:

> Lord Jesus Christ, Son of the living God,
> who by the will of the Father
> and the work of the Holy Spirit,
> through your Death gave life to the world,
> free me by this your most holy Body and Blood,
> from all my sins and from every evil;
> keep me always faithful to your commandments,
> and never let me be parted from you.

Or:

> May the receiving of your Body and Blood,
> Lord Jesus Christ,
> not bring me to judgment and condemnation,
> but through your loving mercy
> be for me protection in mind and body,
> and a healing remedy.

The Priest genuflects, takes the host and, holding it slightly raised above the paten or above the chalice, while facing the people, says aloud:

> Behold the Lamb of God,
> behold him who takes away the sins of the world.
> Blessed are those called to the supper of the Lamb.

And together with the people he adds once:

> Lord, I am not worthy
> that you should enter under my roof,
> but only say the word
> and my soul shall be healed.

The Priest, facing the altar, says quietly:

> May the Body of Christ
> keep me safe for eternal life.

And he reverently consumes the Body of Christ.

Then he takes the chalice and says quietly:

> May the Blood of Christ
> keep me safe for eternal life.

And he reverently consumes the Blood of Christ.
After this, he takes the paten or ciborium and approaches the communicants.
The Priest raises a host slightly and shows it to each of the communicants, saying:

> The Body of Christ.

The communicant replies:

> Amen.

And receives Holy Communion.
If a Deacon also distributes Holy Communion, he does so in the
same manner.
If any are present who are to receive Holy Communion under both kinds, the
rite as described in the proper place is to be followed.
While the Priest is receiving the Body of Christ, the Communion
Chant begins.
When the distribution of Communion is over, the Priest or a Deacon or an
acolyte purifies the paten over the chalice and also the chalice itself.
While he carries out the purification, the Priest says quietly:

> What has passed our lips as food, O Lord,
> may we possess in purity of heart,
> that what has been given to us in time
> may be our healing for eternity.

Then the Priest may return to the chair. If appropriate, a sacred silence may
be observed for a while, or a psalm or other canticle of praise or a hymn may
be sung.
Then, standing at the altar or at the chair and facing the people, with hands
joined, the Priest says:

> Let us pray.

All pray in silence with the Priest for a while, unless silence has just
been observed. Then the Priest, with hands extended, says the Prayer after
Communion, at the end of which the people acclaim:

> Amen.

What the Church Wants Us to Understand

The prayers asking forgiveness, peace, and unity in the preparatory rites for Communion are echoed again, now more pointedly, in the words surrounding Holy Communion. The rite of reception begins with prayers of preparation, followed by the actual reception of the Body and Blood of Christ, after which the sacred vessels are purified, and concludes with the Prayer after Communion.

First, as an example to those gathered, the priest prepares himself quietly for the reception of Holy Communion. Using one of two prayer formulas, both of which have existed in the Roman Church by the eleventh century,[15] the priest "says quietly" (*dicit secreto*) a prayer to Christ for forgiveness, faithfulness, and union (as in the first option), or salvation, protection, and healing (as in the second option). He prays, in other words, for his Communion to be just that, a *communion* with the Logos, which is his (and our) transformation and divinization.

The words of the Communion Rite, like each liturgical word, testify *to the* Word, Christ the Incarnate Logos.

The presiding priest, as a "mouthpiece" of Christ the Head, speaks often for Christ, both on behalf of the Church to God and for God to the Church (as we discussed in chapter 5, the often-used response "And with your spirit" signifies this position as mediator). Nevertheless, because the priest also prays as an individual in need of redemption as much as any other, he also "speaks for himself" at times. A priest's private prayers (prior to the Gospel, at the Preparation of the Gifts, and before and after Communion) foster his own conscious participation in the work of Christ, and his prayer at these times is an example to all present.

Next, while showing the host (either above the paten or above the chalice), the priest says: "Behold the Lamb of God, behold him who takes away the sins of the world. Blessed are those called to the supper of the Lamb." The first part of the exhortation (as noted in the previous section on the *Agnus Dei*) sounds the testimony of John the Baptist, "the voice of one crying out in the desert" (John 1:23). The remaining words of the invitation are those of a heavenly author. John reports that "the angel said to me, 'Write this: Blessed are those who have been called to the wedding feast of the

Lamb'" (Revelation 19:9). What's more, the angel adds: "These words are true; they come from God" (ibid.). The words of the Communion Rite, like each liturgical word, testify to *the* Word, Christ the Incarnate Logos. Both priest and people respond scripturally, speaking to Christ after the example of the good centurion who, upon seeking the Lord's favor in healing his servant, says: "Lord, do not trouble yourself, for I am not worthy to have you enter under my roof . . . but say the word and let my servant be healed" (Luke 7:6–7). The Roman Rite has adapted the centurion's words to the present liturgical context, changing "my servant" to "my soul" (*anima mea*), and when the Lord "says the word" it is healed and filled with grace. Left unchanged, however, is the word *roof* (*tectum*), signaling our own personal abode into which the Lord will enter (even though the Lord never did enter the centurion's house).

The zenith of active participation is the worthy reception of the body, blood, soul, and divinity of Christ in the consecrated bread and wine. This supernatural food is unlike any other, for (to cite Saint Augustine once again) rather than incorporating this food into our bodies, we are changed into it, which is to say, Christ. It is the essence of sacrifice, Cardinal Ratzinger has clarified, that the giver be represented in his gift. Christ has done this for us by taking mankind to himself in the Incarnation and then offering us with himself upon the cross to the Father. What remains to be accomplished is our identity with Christ (who is our gift and offering), so that true union, divinization, and loving transformation become a reality.[16] In communing with the Logos, our identity with him ("the 'logicizing' of my existence")[17] is made possible:

> The ancient world had dimly perceived that man's real food—what truly nourishes him as man—is ultimately the *Logos*, eternal wisdom: this same *Logos* now truly becomes food for us—as love. The Eucharist draws us into Jesus' act of self-oblation. More than just statically receiving the Incarnate *Logos*, we enter into the very dynamic of his self-giving. The imagery of marriage between God and Israel is now realized in a way previously inconceivable: it had meant standing in God's presence, but now it becomes union with God through sharing in Jesus' self-gift, sharing in his body and blood. (DCar, 13)

The words employed in the preparatory rites for Communion (if said and heard rightly) prepare our hearts for this union with the eucharistic Christ. At the center of the Church's liturgical texts is Christ, whose voice resonates for us today through the scriptures and in the tradition of the

Church. Active participation in the liturgical vernacular of the Roman Rite draws us into union with the Word.

Following Communion, so that the Word may resonate most fully, the Church recommends that the faithful "praise God in their hearts and pray to him" in silence (GIRM, 45) or in song (GIRM, 88). The sacred vessels may also be purified at this time by the priest, deacon, or instituted acolyte.[18] While the priest purifies the vessels, he prays for his own purification in a low voice: "What has passed our lips as food, O Lord, may we possess in purity of heart, that what has been given to us in time may be our healing for eternity." In the elevated tones of prayer and poetry, the prayer here as elsewhere utilizes classical rhetorical devices, including the unnatural pairing of *catechresis* (where the *food* passing our lips is "ingested" in the *heart*) and the unequal coupling of *antithesis* ("in time . . . for eternity"). These techniques help the texts signify the reality at hand—that purifying the sacred vessels is unlike cleaning mundane dishes. The action reflects the body and soul's own purification caused by their encounter with the Lamb of God.

Finally, the Communion Rite and, in a sense, the entire prayer of the people, concludes with the Prayer after Communion, in which the priest "prays for the fruits of the mystery just celebrated" (GIRM, 89). Like the Opening Prayer and the Prayer over the Offerings (the other Presidential Prayers), the style of the Prayer after Communion expresses in concise and compact terms (which is the Roman way) the divine truths of faith. The vernacular rendering, furthermore, is patently sacred, elevating those who hear it into the City of God:

> Look with kindness upon your people, O Lord,
> and grant we pray,
> that those you were pleased to renew by eternal mysteries
> may attain in their flesh
> the incorruptibile glory of the resurrection.
> Through Christ our Lord.[19]

The worthy reception of Communion is participation *par excellence*, for the Incarnate Logos gives himself not only in words, but also under sacramental species. In the Mass of the Roman Rite, the Sacrifice of the Word is a living reality, and by communicating with the Word we too become men and women "fully alive."

Concluding Rites

If they are necessary, any brief announcements to the people follow here.

Then the dismissal takes place. The Priest, facing the people and extending his hands, says:

The Lord be with you.

The people reply:

And with your spirit.

The Priest blesses the people, saying:

May almighty God bless you:
the Father, and the Son, ✠ and the Holy Spirit.

The people reply:

Amen.

On certain days or occasions, this formula of blessing is preceded, in accordance with the rubrics, by another more solemn formula of blessing or by a prayer over the people.

Then the Deacon, or the Priest himself, with hands joined and facing the people, says:

Go forth, the Mass is ended.

Or:

Go and announce the Gospel of the Lord.

Or:

Go in peace, glorifying the Lord by your life.

Or:

Go in peace.

The people reply:

Thanks be to God.

Then the Priest venerates the altar as usual with a kiss, as at the beginning. After making a profound bow with the ministers, he withdraws.

What the Church Wants Us to Understand

The Concluding Rites contain any brief announcements deemed necessary, the greeting of the priest and the response of the people, a prayer of blessing, and the dismissal (GIRM, 90). Like the Introductory Rites opening the Mass, the Concluding Rites give a formal end to the celebration, yet the words they contain call participants to offer a "living sacrifice" to God in the world (see Romans 12:1).

So that the Communion Rite maintains its integrity, any announcements follow the Prayer after Communion rather than precede it. Then, using the customary words of the Roman Rite, the priest greets the people, "The Lord be with you," to which they respond, "And with your spirit," thus paralleling the opening dialogue of the Mass. The priest then blesses the people, using one of three blessing prayers: a simple blessing, a Prayer over the People, or a solemn blessing. First, the simple blessing ("May almighty God bless you: the Father, and the Son, ✠ and the Holy Spirit") most closely resembles the Sign of the Cross preceding the Greeting of the Introductory Rites, thus adding to their corresponding structure. Liturgical history shows that the final blessing was not originally a part of the Concluding Rites but was given instead by the Pope (and bishops and then by priests) to the faithful who asked for a blessing on his way back to the sacristy after the dismissal, much as a bishop blesses today on his way from the sanctuary through the aisle of people.[20]

Second, the Prayer over the People begins with the deacon's (or priest's) invitation to "Bow your heads for the blessing," an invitation found in the fourth-century document, *Apostolic Constitutions*.[21] Then, after a pause for silent prayer, the priest says the prayer, for example:

> Be near to those who call on you, Lord,
> and graciously grant your protection
> to all who place their hope in your mercy,
> that they may remain faithful in holiness of life
> and, having enough for their needs in this world,
> they may be made full heirs of your promise for eternity.
> Through Christ our Lord.

R.:   Amen.

> And may the blessing of almighty God,
> the Father, and the Son, ✠ and the Holy Spirit,
> come down on you and remain with you forever.

R.:   Amen.[22]

The Latin Church's tradition associates Prayers over the People in a particular way with penitents and penitential seasons, and as a result the third edition of *The Roman Missal* provides Prayers over the People for weekdays during the Lenten season.

The solemn blessing, finally, elaborates further the divine benediction in a manner proper to the feast or season. After the deacon calls upon the people to bow their heads, the priest continues:

> May almighty God bless you in his kindness
> and pour out saving wisdom upon you.

R.:   Amen.

> May he nourish you always with the teachings of the faith
> and make you persevere in holy deeds.

R.:   Amen.

> May he turn your steps towards himself
> and show you the path of charity and peace.

R.:   Amen.

> And may the blessing of almighty God,
> the Father, and the Son, ✠ and the Holy Spirit,
> come down on you and remain with you for ever.

People: Amen.[23]

Blessing literally means "good word" (*bene-dictio* in Latin; *eu-logia* in Greek). The entire Mass is a benediction and eulogy: Christ the Logos is spoken to us by the Father, and reciprocated to the Father by us. The final blessing encapsulates the entire movement of the Mass, and the Father "eulogizes" us again, speaking his "good Word" to "logicize us" and send us out into the world to transform it according to the Logos, making the city of man more closely resemble the City of God.

It is in this same spirit that the priest then dismisses the people, sending them on a mission to extend the Sacrifice of the Word in the world. Rooted first in the secular dismissal of civic gatherings,[24] the dismissal of the Roman Rite (*Ite, missa est,* "Go forth, the Mass is ended") verbalizes our missionary mandate from Christ to "Go and make disciples of all nations" (Matthew 28:19). An authentic encounter with Christ, says Pope John Paul II, leads one to a conversion, and then impels one to evangelization, which is the telling the Good News to the world (see, for example, *Ecclesia in America*, 8). The liturgical encounter with Christ the Word is the most perfect encounter possible for us on this side of heaven. The Pope calls the liturgy "the outstanding moment of encounter with the living Christ,"[25] the "deepest and most effective answer to this yearning for the encounter with God."[26] So that the "People of God might be helped to understand more clearly this essential dimension of the Church's life" (SCar, 51), that is,

> The entire Mass is a benediction and eulogy: Christ the Logos is spoken to us by the Father, and reciprocated to the Father by us.

from encountering Christ to proclaiming him, Pope Benedict XVI has expanded the possible formulas for the dismissal:

Go forth, the Mass is ended. (*Ite, missa est.*)

Go and announce the Gospel of the Lord. (*Ite ad Evangelium Domini annuntiandum.*)

Go in peace, glorifying the Lord by your life. (*Ite in pace, glorificando vita vestra Dominum.*)

Go in peace. (*Ite in pace.*)

These dismissal options sound clearly the Mystical Voice of the risen Christ, united now to his Body, the Church, calling each member to "Go out" and offer his or her entire self "as a living sacrifice, holy and pleasing to God, your spiritual worship" (Romans 12:1).

Summary

Christ is the Logos, but he is also the Logos *incarnatus*, and in the Liturgy of the Eucharist his incarnate self is made substantially present under the forms of bread and wine. Christ's presence under these elements is wrought by words: words rooted in the traditions of the Chosen People, words made powerful by his own use and command, and words thereupon spoken by him and his Mystical Body. In the West, Christ's words have "crystallized"[27] in the Roman Rite of the Latin Church, and they are present to the faithful today as the outstanding means to hear the Word, speak with him to the Father in the Spirit, and become like him in every dimension of the Christian life in the world through the sanctifying work of his Spirit.

Endnotes

1. Pope St. Pius X, who first used the term *active participation* in an ecclesial document, is also the patron saint of first communicants.

2. See also Joseph Ratzinger, *The Spirit of the Liturgy*, trans. John Saward (San Francisco: Ignatius Press, 2000), Part One, Chapter III: "From Old Testament to New: The Fundamental Form of the Christian Liturgy—Its Determination by Biblical Faith."

3. See Robert Cabié, *The Eucharist*, ed. Aimé Georges Martimort, trans. Matthew J. O'Connell (Collegeville: Liturgical Press, 1986), 108; Johannes H. Emminghaus, *The Eucharist: Essence, Form, Celebration*, trans. Linda M. Maloney, revised and edited by Theodor Mass-Ewerd (Collegeville: Liturgical Press, 1997), 192.

4. See Cabié, *The Eucharist*, 108.

5. *De Sacramentis*, IV, 24; *On the Mysteries and On the Sacraments by Saint Ambrose*, trans. T. Thompson, ed. with Introduction and Notes by J. H. Strawley (London: SPCK, 1950), 104.

6. In Cabié, *The Eucharist*, 109; see also Joseph A. Jungmann, *The Mass: An Historical, Theological, and Pastoral Survey*, trans. Julian Fernandes, ed. Mary Ellen Evans (Collegeville: Liturgical Press, 1976), 205.

7. See Emminghaus, *The Eucharist*, 193, Jungmann, *The Mass: An Historical, Theological, and Pastoral Survey*, 206.

8. Ratzinger, *The Feast of Faith: Approaches to a Theology of the Liturgy*, trans. Graham Harrison (San Francisco: Ignatius Press, 1986) 26.

9. See Jungmann, *The Mass: An Historical, Theological, and Pastoral Survey*, 209; Cabié, *The Eucharist*, 114. Pope Benedict XVI, following the XI General Assembly of Bishops on "The Eucharist: Source and Summit of the Life and Mission of the Church," called for consultation among the Roman Rite Bishops of the Church on possibly moving the sign of peace in the Roman Mass from before Communion to before the Preparation of the Altar.

10. See Emminghaus, *The Eucharist*, 195.

11. W. Jardine Grisbrooke, editor and translator, *The Liturgical Portions of the Apostolic Constitutions: A Text for Students*, (Nottingham, UK: Grove Books, LTD, 1990), 30.

12. In Cabié, *The Eucharist*, 23–24.

13. In Cabié, *The Eucharist*, 111.

14. See Emminghaus, *The Eucharist*, 200.

15. See Cabié, *The Eucharist*, 166–67.

16. See Ratzinger, *The Spirit of the Liturgy*, 173.

17. Ibid., 58.

18. "Nevertheless, it is also permitted to leave vessels needing to be purified, especially if there are several, on a corporal, suitably covered, either on the altar or on the credence table, and to purify them immediately after Mass, after the Dismissal of the people" (GIRM, 163).

19. Prayer after Communion for Tuesday of the Fifth Week of Easter.

20. See Jungmann, *The Mass: An Historical, Theological, and Pastoral Survey,* 213; Cabié, *The Eucharist* 169; Emminghaus, *The Eucharist,* 213. And as Emminghaus observes further, until 1967 the Blessing *followed* the dismissal.

21. See Jungmann, *The Mass: An Historical, Theological, and Pastoral Survey,* 212.

22. *The Roman Missal,* Prayers over the People, 19.

23. Solemn Blessing for Ordinary Time III.

24. See Jungmann, *The Mass: An Historical, Theological, and Pastoral Survey,* 214; Cabié, *The Eucharist,* 123.

25. John Paul II, *Ecclesia in America,* n. 35.

26. John Paul II, *Spiritus et Sponsa,* n. 12.

27. See Ratzinger, *The Spirit of the Liturgy,* 161.

Chapter 8

Liturgical Catechesis for Active Participation

Mystagogical Catechesis

This book began with the challenge to "have the courage to face silence and in it to listen afresh to the Word. Otherwise we shall be overwhelmed by 'mere words' at the very point where we should be encountering the Word, the Logos, the Word of love, crucified and risen, who brings us life and joy."[1] It is our conviction that the English-language *Roman Missal*, when prayed with sympathetic tongues and heard with receptive ears, has the power to lead us to encounter "the Word, the Logos, the Word of love."

How is "a well-trained tongue" acquired, and where will we find "ears that we may hear" (see Isaiah 50:4)? While *Sacrosanctum concililum* speaks often of the "ease" with which the laity are to participate in Mass (e.g., SC, 50, 59, 79, 90, 92), it cannot be denied that liturgical participation requires training, or *askesis*. As we saw in the first chapter, one of the liturgy's etymological constituents is *ergon*, meaning "work." The only "spectator" in the liturgy is God the Father: all others (Son and Holy Spirit, angels and saints, ordained and lay) have *work* to do, and for those of us on earth, a constant effort and lifetime of training is required.

Two principal elements contribute toward a full engagement and conscious participation in the Church's liturgy. The first is an appreciation of the sacramental nature of the liturgy as sign and reality; the second requires a sacramental perspective through the realignment of our senses to the liturgy's supernatural and sacramental character. Put another way, supernatural ears do not hear "mere words" but hear "the Word." To be unconscious of the sacramental nature of the liturgy results in liturgical deafness, and failure to realign our senses to the liturgy's supernatural character, we risk being frustrated and confused.

What, then, is the sacramental nature of the liturgy that we need to appreciate? It is that Christ, who once carried out his salvific work in the flesh, now continues this same work *in the Church and the sacraments*. Today, in what the *Catechism of the Catholic Church* calls "the age of the Church," Christ ". . . manifests, makes present, and communicates his work of salvation through the liturgy of his Church, 'until he comes.' In this age of the Church Christ now lives and acts in and with his Church, in a new way appropriate to this new age. *He acts through the sacraments . . .*" (CCC, 1076, emphasis added).

The sacramental age here described presents two dimensions: the unseen reality, which is Christ and his grace, and the sensible symbols that mediate his presence.

The invisible reality found behind each sacrament and sacramental (what theology calls the *res*) is ultimately Jesus Christ and the grace of his Paschal Mystery: "In the liturgy of the Church, it is principally his own Paschal mystery that Christ signifies and makes present" (CCC, 1085). In our current examination, Christ's particular identity as Logos is emphasized, for his Logical work is at the core of salvation history:

1. Jesus Christ is the divine Word of the Father;

2. Through the Word all things were made;

3. The Word calls mankind together through the Chosen People, after man sinned by disobeying God's Word;

4. The Incarnate Word reunites heaven and earth in his obedient and loving "yes" to the Father from the cross; and

5. The Word continues to call us and unite us with himself in his Church, allowing us to enter into the eternal dialogue of love within the Trinity.

Our salvation is Word-based, which is to say it is Christ-based: he is the reality of every sacramental encounter.

Yet in this "age of the Church," the time between Christ's Paschal Mystery and its full consummation in heaven, the reality of Christ the Word is encountered in sacramental signs and symbols. First among these is the Church herself, the Mystical Body of Christ. As the "universal sacrament of salvation" (see LG, 9), the Church is "the visible plan of God's love for humanity."[2] By her observable actions in the world, the Mystical Body makes present Christ and his saving work.

Christ the Logos is also encountered in the Church's sacramental liturgy, in which "the sanctification of man is signified by signs perceptible to the senses, and is effected in a way which corresponds with each of these signs" (SC, 7). A sacramental liturgy exists as a rite or ritual, which is "the practical arrangements made by the community, in time and space, for the basic type of worship received from God in faith."[3] These practical arrangements include objects, actions, postures, ministers and the assembly, time, music, images, architecture, and words, each of which by itself mediates the presence of Christ, and all of which together "weave" the face of Christ (CCC, 1145). As "masterpieces of God" (CCC, 1091), the sacraments portray the risen and glorified Christ in a way that is accessible to human nature. The external and sensible dimension of the sacrament is the most efficacious means to encountering God. Because sacraments are both supernatural reality *and* natural sign, it is possible for us to say heaven *and* earth, grace *and* nature, God *and* man.

Of particular emphasis in this book is the sacramentality of words, especially those of *The Roman Missal*. Like every sacramental sign, liturgical words mediate Christ and the saving grace of his Paschal Mystery. Yet, unlike other sacramental signs, words possess a special affinity with Christ, who is *the* Word. Christ the Logos is sacramentalized by each ritual component and by the rite as a whole, but words have a privileged place within the rite since they, by their nature, correspond to Christ, who is also Word.[4] Sacramental words "sound like" the divine Word,[5] and the Church's Mystical Voice (which is to say, Sacramental Voice) at prayer is an encounter with Christ the Word. Consequently, the sacramental language of *The Roman Missal*, while reflecting in many ways our natural speech, is unlike any other language. The *Missal's* words (cultivated from the soils of human culture, God's dialogue with Israel, the Paschal Sacrifice of the Incarnate Word, and the language of the Sacred Scriptures) are an efficacious and real encounter with "the Word, the Logos, the Word of love." The *Missal's* words speak as they do because the Word speaks in a unique way in the Latin Church. When sacramental words are manipulated to speak differently, they distort the meaning of the Word to us. An appreciation of the liturgy's sacramental nature sees the grace of the living Christ conveyed through sacramental signs and symbols. Logically speaking, this means that the Word of God is heard and encountered in the language of the Church's rites, and especially in the rites of the Mass.

After coming to an awareness of the sacramental character of the liturgy, we must still acquire "sacramental senses" to achieve true and actual participation in the Mass. Undoubtedly, we can gain some insights from viewing the liturgy historically, psychologically, sociologically, or rubrically, but to perceive the heart of the mystery requires this sacramental (or what we also call mystagogical) perception. Mystagogy (as discussed in chapter 2) means "to lead into the mystery," by "proceeding from the visible to the invisible, from the sign to the thing signified, from the 'sacraments' to the 'mysteries.'"[6] To perceive only that which is naturally visible and outwardly signified is to see only part of the picture. Seeing only bread in the priest's hands, hearing nothing more than the voices of our neighbors in the choir, or smelling only the smoking incense of the acolyte's thurible, is perceiving the visible without the invisible, the sign without the signified, and the "sacrament" without the "mystery." Full participation in the person and work of Christ calls our natural senses to a supernatural plane, where seeing the appearance of bread means seeing the Body of Christ, hearing the choir surrounds us with the song of the angels, and smelling the incense takes us to the altar of the Lamb. Full, conscious, and active participation *presupposes* that we perceive the liturgy in this way—that is, sacramentally—for to see it in any other is inadequate. Likewise, to hear the words of the Mass clearly and rightly is to hear them sacramentally, where we hear the real Word in them.

Mystagogical sensing presupposes two conditions: one, that the ritual authentically sacramentalizes the reality it seeks to convey and two, that our senses have been formed properly to perceive this reality. The mind of the Church (from *Sacrosanctum concilium* through the subsequent interventions of the Popes, to the promulgation of the English-language edition of the third *Roman Missal*) sees the English translation of the Mass as an authentic verbal expression of the reality of Christ. The *Missal*'s words are, "according to the Logos," consonant with the one who is the ultimate Word. Because the words of the Mass are authentic signs, it is possible for us to perceive

> After coming to an awareness of the sacramental character of the liturgy, we must still acquire "sacramental senses" to achieve true and actual participation in the Mass.

them mystagogically and, through them, to participate actively in Christ's voice of praise to the Father. Let us be clear: our actual participation succeeds or fails on the authenticity of the sacramental sign. Without true sacramental signs, real participation is impossible.

To lead us from what we hear externally in the rite to what is spoken inaudibly by the Mystical Voice of Christ and his Body, our perception is sharpened by discovering the roots of the sacramental signs. Unlike artificial signs, which are created by mutual consent and are therefore changeable, sacramental signs are generated from more fixed sources of meaning: nature and creation, human culture and society, God's covenants with the Chosen People of the Old Testament, the Person and work of the Incarnate Christ, the eternal liturgy of heaven in which we participate and anticipate today, and the use the Latin Church has made of these throughout her history. The liturgy is organic, rooted, and growing from a rich and multi-layered soil. To uncover these roots, mystagogical catechesis looks at each of the liturgy's signs and symbols in the categories mentioned above. The same sources also reveal the meaning of liturgical language. Indeed, the meaning of the words of the Mass are heard clearly when their natural, human, and Christological origins are uncovered.

It has been our intention to provide a verbal mystagogy of the words of the Mass. Nevertheless, obtaining sacramental senses requires not simply information but, above all else, the formative power of the liturgy. Liturgical and mystagogical catechesis is experiential, where the whole person (intellect, will, and body) encounters the saving grace of Christ and, having encountered him, becomes like him (see 1 John 3:2). Our transformation in Christ (what has been called divinization and logification through mystagogical participation) is an ongoing process. Like Saint Paul, in the present age of the Church "we see indistinctly, as in a mirror, but then face to face" (1 Corinthians 13:12). In the end, mystagogical catechesis is not primarily educational but *formational*, not the simple teaching of divine data but the transformation of the whole person through a living encounter with Christ. We are led in the process of mystagogy from the sacramental words to the Word himself, always with the grace of God and under the direction of the Church.

The *Questions and Answers* section that follows is written with this mystagogical outlook in mind. To understand and fully participate in the liturgy, or to be a "mystagogue" leading others to encounter the Logos in the words of the Mass, sacramental and mystagogical catechesis is paramount. The

Mystical Body has Christ as her Head, and together Christ and his Church proclaim a Mystical Voice of praise to God the Father. Mystagogical ears hear this voice today. Christ *is* in the words of the Mass: we come to recognize his voice for our own sanctification and for the greater glory of God.

Questions and Answers

1. Why do words matter?

Words are sacramental, which means they contain and convey the reality they speak.

Homo sapiens is a talking animal, communicating with the senses, by word of mouth, pen and paper, telephone, electronic message, magazine, radio, television, and image. So voluminous is this communication, we often speak of "information overload." We also acknowledge with a common expression this inflation of language—"talk is cheap," and as a result we often "pay lip service" to it. Liturgical language, on the other hand, is never "cheap," by no means wasted, and in no way empty. As sacramental signs, the words of the Mass in some way cause, contain, and convey their meaning: ultimately, these signs must point us to the reality, which is Christ himself. By virtue of the sacramental connection between sacramental words and their supernatural reality, when the Church speaks her Mystical Voice, she says what she believes and means what she says.

What does she mean? Better yet, *whom* does she mean? She means Christ, her Spouse, the eternal Son of God, and our Redeemer. In the Word made flesh, Jesus undoes our own disobedience (literally, our "not listening") to the voice of God by his own perfect obedience, thus allowing men and women to enter into the eternal dialogue of love within the Trinity. When the Church speaks, she joins her Mystical Voice with that of Christ her Head, speaking with him his "yes" to the Father's design. The sacramental words of the Mass, cultivated from divine and human sources, are the words of the Lord and his Church in this dialogue of Trinitarian love. The words of the Church speak this divinized language; when words become individualized or idiosyncratic, they speak a language that is not her own, thus symbolizing a different reality.

The precision of the Church's sacramental language, consequently, expresses the reality of Christ the Logos and fosters a supernatural—and Logical—response from us. When the Church determines the words of the Mass, it is not a matter of mere semantics, for her sacramental words must correspond to *the Word* they signify. To use obscure, novel, or imprecise language causes, in the end, an obscure, novel, or imprecise reality. As there are rules governing any language, the "grammar" that defines the Church's mystical language is determined by Church doctrine and history. Catholic belief and Catholic language are closely related. Words mean things; and in the Church's liturgy, they mean Christ.

2. Why is the language at Mass different from everyday language?

The language of the Mass sounds different from our everyday language because the Mass is different from everyday activities.

A *culture* is the product (i.e., it is "cultivated") of the history and values of a people as expressed in daily life. American culture, for example, results in part from our Revolutionary history and the importance of individual freedom and self-reliance as lived out in the American "work ethic" and ritualized in the annual observations of Independence Day, Labor Day, and Thanksgiving. To divorce the lived expression of a people from the history results in mere nostalgia and sentimentality, while neglecting the historical and valuable from the enactment leaves only an empty ritualism. Families, too, have a "culture." "The Joneses," for example, are the product of their own history and values as carried on in actual events: the story of great, great, grandfather Jones coming from the "old country" and settling in upstate New York is relived in its retelling at the annual family reunion. The Church has her own unique culture, one founded on a particular set of values and history—the Ten Commandments, the Incarnation, the teachings of Christ, and the Apostolic mission. These components of our religious patrimony are relived (literally: they really do "come to life again") in the observance of the liturgical year and the Church's ritual celebrations.

Language itself is culturally bound. A nation, family, or religion speaks according to its history, values, and actions. The group's origin, what it holds dear, and how it lives all contribute to the way it speaks: its grammar, syntax, tone, tempo, emphasis are proper to each linguistic culture. The topics of discussion, whether there is economy or prodigality in expression, whether the notions are concrete or abstract, words prosaic or words extraordinary: these are all rooted in the cultural milieu. Americans speak differently from Brazilians; the Joneses, differently from O'Briens; Catholics, differently from Lutherans. While the universal faith speaks to every time and place, Catholics at prayer speak in a way consonant with their own culture.

What these cultural and linguistic differences mean in practice is that the language of the faith differs from the language of Main Street. One stems from Ecclesial culture and the other from American culture. While there is a "double exchange" in the inculturation process, it is the eternal and authentic culture of the Church that plays the dominant part. Liturgically speaking, our language tends more toward the heavenly than toward the earthly. God became human, after all, so that we might become God (in our reprise of Saint Athanasius); in the arena of language, we might say that God speaks like humans, so that humans might speak like God. It should not surprise us, then, that the liturgical language of the Church has a different tenor than the everyday language of the world.

> **In the Paschal Sacrifice of the Incarnate Word, the Son of God, on our behalf, responds perfectly…to the Father's invitation to divine communion.**

3. Why is the contribution of my own voice important to the larger prayer of the Church?

Christ's voice of loving and obedient praise to the Father is perfect, yet he awaits us to join our voices to his own.

As Adam's deafness to the voice of the Father caused sin and death, so another's obedience won for the many sanctity and eternal life (see Romans 5:15). The Church's theology recognizes the Second Person of the Trinity as the Father's Word and sees the story of salvation as the narrative of human dialogue with and through the same Word. In the Paschal Sacrifice of the Incarnate Word, the Son of God, on our behalf, responds perfectly, unreservedly, and completely to the Father's invitation to divine communion. Jesus Christ is a uniquely positioned mediator, for as God he can speak for the Father (indeed, he is the very voice of the Father), and as man (the perfect Adam) he hears and listens to the Father's voice. Completing the dialogue, which means literally "speaking across," Jesus can, as man, speak on our behalf to God, and as God he can receive our pleas. Only Jesus (the God-Man, Word and flesh) can effect perfect reconciliation between the human and the divine.

Nevertheless, our own voices must join with Christ's because God forces none to be saved, and it is for individuals to decide to serve the living God. Adam chose himself over God and followed his own path through sin to death. Jesus, the Second Adam, "Who, though he was in the form of God, did not regard equality with God something to be grasped," (Philippians 2:6) chose the Father's will over his own and clears for us the path from sin, through the cross, to eternal life. Our own voices, as a result, must resound with the voice of the Word, Jesus Christ. The Sacrifice of the Word is perfect, filling the halls of heaven. It awaits, nevertheless, ourselves and our own voices to attain "mature manhood, to the extent of the full stature of Christ" (Ephesians 4:13). The Christian acts like Christ, loves and thinks like Christ, and *sounds* like Christ, speaking like him and with him in a perfect hymn of praise to God the Father in the Holy Spirit.

4. What does the liturgy have to do with Christian life?

The Church's liturgy is the heart of the Christian's life: our freely entering into right relationship with God is the precondition for the Christian life in the world.

Prior to the Fall, Adam and Eve's relationship with God translated into a harmony within the individual soul, between husband and wife, and even toward nature. After the Fall, when this right relationship with God was disrupted, human beings lost the harmony within themselves. The theological tradition calls this concupiscence. The idea echoes Saint Paul's struggle: he does not do the good he wants, but does the evil he does not want (see Romans 7:19). Another casualty of the Fall is harmony between spouses. When God asks Adam why he ate of the tree, Adam turns on his wife: "The woman whom you put here with me—*she* gave me fruit from the tree" (Genesis 3:12). Nature turns on him, too: "Cursed be the ground because of you! In toil shall you eat its yield all the days of your life. Thorns and thistles shall it bring forth to you" (Genesis 3:17–18). In short, as the ruptured relationship with God leads to a life of sin and death, so right relationship with God brings us to sanctity and eternal life.

God did not leave us to our own devices or our own attempts to mend our relationship to him. In fact, due to our fallen nature, we could do nothing but die. Therefore, out of love for man, God called him into a series of covenants. The covenant offered by God to the Chosen People on Mt. Sinai, for example, seeks to rectify each one's broken relationship: with God, with others, and within himself.[7] The first and most important relationship to fix, the one without which no other can be mended, is with God. Human relationship to God must be that of "right worship" and praise (*ortho-doxa,* in Greek), and God himself determines how we relate to him. Christ has shown us "the way to the Father," demonstrated that *ortho-doxa* means handing oneself over without reservation to God the Father. His sacrificial act is made present for us today in the liturgy of the Church, which is for us the occasion to participate in it, to become coworkers with Christ in his voice of perfect praise to the Father. By joining with him, we ourselves, through Christ's saving grace, participate in the restoration of our relationship to God and, as a result, we can live rightly in the world: overcoming concupiscence within ourselves, creating families that reflect the love of the Trinity, and offering peace and comfort to all, especially the most vulnerable and those most in need.

The liturgical celebration is therefore the foundation of a *liturgical life,* that is, one lived in constant union with God and, as a result, in sacrificial union with others. "I urge you," Saint Paul writes, "by the mercies of God, to offer your bodies as a living sacrifice, holy and pleasing to God, your spiritual worship" (Romans 12:1). By participating in the sacrifice of Christ on the altar, we are enabled by grace to participate in the sacrifice of Christ in every aspect of our lives.

5. How is today's English-language liturgy a fruit of Vatican II?

The Mass and other sacramental celebrations reformed by the Church, both in their typical Latin editions and in their English translations, are the authentic embodiment of the teachings and spirit of the Second Vatican Council.

The Second Vatican Council's *Constitution on the Sacred Liturgy* saw that the "full and active participation by all the people is the aim to be considered before all else" (SC, 14). So that this paramount goal could become reality, *Sacrosanctum concilium* offered a number of principles to guide the liturgy's reform, among them the desire "for legitimate variations and adaptations to different groups, regions, and peoples" on the one hand, and the preservation of the "substantial unity of the Roman Rite" (SC, 38), on the other. As one case in point, the document allows "the use of the mother tongue," vernacular, while at the same time clearly esteems and seeks to preserve the Latin language (SC, 36).

Most of the liturgical books were translated from Latin to the vernacular in a short period of time. In 1969, the Consilium (a precursor to today's Sacred Congregation for Divine Worship and the Discipline of the Sacraments) provided theoretical and practical guidelines in the document "On the Translation of Liturgical Texts for Celebrations with a Congregation"

(*Comme le prévoit* in its original French title). Giving priority to the underlying message of a liturgical text and placing less emphasis on the precise rendering of the actual texts (see numbers 7–9, for example), *Comme le prévoit* helped give the English-speaking Church an immediate way to participate in the prayers of the Mass.

Twenty-five years after the *Constitution on the Sacred Liturgy*, Pope John Paul II acknowledged the graces and benefits of the liturgical reform and sought to inspire the Church to a deeper appreciation of the liturgy, which would bring it to its full fruition. About liturgical translations, he says: "But now the time has come to reflect upon certain difficulties that have subsequently emerged, to remedy certain defects or inaccuracies, to complete partial translations . . . , to ensure respect for the texts approved and lastly to publish liturgical books in a form that both testifies to the stability achieved and is worthy of the mysteries being celebrated" (VQ, 20). Two subsequent documents authorized by the Holy See (*Varietates legitimae*, "On Inculturation and the Roman Liturgy," and *Liturgiam authenticam*, "On the Use of Vernacular Languages in the Publication of the Books of the Roman Liturgy") carried forward the wishes of the Second Vatican Council to completion.

As a result, a "hermeneutic of continuity," as identified by Pope Benedict XVI, can be traced from the current English-language liturgical books to the Second Vatican Council. The thread connecting our current *Missal* to the Council passes through the documents and directions of intervening popes, especially the documents guiding the proper implementation of the *Constitution's* principles, *Varietates legitimae* and *Liturgiam authenticam.*

6. How do other ritual elements, like music and gesture, relate to liturgical language?

Each ritual component of the liturgy (whether language, music, or gesture) is woven together in a full sacramental expression of Christ: together they "speak" of Christ and to Christ.

A liturgical rite is made up of many elements—including objects, gestures, time, architecture, music, and words. Both individually and together, these elements signify Christ the Logos. Sacramental words share a special affinity for the Word, and when informed by scripture and the Church's own liturgical tradition, they express the Word and foster his likeness in us.

Other ritual elements take *the Word* as their standard and form a ritual expression that evokes him. Music, for example, is an especially fitting sacramental sign. As sung music combines both words and breath, they sacramentalize *the Word*—Christ—and *the Breath*—the Holy Spirit—in their eternal hymn of praise to the Father. Authentic liturgical music, which Pope Benedict describes as the "new tongue" singing a new song, is "in harmony" with the Logos and with the Spirit.[8]

Gestures also say with the body what words do with the mouth. Following the model of the Incarnation (God's love in human flesh), we put into our bodies what we believe. When the priest greets the people with "The Lord be with you" or wishes "The peace of the Lord be with you always," he extends his hands toward the people, as if embracing them. He likewise raises his hands when inviting the people to "Lift up your hearts." Each of the faithful strikes his or her breast when confessing sinfulness "through my fault, through my fault, through my most grievous fault," signifying in gesture the compunction of heart which the words of the *Confiteor* express. All bow at the words in the Creed, "And by the Holy Spirit was incarnate of the Virgin Mary," communicating with the body our wonder at Christ's divine condescension. All communicate through a bodily sign of peace what is also conveyed in words at the same moment of the Sign of Peace.

> What these cultural and linguistic differences mean in practice is that the language of the faith differs from the language of Main Street.

In the end, ritual language *embodies* the reality of the Word, Christ himself. The faithful do not restrict themselves to a "logical" worship, using only words; they also employ "incarnational" worship with their bodies, since Jesus himself is both *Logos* and *incarnatus*. Liturgy then truly becomes the "spiritual worship" called for by Saint Paul, divinizing the whole human being, "logifying his existence," and making him like the standard, the Logos.[9]

7. How does the Liturgy form us?

Liturgical formation is mystagogical, leading us to encounter Christ present and active in sacramental signs.

As we stated in the Introduction to this book, because Christ's work in the "age of the Church" is sacramental, our participation in his work is likewise sacramental. A sacrament possesses two dimensions: the inward and unseen reality, which is Christ and his saving grace, and the outward and perceptible sign, which is engaged by our human senses. As we learned, myst-agogy (which means "to lead," from the Greek *agogue*, into "the mystery," from *mystes*) leads the faithful from the sacramental sign to its inward real-ity, Jesus Christ. Pope John Paul II calls upon pastors to be mystagogues:

> Pastors should be committed to that *"mystagogical" catechesis* so dear to the Fathers of the Church, by which the faithful are helped to understand the meaning of the liturgy's words and actions, to pass from its signs to the mystery which they contain, and to enter into that mystery in every aspect of their lives. (MND, 17)

The first requirement of mystagogy is a beautiful and fully expressive celebration faithful to the text and rubrics in the rite; these latter have grown from the Church's liturgical tradition. Speaking about the Mass, Pope Benedict says, "the best catechesis on the Eucharist is the Eucharist itself, celebrated well" (SCar, 64). The rite which is perceived, in other words, must be *fully perceptible*. By analogy, it is impossible to "read" when the "text" is illegible. The second requirement of mystagogy is "sacramental perception," where one senses not only the sacramental sign, *but also* the inward reality. Even entering the Church prior to Mass can be a mystagogical experience as we penetrate the outward signs to see the realities they point to beyond themselves: walking through the doors of the church we recognize our pas-sage into the Heavenly Jerusalem; signing with holy water wraps us in the Trinity and clothes us with eternity as we recall Baptism; and walking down the aisle finds us pilgrims in an eschatological procession which leads us to the altar of the Lamb in heaven.

Linguistically, our ears also acquire a mystagogical and sacramental orientation, for ultimately every liturgical word speaks of *the* Word. To "attune" our ears in order to hear this reality requires the leadership of a mystagogue, one who can teach us to hear the Word in the sacramental words of the Mass. The mystagogue's method adopts that of God himself as revealed in salvation history. The meaning of sacramental words "is rooted in the work of creation and in human culture, specified by the events of the old covenant and fully revealed in the person and work of Christ" (CCC, 1145), and these sources inform the liturgy's words and inform those who speak them. In short, liturgical formation is mystagogical, where hearing words is to hear the Word. A well-celebrated liturgy "speaks" its words clearly; mysta-gogical ears, which perceive words at their roots, hear the Word in them.

8. As a priest or deacon, how can I preach about the words of the Mass?

Preaching is a privileged occasion to uncover the riches and beauty of the Mass' sacramental language and in it to encounter the Word of the Father.

The homily is a "living explanation" of the "mystery of Christ," and the mystery of Christ is the meaning of every sacramental sign. (*Introduction* to the *Lectionary for Mass*, 25; SC, 35). As with every text of the Mass, the homily nurtures the Christian life, transforming its hearers into the likeness of Christ the Word. The *General Instruction of the Roman Missal* gives three categories of texts on which the homily may expound: 1) the readings from Sacred Scripture, 2) a text from the Ordinary of the Mass, or 3) a text from the Proper of the Mass (GIRM, 65).

Ordinary texts of the Mass include the dialogues and responses, the texts of the Penitential Rite, the Gloria, Profession of Faith (Creed), the Eucharistic Prayers, and the texts of the Communion Rite and Concluding Rites. Each of these words is a part of the Church's living voice of prayer (LA, 7) and, as sacramental, leads us to encounter Christ himself. For example, a thoughtful explanation of "And with your spirit" will lead to an appreciation of the ordained priesthood, the baptismal priesthood, and even the mystery of the Church herself. To uncover the meaning of "consubstantial with the Father" is to encounter Christ, the Second Person of the Holy Trinity. Meditation upon the *Sanctus* anticipates the heavenly altar around which the assembly will soon gather.

Proper texts consist of the Presidential Prayers (Opening Prayer, Prayer over the Offerings, and Prayer after Communion), the antiphons at the entrance and at Communion, as well as certain prefaces, sequences, or other texts that are used at particular celebrations. Like the Ordinary texts, the Proper Prayers of the Mass speak with the voice of the whole Church, and to preach upon them is to introduce the faithful to the Mystical Voice of the Church who prays at all times and in all places. The proper chants of the Mass are nearly always taken from Sacred Scripture; they sometimes connect different celebrations in the liturgical calendar. "We should glory in the cross of our Lord Jesus Christ," for example, comes from Saint Paul and links Holy Thursday with the September fourteenth celebration of the Exaltation of the Holy Cross. The Collects in the sanctoral cycle are woven together with biographical allusions that make profound connections between the life of a saint and the mystery of salvation. These provide a rich treasury for liturgical prayer and Catholic spirituality.[10]

9. What can be done musically to foster active participation in liturgical language?

Sung texts in Mass are memorable, foster unity of voices, and engage the whole person.

Because words are sacramental, they have the potential to become more efficacious in song. Jesus not only *speaks* to us and to the Father, but his "tone of voice" is elevated into song: "Christ Jesus, high priest of the new and eternal covenant, taking human nature, introduced into this earthly exile that hymn which is sung throughout all ages in the halls of heaven. He joins the entire community of mankind to himself, associating it with His own singing of this canticle of divine praise" (SC, 83). Our liturgical dialogue of love with the Trinity, mediated by the Logos, is perfected by the Breath, which is the Holy Spirit.

Of the many parts that can be sung at the Mass, the Church insists that foremost are "those which are to be sung by the Priest or the Deacon or a reader, with the people replying, or by the Priest and people together" (GIRM, 40). In short, the Church holds that the faithful should *sing the Mass itself,* almost as a single continuous sacrifice of praise. In particular, the dialogues and responses, orations, and the Ordinary of the Mass (e.g., Kyrie, Gloria, Holy, Holy, Holy, etc.) are deemed the chief texts to be chanted because in large part they fully animate the Body of Christ in its "canticle of divine praise" to the Father.

Chanting these texts is also an eminently practical way to foster participation. First, music makes the text more memorable (try to recite without accompanying music, for example, the "Star Spangled Banner"). By committing the liturgy to memory in this way (by taking the texts to heart), we can participate with ease from Mass to Mass, the texts having become a part of ourselves. Second, music helps through its rhythm and meter. These elements allow a larger number of voices to pray together, thus manifesting the unity of the Church by the unity of her Mystical Voice. Third, music fosters the effective communication of the meaning of a text. In fact, *sung* texts sacramentalize clearly that their meaning is Christ. Even on a natural plane, the use of music helps heighten the meaning of an occasion. What birthday would feel complete without at least one refrain of "Happy Birthday"? How else can a civic or sporting event begin except with the National Anthem?

Even a romantic moment seems imperfect without a love song playing in the background. Finally, music's emotive quality engages the whole person, letting his or her words issue not only from the head but also from the heart and soul. From the incarnational perspective of Catholic liturgy, sung prayer reveals the deeper meaning of the words by the intimate cooperation of spirit in flesh.

10. What can I do outside the context of Mass to foster participation in the liturgy?

Full participation in the sacramental liturgy requires preparation, which takes place before the Mass begins and after the celebration has ended.

In the pursuit of a deepening sacramental engagement, the formation that needs our attention is that which occurs outside the context of liturgical celebration. Although the Eucharistic Liturgy is the most supreme means to encounter Christ, it is not the only place where we meet him. Scripture, the Liturgy of the Hours, devotion to the saints, care for the poor, meditation on the mysteries of the Rosary, and the life of faith all put us into contact with God. The Mass becomes an even more effective encounter with the Logos when supported by these practices of the Christian's life.

Participation in the Mass in particular can benefit greatly from prayer and work outside of it, whether in the home or in the classroom. Observing the liturgical seasons, for example, contextualizes the Mass's celebration. Time is as much a liturgical sign as are words, and both speak to the mystery of Christ present in the Mass. Private prayer, although different from the corporate prayer of the Mystical Body, prepares our minds and hearts for the liturgical encounter with Christ, while the voice of the Church informs our personal prayer. The saints whose works we study and whose lives we seek to emulate are the same who influenced the Mass we still celebrate today: Saint Augustine, Saint Ambrose, Saint Jerome, Saint Thomas Aquinas. By preaching, writing about the Mass, and praying it with their own lips, these saints have left their mark on it—and indeed, they join us in the Mass today from the sanctuary of the Heavenly Jerusalem. The Liturgy of the Hours complements and extends the celebration of the Mass, and "the whole course of the day and night is made holy by the praises of God" (SC, 84; see also *Laudis canticum*, Pope Paul VI, 1970).

Of particular aid to participation in the Mass is the study of Sacred Scriptures, since almost every word of the Mass, either verbatim or by inspiration, finds a scriptural origin. Knowing the story of Boaz and Ruth is to hear the priest's liturgical greeting, "The Lord be with you," and to understand it in an enriching way. Praying with Isaiah gives a glimpse of the suffering servant who gave his life for the "many" and shows furthermore who the "many" are. Integrating the images of the book of Revelation prepares us to live in the City of God, a glimpse of which is given to us in the sacramental liturgy. A helpful scriptural preparation for conscious participation in the Mass is *lectio divina*. This "divine reading" is a centuries-old tradition that is strongly encouraged in our time. In essence, *lectio divina* has the reader first

1. read carefully the sacred text;

2. reflect on its meaning;

3. follow with personal prayer to God; and

4. conclude with a period of contemplation, in which the heart dwells with the Word and seeks to become like him.

Like any worthy activity, the liturgy requires preparation. In particular, parents and teachers can foster Eucharistic participation by extra-liturgical encounters with the Logos, alive in the saints, the seasons, and the scriptures.

11. What does the Church want us to understand when we say or hear the following parts of the Mass?

"And with your spirit." (Response to the Priest's Greeting)

At the greeting during the Introductory Rites, the dialogue prior to the Gospel, at the Preface Dialogue, and for the greeting at the Concluding Rites, the priest (or at times, the deacon) says, "The Lord be with you," and each time the people respond, "And with your spirit." "And with your spirit" (translated from the Latin *Et cum spiritu tuo*) echoes the many greetings and conclusions of Saint Paul's letters: "The grace of our Lord Jesus Christ be with your spirit" (for example, Galatians 6:18). As the priest greets us in the person of Christ the Head, the people's response acknowledges his spiritual conformity to Christ. The "spirit" refers "not to the soul of the priest but to the Spirit he has received through the laying on of hands."[11]

"Through my fault, through my fault, / through my most grievous fault." (Penitential Act)

At the beginning of Mass, the Church's members admit their sinfulness and invoke the prayers of others for forgiveness before God. To signify the gravity of sin (and to fully appreciate the reconciliation won by Christ now offered in the Mass), individuals confess they have "*greatly* sinned," and done so "through my fault, through my fault, / through my most grievous fault." Multiplying "through my fault" three times magnifies the confession of sin in a way that the threefold *Sanctus* expresses the divine holiness or *Agnus Dei* emphasizes the redemptive sacrifice of the Paschal Lamb. Finally, *Mea culpa, mea culpa, mea maxima culpa* has become an expression familiar to "the general human patrimony" (LA, 56), which, in part, explains its literal translation in the English *Roman Missal*.

"We praise you, / we bless you, / we adore you, / we glorify you, / we give you thanks for your great glory." (*Gloria*)

As the doxology ("Glory be to the Father, and to the Son, and to the Holy Spirit") glorifies God, albeit in an abbreviated way, the larger doxology of the *Gloria* praises the Trinity in a more fully developed way. An early Christian hymn, the *Gloria* opens with the words of the angels on the night Christ was born (Luke 2:14) and then glorifies the Trinity in a series of invocations similar to those once reserved to ancient emperors: "We praise you, / we bless you, / we adore you, / we glorify you, / we give you thanks for your great glory" (*Laudamus te, benedicamus te, adoramus te, glorificamus te, gratias agimus tibi propter magnam gloriam tuam*). The entire Mass makes present Christ's perfect sacrifice of praise, and in the *Gloria* the Church prepares her members to enter fully and consciously into the worship of God.

"I believe in one God." (Creed)

The Niceno-Constantinopolitan Creed begins *Credo in unum Deum*, "I believe in one God." Like the Apostles' Creed, the Niceno-Constantinopolitan Creed originated as a baptismal formula in which the individual professed his or her own belief in the tenets of faith. Meaning literally "I give my heart" (from the Latin *cor*, "heart," and *do*, "I give"), the *Credo*, or Profession of Faith, symbolizes the personal conformity to God's divine truth. When spoken by the whole Mystical Body, "I believe" is a confession "coming from the person of the whole Church, united by means of the Faith" (LA, 65, quoting Saint Thomas Aquinas). The "I" therefore unites the members to each other in the one Church, and ties each member of the Church to the eternal truths of God.

"Consubstantial with the Father." (Creed)

Consubstantialem in Latin, *homoousious* in Greek, "consubstantial with the Father" signifies the identity the Son shares with the Father in the one divine nature. The Church took up the question of Christ's divinity at the Council of Nicaea 325 in response to Arius and his followers who claimed that Christ was not God. Jesus, they claimed, was not "same in being" or substance (*homo-ousious*) as the Father, but only "like in being" (*homoi-ousious*). In response, the Council defined and confirmed that Jesus *is* God, that he is of the *same* being as God the Father (there is not an *iota's* difference in their being, as the term *homoi-ousious* claimed). Since Nicaea, the Church has gone to great pains to see that her "rule of language" is consonant with her "law of belief." The Church expresses her doctrine in a language suitable to the contents of the faith. Changing the language may change the faith (and vice versa), as Nicaea's *iota* controversy demonstrates: this one little letter separated Christ from his rightful divinity. *Consubstantial*, meaning "one in being," not only conveys the contents of the faith, but does so in a way faithful to the tradition of the Latin Church.

"My sacrifice and yours." (Preparation of the Gifts)

In concluding the Preparation of the Gifts, the priest asks the people to pray that "my sacrifice and yours (*meum ac vestrum sacrificium*) may be acceptable to God, the almighty Father." Since the sacrifice of Christ is singular, and since there is only one sacrifice being offered by the priest and people, it is not incorrect for the priest to call the sacrifice "ours." On the other hand, by calling it "my sacrifice and yours" the Church adds another layer of meaning that brings out the complementary character of priest and people. Because the priest offers the sacrifice of the Mass in a sacramentally unique way (in the person of Christ the Head), the prayer was originally a petition by the priest to his assistants to pray that he may be worthy and that his offering be pleasing to God. However, as the offering is made not simply by the priest but also by the people, albeit in an essentially different way, the people are also included in the prayer: "my sacrifice *and yours*." This invitation to prayer acknowledges the difference between priest and people, and at the same time sacramentalizes the complementary participation in the one priesthood of Christ. The people, moreover, acknowledge the same theological truth in their response: "May the Lord accept the sacrifice at *your* hands" (versus "our hands").

"For you and for many." (Words of Institution)

At the words of consecration over the chalice, the priest, using the words of Christ as recorded in the Gospel accounts of Saint Matthew and Saint Mark, says the blood of the new and eternal covenant "will be poured out for you and for many" (*pro multis* in the Latin tradition). Their reference to "the many" recalls the "suffering servant" of the prophet Isaiah: "Through his suffering, my servant shall justify *many*, and their guilt he shall bear . . . , and he shall take away the sins *of many*, and win pardon for their offenses" (53:11–12). While it is the clear teaching of the Church that Christ offered himself for the whole world (see John 11:52; 2 Corinthians 5:14–15; Titus 2:11; 1 John 2:2), "for many" (words that are Jesus' own) brings forth an image of the "lamb led to the slaughter" (Isaiah 53:7) in clearer fashion. "For many" also signifies the necessity of our own efforts in redemption, that we are *coworkers* with Christ, and that salvation does not happen to us without our willing participation in Christ's grace. Thus, "for many" indicates on the one hand that Christ did die for all but, on the other hand, that his saving death must become a "living sacrifice" in us.

"Lord, I am not worthy / that you should enter under my roof." (Preparation for Communion)

Prior to Communion, the priest shows the consecrated host to the people and, in scripture's words, calls the people to "Behold the Lamb of God." As a prayer of humility, both priest and people respond, "Lord, I am not worthy that you should enter under my roof, but only say the word and my soul shall be healed." Like the priest's invitation, the response is scriptural, citing the centurion who had requested healing for his servant. Not considering himself or his household worthy to receive Jesus, the humble and faithful centurion asks him only to "say the word and let my servant be healed" (Luke 7:6–7). This prayer of humility prior to Communion resonates with each preparation rite for Communion that seeks forgiveness (the Lord's Prayer and embolism), peace (the kiss of peace), and unity (the fraction). The prayer signals once again the proper disposition of our heart (*Domine, non sum dignus*) and prepares us to receive Jesus with the faith and humility of the centurion. It also, like the centurion's servant, foresees the healing we can expect from receiving Jesus worthily and faithfully.

"Go in peace, glorifying the Lord by your life." (Dismissal)

Saint Paul beseeches us to "offer our bodies as a living sacrifice" (Romans 12:1), and this is the spirit in which the Mass concludes. The Paschal Sacrifice of the Word made present in the form of bread and wine is now to become present and active in the form of our daily lives in the world. So important, in fact, is this mission sending us into the world that the *missa* gives the entire celebration its name, "Mass." To make clear the connection between the celebration of the Mass and the transformation of our lives, three dismissal formulas are added to the traditional "Go forth, the Mass is ended" (*Ite, missa est*): 1) "Go and announce the Gospel of the Lord," 2) "Go in peace, glorifying the Lord by your life," and 3) "Go in peace." The ending of the Mass is the beginning of a transformed life of "living sacrifice:" *Go!*

12. Where can I go for more information about the Mass?

Local conferences of bishops have the authority to approve vernacular translations, and their translations are further confirmed by the Holy See (SC, 36). Assisting the United States Conferences of Catholic Bishops (USCCB) is its permanent Committee on Divine Worship (BCDW), which is composed of USCCB member bishops, and assisted further by a full-time Secretariat. The BCDW and its Secretariat serve bishops, pastors, liturgists, catechists, and all the faithful by providing current information and catechetical resources on the Mass and its English-language *Roman Missal*. The BCDW publishes a *Newsletter*, produces materials available through USCCB publishing, and provides extensive resources on the liturgy and *The Roman Missal* through their well-developed Web site: www.usccb.org/liturgy. See also their Web site on the *The Roman Missal:* usccb.org/romanmissal.

Liturgy Training Publications (LTP) offers a wide variety of resources in English and Spanish to help form liturgical leaders and participants in a proper understanding of the Church's liturgy. LTP offers a number of resources on *The Roman Missal*. See their helpful Web sites for more products and services: www.RevisedRomanMissal.org and www.LTP.org.

The Liturgical Institute (Mundelein, IL) promotes the Church's liturgical life through prayer and education. It offers four degree programs, conferences, workshops and maintains a publishing imprint, Hillenbrand Books. For more information on the Institute, visit www.liturgicalinstitute. org; for information on *The Roman Missal*, see mbmv.org. View the video at http://www.youtube.com/user/liturgicalinstitute.

> O God, who willed that your Word
> should take on the reality of human flesh
> in the womb of the Virgin Mary,
> grant, we pray,
> that we who confess our Redeemer to be God and man
> may merit to become partakers even in his divine nature.

Who lives and reigns with you and the Holy Spirit,
one God, for ever and ever.
Amen.

—Collect for the Solemnity of the Annunciation

Endnotes

1. Joseph Ratzinger, *The Feast of Faith: Approaches to a Theology of the Liturgy,* trans. Graham Harrison (San Francisco: Ignatius Press, 1986), 73.

2. Pope Paul VI, in CCC, 776.

3. Ratzinger, *The Spirit of the Liturgy,* trans. John Saward (San Francisco: Ignatius Press, 2000), 160.

4. See Ratzinger, *A New Song for the Lord: Faith in Christ and Liturgy Today,* trans. Martha M. Matesich (New York: The Crossroad Publishing Company, 1996), 121: "The 'Word' to which Christian worship refers is first of all not a text, but a living reality: a God who is self-communicating meaning and who communicates himself by becoming a human being."

5. This fundamentally is the meaning of Cardinal Ratzinger's expression "according to the Logos" described throughout *Mystical Body, Mystical Voice.* A church building is "in accord with the Logos" when it represents the heavenly realities and ultimately the Logos, Christ, thus sacramentalizing him and his saving grace. To say that liturgical words are "in accord with the Logos" expresses something more than a sacramental connection, since the resemblance is between words.

6. CCC, 1075; see also *Spiritus et Sponsa,* 12; *Mane nobiscum Domine,* 17; *Sacramentum caritatis,* 64.

7. See Ratzinger, *The Spirit of the Liturgy,* Part I, Chapter I.

8. See Ratzinger, *The Spirit of the Liturgy,* 140, 151.

9. See Ratzinger, *The Spirit of the Liturgy,* 151.

10. See Columba Marmion, *Christ in His Mysteries,* trans. Alan Bancroft (Bethesda, MD: Zaccheus Press, 2008).

11. "Narsai of Nisibis," in Robert Cabié, *The Eucharist,* ed. in Aimé Georges Martimort, trans. Matthew J. O'Connell (Collegeville: Liturgical Press, 1986), 51.

The Translation Process

The work of translation today is a lengthy and cooperative effort. The third edition of the English-language *Roman Missal*, for example, was ten years in the making. The translation process involved bishops and their own consultors, both priests and laity; experts in literature, language, poetry, history, sacred scripture, and music; as well as members of the Holy See and their own international team of experts.

In this Appendix, we will briefly examine the different bodies and organizations involved in the translation to see the great care and pastoral concern of all involved in the translation process.

Bishops' Conferences

A fundamental responsibility that derives from a bishop's pastoral office is that he is custodian of the Sacred Liturgy. In keeping with the norms put forth in *Sacrosanctum concilium*, it is for local bishops' conferences to bear the responsibility of determining whether the vernacular ought to be introduced into the liturgy and, if so, the extent of its inclusion (SC, 22, 36); their decisions are further recognized and approved by the Holy See. If the conference of bishops desires to incorporate the vernacular, it falls to that conference to provide a translation, approved by a two-thirds majority in secret balloting (LA, 79). The translation is then submitted to the Holy See for approval, or *recognitio*. Each bishop member of the conference, *Liturgiam authenticam* says, ". . . must commit himself to this as a direct, solemn, and personal responsibility" (LA, 70).

Bishops' Committee on Divine Worship

The Bishops' Committee on Divine Worship (BCDW) assists members of the United States Conference of Catholic Bishops (USCCB) in their liturgical work. This permanent committee is composed of bishop members of the USCCB, assisted by expert consultants, and served by its secretariat or staff. The BCDW assists the USCCB in its communication with the International

Commission on English in the Liturgy (ICEL), the distribution and collection of translation materials to bishops, and in directing the discussion and approval of proposed texts.

International Commission on English in the Liturgy

The International Commission on English in the Liturgy (ICEL) is entrusted by English-speaking bishops' conferences with the task of preparing the actual translations for use in Roman rite liturgies. ICEL has 11 "full member" conferences (Australia, Canada, England and Wales, India, Ireland, New Zealand, Pakistan, the Philippines, Scotland, South Africa, and the United States of America), and each conference is represented by one of its own bishops to ICEL. It should be emphasized that ICEL itself has no authority to submit or approve a translation, as these responsibilities belong to the conference of bishops and the Holy See.

Sacred Congregation for Divine Worship and the Discipline of the Sacraments

In the work of translations, it is the task of the Sacred Congregation for Divine Worship and the Discipline of the Sacraments (CDWDS) to recognize (what is called granting the *recognitio*) the lawfully approved texts submitted by a bishops' conference. Working under the authority of the Pope, the CDWDS oversees all liturgical matters, and with his authority directs the celebration of the liturgy according to the Magisterium, especially as articulated in the documents of the Second Vatican Council. The CDWDS does not normally produce translations of its own, for this is the work of bishops' conferences, but it does confirm them before they can be used. Approving texts in this way assures that texts correspond with the law of faith and the law of prayer, and also "expresses and effects a bond of communion between the successor of blessed Peter and his brothers in the Episcopate" (LA, 80).

Vox Clara Committee

At times the CDWDS does need to produce its own translations; for example, when resources are lacking in particular episcopal conferences to do so (LA, 84) or when a translation is needed in the city of Rome or by one of the dicasteries of the Holy See (LA, 76). To assist the CDWDS in its own translations, as well as to give consultation on English translations submitted by bishops' conferences, the CDWDS established the *Vox Clara* Committee in 2002. Composed largely by English-speaking bishops from throughout the world, the Committee meets about three times each year.

Process

The third edition of the English-language edition of the *The Roman Missal* has come about through many phases and with the help of each of the above-mentioned groups. Here, roughly, is its story:

Pope John Paul II promulgated the third typical edition of *The Roman Missal* (*Missale Romanum, editio typica tertia*) in 2002, in Latin. This *Missal* was subsequently divided into 12 sections for the purposes of translating:

1. Order of Mass I

2. Proper of Seasons

3. Order of Mass II

4. Ritual Masses

5. Masses for Various Needs and Intentions

6. Votive Masses and Masses for the Dead

7. Proper of Saints I and Common of Saints

8. Proper of Saints II

9. Propers for the Dioceses of the United States of America

10. Antiphons

11. Introductory Material

12. Appendixes

For the most part, ICEL translated a section and sent the first draft to its member conferences in what is called a "green book." The green book was then distributed to the individual bishops of the USCCB, who submitted their evaluations to the BCDW. The BCDW collated and summarized the green book comments from the bishops and returned them to ICEL. At that point, ICEL, in light of comments from 11 member conferences, produced a second version of one of the 12 sections and sent it once again to each of its member conferences as a "gray book." Similar to before, the gray book translation was sent to member bishops who, in the United States, submitted their comments to the BCDW for discussion at the next plenary session of the USCCB. Prior to the plenary meeting, the BCDW considered the gray book evaluations and adjusted the text accordingly, where it saw fit. At the next meeting of the full body of bishops, the proposed amendments to the gray book were discussed and voted upon, as was the section as a whole, which had to receive a two-thirds majority to pass. If the text failed, it would be reconsidered at the next meeting. If it passed, the section would be forwarded to the CDWDS, which may consult the *Vox Clara* Committee, and the *recognitio* may then be granted.

For example, the green book of the Proper of Seasons was sent from ICEL to the USCCB on March 1, 2006. Consisting of 670 pages, the green book contained the Latin text of the typical edition on one side and the proposed English translation on the other. Comments on the green book translation were returned to ICEL on June 22, 2006. After considering feedback from the conferences, the translation was changed, and a 288-page gray book was sent from ICEL to the USCCB on June 28, 2007. These gray book copies were distributed to the United States Bishops, and the BCDW collected and considered the bishops' gray book responses in January of 2008 in preparation for the June 2008 plenary meeting. At the June 2008 meeting, the Proper of Seasons was debated but failed to obtain its two-thirds majority. When the vote of absent bishops had been solicited by mail, the vote was still short. As a result, consultation was sought again from United States Bishops before presenting the text in November 2008, at which time the Proper of Seasons obtained the necessary two-thirds majority vote.

Not all sections underwent precisely this same process. The Antiphons, Introductory Material, and Appendices, after the production of the gray books, were completed by the CDWDS rather than the United States Bishops as a time-saving measure. In addition, the Eucharistic Prayers for Masses with Children are to be treated separately by the CDWDS and not as a part of the English translation of the *The Roman Missal*. Once each section of the *Missale Romanum* was granted the *recognitio*, a period of time was allowed to produce the ritual editions and catechize clergy and the faithful.

History of *The Roman Missal* since the Second Vatican Council

The English-language *Roman Missal* resulting from the *Constitution on the Liturgy*, the apostolic letter on the 25th Anniversary of *Sacrosanctum concilium*, and *Liturgiam authenticam* is the third edition of the *Novus Ordo* since the Second Vatican Council. The following is an abbreviated account of its genesis:[1]

January 1959: John XXIII announces his intention to call together an ecumenical council.

October 1962: Opening of the Second Vatican Council.

December 4, 1963: Paul VI promulgates *Sacrosanctum concilium*.

April 3, 1969: Paul VI, in the apostolic constitution *Missale Romanum*, promulgates the *Novus Ordo Missal* for use as early as November 30, 1969, the First Sunday of Advent.

November 13, 1969: The United States Bishops approve the English-language Order of Mass; this same Order of Mass is confirmed by the Holy See on January 5, 1970.

February 4, 1974: English translation of the first edition of the *The Roman Missal* published.

March 27, 1975: *Missale Romanum, editio typica altera* promulgated. This second edition of the *The Roman Missal* contains additional prayers and some modifications to texts in the first edition.

March 1, 1985: Second edition of the *The Roman Missal* in English approved. The second edition in English kept for the most part the same translation published in 1974, adding only prayers for recently canonized saints, Eucharistic Prayers for Masses with Children, and Eucharistic Prayers for Reconciliation.

November 1987: Revision of the texts of the English language *Roman Missal* begins.

December 4, 1988: *Vicesimus quintus annus*, the apostolic letter on the 25th anniversary of *Sacrosanctum concilium*.

March 29, 1994: *Varietates legitimae*, the Fourth Instruction on the Proper Implementation on *Sacrosanctum concilium* promulgated, addressing the subject of inculturation.

November 1996: Revisions to the Second edition of the *The Roman Missal* are approved by the United States Bishops. The Holy See declines to grant its *recognitio* in light of the forthcoming third edition.

April 10, 2000: *Missale Romanum, editio typica tertia* announced, and its *General Instruction* released.

April 25, 2001: *Liturgiam authenticam*, the Fifth Instruction on the proper implementation on *Sacrosanctum concilium* promulgated, addressing vernacular translations of liturgical texts.

March 18, 2002: *Missale Romanum, editio typica tertia* promulgated by John Paul II.

December 4, 2003: *Spiritus et Sponsa*, the apostolic letter on the 40th anniversary of *Sacrosanctum concilium*.

February 2004: English language draft of the Order of Mass presented to English-speaking bishops' conferences by ICEL.

June 2006: English language Order of Mass approved by United Stated Bishops.

June 23, 2008: English language Order of Mass given *recognitio* by CDWDS.

November 18, 2009: United States Bishops approve remaining texts of *The Roman Missal* and submit them to the CDWDS for approval.

March 25, 2010: The Holy See grants *recognitio* to the entire English-language *Roman Missal*, third edition.

Endnote

1. See www.usccb.org/romanmissal/.

Bibliography

Bulzaccelli, Richard H., "The Εσχατος Αδαμ and the Meaning of Sacrifice in the Theology of Joseph Ratzinger/Benedict XVI," *Antiphon* 13.1 (2009).

Cabié, Robert, *The Eucharist,* in *The Church at Prayer,* Aimé Georges Martimort, ed. trans. Matthew J. O'Connell (Collegeville: Liturgical Press, 1986).

Crouan, Denis *The History and the Future of the Roman Liturgy,* trans. Michael Miller (San Francisco: Ignatius Press, 2005).

Emminghaus, Johannes H. *The Eucharist: Essence, Form, Celebration,* trans. Linda M. Maloney, revised and edited by Theodor Mass-Ewerd (Collegeville: Liturgical Press, 1997).

Jungmann, Joseph A., *The Mass of the Roman Rite: Its Origins and Development,* trans. Francis A. Brunner, 2 vols. (New York: Benzinger, 1951).

———, *The Mass: An Historical, Theological, and Pastoral Survey,* trans. Julian Fernandes, ed. Mary Ellen Evans (Collegeville: Liturgical Press, 1996).

Malone, Richard, "Eucharist: Sacrifice According to the Logos," *Antiphon,* 13.1 (2009).

Pesarchick, Robert. A., "Worship in accord with the Logos'—Incarnation, Liturgy, and Inculturation," *Antiphon,* 13.1 (2009).

Ratzinger, Joseph, *The Feast of Faith: Approaches to a Theology of the Liturgy,* trans. Graham Harrison (San Francisco: Ignatius Press, 1986).

———, *God Is Near Us: The Eucharist, the Heart of Life,* ed. Stephan Otto Horn and Vinzenz Pfnür, trans. Henry Taylor (San Francisco: Ignatius Press, 2003).

———, *The Spirit of the Liturgy,* trans. John Saward (San Francisco: Ignatius Press, 2000).

———, *A New Song for the Lord: Faith in Christ and Liturgy Today,* trans. Martha M. Matesich (New York: The Crossroad Publishing Company, 1996).

———, *In the Beginning . . . : A Catholic Understanding of the Story of Creation and the Fall,* trans. Boniface Ramsey (Grand Rapids, MI: Eerdmans Publishing Co., 1995).

———, *Introduction to Christianity*, trans. J. R. Foster (San Francisco: Ignatius Press, 1990).

Urs von Balthasar, Hans, "God has Spoken in Human Language," in *The Liturgy and the Word of God* (Collegeville: Liturgical Press, 1959).

Index